HOW TO DESIGN YOUR OWN DRESS PATTERNS

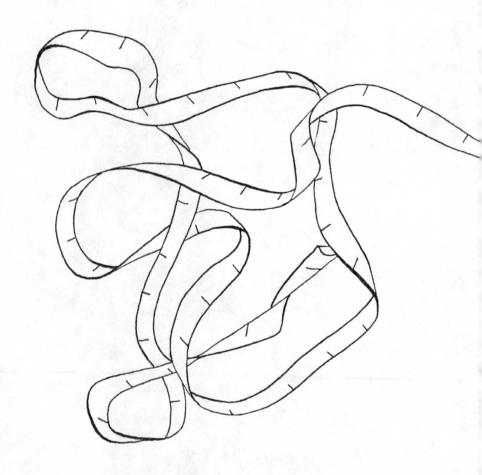

INTRODUCTION

We women who sew are a special breed. In us the creative urge takes on unique forms. We see possibilities in practically every scrap and remnant. A trip to a fabric counter brings on a state of euphoria impossible to induce even with happiness pills. An unusual button or a yard of extraordinary trimming may set off a chain reaction which ends only when a dress or suit or coat is built around this rare find. There is always a drawer or closet or box bulging with odd lengths of cloth which we couldn't resist buying. These grow old along with us before we can bring ourselves to cut into this heavenly stuff. (It may be years before a pattern comes along that is really worthy of it!) A color, a texture, a style line can bring the same inspired glint to the eyes of Miss Eighteen or Mrs. Eighty. Before the hem of one dress is finished, we are already dreaming up something new.

Most of us sew because we love clothing of great beauty and because we enjoy the experience of creating. However, creativity is often blocked by dependence on commercial patterns. As the hours of looking through pattern books mount, so does our frustration. The creative artist in us has visualized something which we cannot find for all our looking. What we are really searching for is our own design idea, which, of course, is not there. So we begin apprehensively to take liberties with patterns. We timidly attempt to combine one pattern with another. But we are too fearful to make much progress. How we wish we knew more about patterns! How we wish we could make our own!

This book is intended for the woman who had reached this stage in her dressmaking activity. The principles of pattern construction are really neither too mysterious, too numerous, nor too difficult for the home sewer. Any woman who can work her way through the labyrinthian directions for sewing which accompany the commercial pattern can surely learn the comparatively simple and clear rules for pattern making.

I am neither an inventor nor a discoverer, except in such manner as all teachers are partly both. I did not originate the principles which govern pattern construction. I am greatly indebted, in fact, to those who did develop the theory and who laid down the rules long before I was even aware that this information existed.

I am a teacher. The teacher's job, it appears to me, is to make her subject clear, its mastery attainable, and its learning a delight. Any measure of success I have been able to achieve in this book (and in my classroom) I hope can be considered a contribution to this field.

The exercises in each chapter of this book were originally used as lecture-demonstrations for classes at the Junto School in Philadelphia and the Adult Evening Program in Cheltenham, Pennsylvania. I am grateful to both of these schools for the privilege and opportunity of testing a favorite theory—that technical and professional material can be successfully translated into simple and easy methods for the amateur.

Philadelphia, Pennsylvania   Adele Pollock Margolis
1959

CHAPTER *1*

There's an art to a dart

IN THE BEGINNING

In the long history of dress and clothing design, the mass-produced garment which closely fits the figure is a comparatively recent development. In very early times, the fig leaf, the tiger skin, the bark cloth, the linen were draped over the body and held in place, variously and decoratively.

Until the first World War, even the fitted models were draped rather than drafted. Patterns were preserved in precious muslins which manufacturers as well as "little dressmakers" "took" from a completed model, generally imported from Paris. (Remember all those wonderful stories of that very clever little dressmaker who arrived at the beginning of the season with her muslin patterns and whipped up the family wardrobe while in brief residence?) This highly personalized method produced too many individual interpretations and variations from a standard size. It was hardly a method which could be profitable for a young country discovering its genius for mass production. One other factor served to stimulate the American search for a new method of reproducing patterns. The customary practice of duplicating Parisian models, temporarily (and of necessity) abandoned during the war, was never fully resumed at its conclusion because it was a costly method. American manufacturers needed a simplified, standardized, and cheaper method compatible with the magnitude of quantity production.

In each of the important clothing factories, pattern makers went to work, tirelessly and very secretly (top-drawer stuff, each firm being most careful not to divulge its secrets). Many methods were tried. After a while the results of the research disclosed certain common features. Steady improvement was made until a fairly standardized procedure was developed whereby a flat pattern could be devised from a sketch.

As you can see, this is a field so recent that it is still very much in the process of experimentation and development. It is so new that there is very little literature on the subject. Most of the people concerned have been too busy making the patterns to write about them.

Undoubtedly, new procedures will emerge as continued research and experiment continue. By now, however, there is a fairly well-established set of basic rules and principles—not too many, but enough to offer possibilities in the hands of the creative artist. These few simple rules and some ways to apply them follow.

LET'S GET STARTED

What will you need to get started?

First of all, the following tools. Some of these are already in your sewing equipment; a few special ones can be purchased at an art store or any dressmaker's supply house or possibly at the well-equipped notions counter of a department store. They are by no means all the tools which a pattern drafter uses but will be sufficient for your purpose.

1. blank paper tough enough to stand use as patterns (wide shelf paper or wrapping paper will do)
2. several pencils (medium soft lead), sharpened to fine points, and a red pencil
3. eraser
4. 12-inch ruler and a yardstick
5. curved ruler, sometimes called a curved stick
6. Dietzgen ✗17 transparent curve, called an armscye
7. any additional transparent French curve (curves and shapes you may want to use in your designs)
8. transparent 45-degree triangle
9. tracing wheel
10. scissors for cutting paper
11. Scotch tape
12. pins
13. tape measure
14. unbleached muslin or cheap cotton material for testing patterns
15. basic pattern or sloper

Note about slopers (also called basic patterns, foundation patterns, or block patterns): These are patterns made from tables of standard measurements for commercial use or from personal measurements for individual use. Directions appear later. Meanwhile, to simplify the learning process, here are quarter-scale models (Fig. 1) with which you can practice. REMEMBER that all dimensions given are for full-scale patterns, while for convenience's sake you are using quarter-scale models. Trace and cut out of heavy paper, Manila tag, or lightweight cardboard.

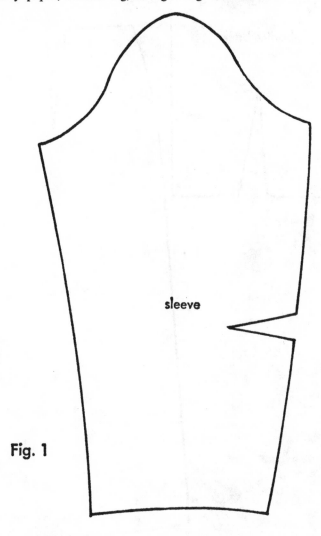

sleeve

Fig. 1

Quarter-scale sloper for your convenience

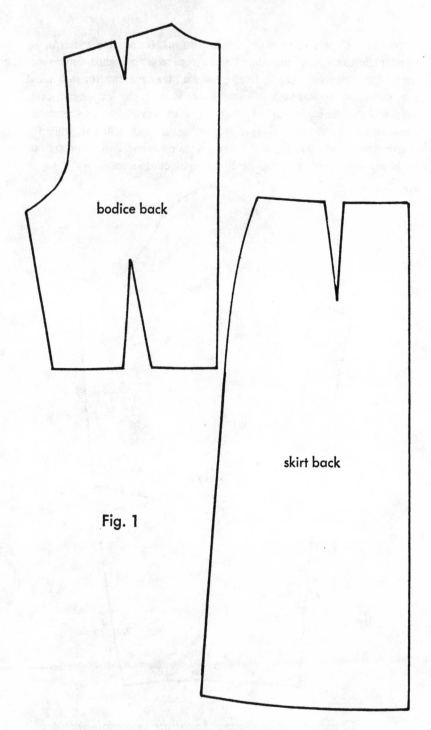

bodice back

skirt back

Fig. 1

Quarter-scale slopers for your convenience

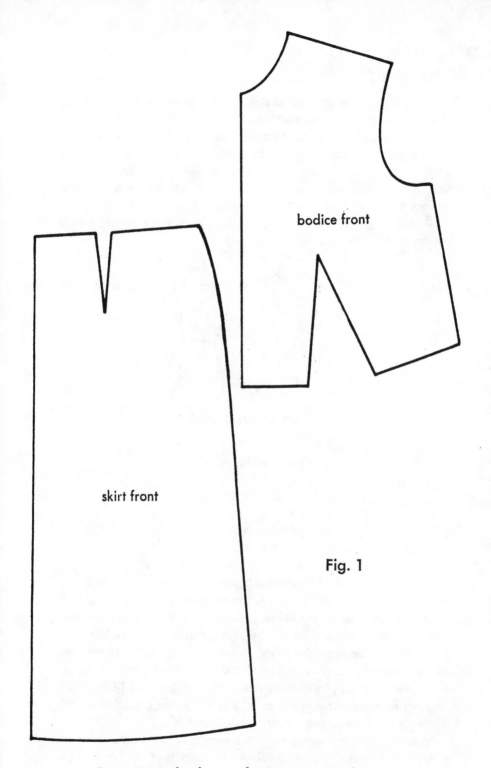

bodice front

skirt front

Fig. 1

Quarter-scale slopers for your convenience

WHY DARTS?

The human figure is three-dimensional; it has height, width, and depth. Within these three dimensions there are further variations, particularly in the female figure. There are curves, both concave and convex; there are tapering and swelling lines. The pattern maker's job is to devise a blueprint from which a flat piece of material may be cut. These flat pattern surfaces indicate how and where to manipulate the fabric so that it will not only fit all these contours but enhance them.

There are eight bulges or high points which have to be reckoned with in pattern making (Fig. 2):

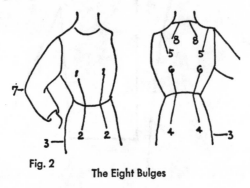

Fig. 2

The Eight Bulges

1. bust
2. abdomen or front hip bone
3. side hip curve
4. buttocks—back hip
5. upper shoulder blades
6. lower shoulder blades
7. elbow
8. dowager's hump (found in mature or round-shouldered figures)

Enough material must be included in the pattern to cover these high points. At the same time, adjoining smaller areas require less material. One flat piece of material must be so worked as to accommodate both. The difference between the larger measurement (high point) and the smaller measurement comes out in what is called "dart control." For example, the full front-bodice measurement for standard size 14 is 18¼", the front waistline on the same size is 14¾". The dart control is the difference between these two measurements—or 3½".

Wherever there is a high point and a smaller adjacent area there will be some dart control. This accomplishes the shaping of the fabric to the curve of the body. In the illustration below, note the dart control on the side seams at the hip curve (Fig. 3a).

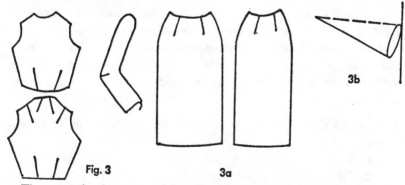

Fig. 3   3a   3b

The very simplest way of handling dart control is by a dart. The material is stitched to take in the amount needed to make it fit the smaller dimension; as it tapers off the high point, it releases enough material to fit the larger dimension (Fig. 3b).

In your basic pattern, dart control appears in one large dart at the waistline.

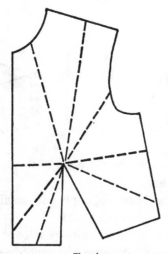

Fig. 4

While the amount of dart control will be constant, the position of the dart may be changed. It may be shifted to any position desired as long as it follows this rule: it must start from some seam and extend to the high point of the curve under consideration. Study this little sketch (Fig. 4). I'm sure you've seen designs which utilize dart control from any of these points.

HOW TO SHIFT THE DART CONTROL

Shifting a dart from one position to another does not change the fit of the garment; it merely changes the shape of the pattern piece. Darts are placed in different positions to vary the design, or style of a garment. Some darts are more flattering to a particular figure than others. The texture of some material lends itself better to some darts than others. The patterned surface of the fabric—figures, stripes, plaids—must also be taken into account.

Let's try to shift the dart control from the waistline dart to an underarm dart

1. Trace the front basic sloper.
2. Cut out the tracing and the dart.
3. On the tracing, locate a point on the side seam about 2½″ down from the armhole. (Remember that in the quarter-scale model this 2½″ becomes ⅝″.) Mark this point A (Fig. 5a).

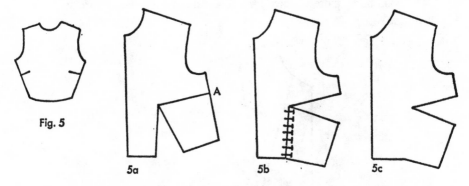

Fig. 5

5a   5b   5c

4. Draw a line connecting the point of the dart with A (Fig. 5a).
5. Slash on this line.
6. Close the original dart; either pin onto another piece of paper or Scotch tape to position (Fig. 5b).

The new dart will appear in the underarm position.

It will automatically contain the proper amount of dart control (Fig. 5c).

Now let's try shifting our waistline dart to a shoulder dart

1. Trace the front basic sloper.
2. Cut out the tracing and the dart control.
3. Locate the center of the shoulder seam and mark the point A (Fig. 6a).
4. Draw a line from the bust point to A (Fig. 6a).

5. Slash on this line.
6. Close the original dart, automatically shifting the control to the shoulder (Fig. 6b).

This has changed the shape of the pattern piece (Fig. 6c) but not the amount of the dart control.

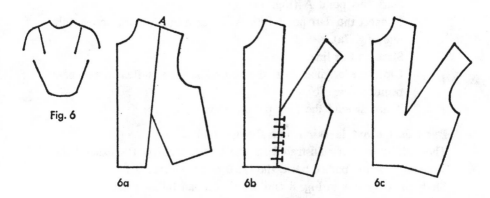

Fig. 6

6a   6b   6c

NOTE: It is not likely that you would use all of the dart control in either the underarm or shoulder position. As you can see, this would distort the grain line of the underarm seam and of the armhole.

The location of point A at the center of the shoulder seam is usual, but it may be placed where it would be more useful or more becoming to the wearer.

This is the French underarm dart

It is a flattering dart for a high, youthful figure and looks particularly well in profile. Here the entire amount of control is thrown into one dart and is used so in the finished pattern.

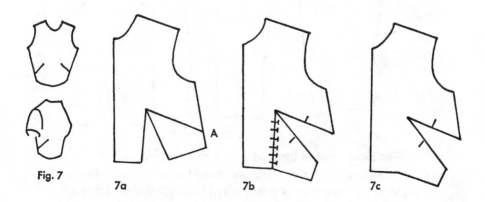

Fig. 7

7a   7b   7c

We start as before:

1. Trace the front basic sloper.
2. Cut out the tracing and the dart.
3. Locate the position of the new dart as follows: measure up 1″ to 2″ on the side seam from the waistline mark this point A (Fig. 7a).
4. Connect the dart point with A. Place a notch mark across this line (Fig. 7a).
5. Slash on this line.
6. Close the original dart; the control is then shifted to the new position (Fig. 7b).
7. Trace around the new pattern shape (Fig. 7c).

Darts dart about in skirts and sleeves, too!

The shifting of darts illustrated for the bodice front works exactly the same way for the bodice back, the skirt, or the sleeve.

Study the diagrams in Fig. 8 and see if you can follow them.

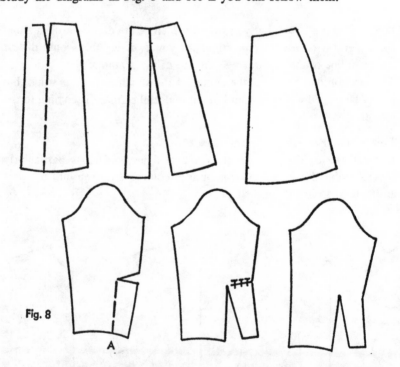

Fig. 8

NOTE: The broken line in the skirt goes from dart point to hem, parallel to the center front line. With a slight correction for flare at the center front, this could be the front gore of a four-gored skirt. (Directions for this will be given you later.) The broken line in the sleeve pattern goes from elbow to wrist. Point A is one quarter of the wrist measurement.

Work these out from the diagrams:
Shift the dart from the shoulder to the back neckline.

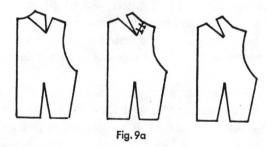

Fig. 9a

Shift the dart to the side seam.

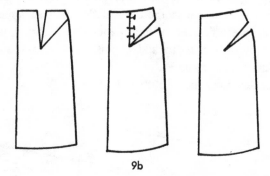

9b

Here are some interesting designs (Fig. 9c). If you saw pictures of them in a fashion magazine or saw the models displayed in a window, could you now determine how the dart control was arrived at? Train yourself to observe dart control. Keep a scrapbook or file of pictures and sketches of designs which display interesting features.

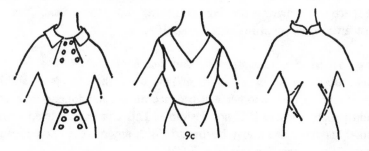

9c

FROM EXERCISE TO PATTERN

There are three types of patterns with which we work in pattern making: first, the basic pattern (all patterns are a variation of this); second, the construction pattern, which is the working pattern (this may go through many changes); and third, the final pattern, which includes all the information you will need to cut and sew your garment.

So far, we have worked with the first two. All of the preceding exercises can be turned into truly final patterns when certain other features are added.

While your construction pattern (which is what all of these were) works with the dart point, the finished dart—the one to be stitched into your garment—almost never does. It is shortened to give a softer effect. To stitch a dart to the actual high point would define it too sharply. A graceful garment should give a sculptured, smooth effect. On p. 30 there is a table of lengths to which darts are stitched. You will also need to correct certain lines which in the construction pattern appear angular and sharp but in the finished or final pattern must appear smooth and continuous. You will need to add certain indicators—notches, grain lines, seam and hem allowances.

Following are directions for all of these features.

How to shorten a dart

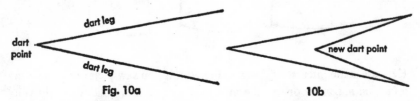

Fig. 10a   10b

The two lines which form the dart are called the dart legs. The point at which they converge is called the dart point (Fig. 10a). To shorten the dart, locate the new dart point at the desired length in the center of the space and draw new dart legs to the original starting place. Dart legs must always be equal in length (Fig. 10b).

How to correct a line after the dart has been shifted

There are many times in pattern making when the process of shifting one section to meet another will produce an angular joining or a protruding section where it is not desirable. This can be corrected with a smoothly curved line drawn freehand or with any of your curved instruments. It will look like this (Fig. 11a):

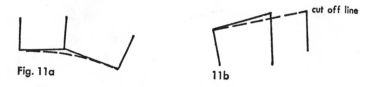

Fig. 11a   11b

Cut off the protruding section with a straight line (Fig. 11b).

Pattern symbols

A finished pattern contains certain symbols which make cutting accurate and pieces easy to put together. Here they are:

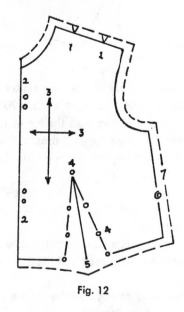

Fig. 12

1. notches
2. fold of fabric
3. grain of fabric—horizontal or vertical—also called the straight of goods
4. punch hole—indicating the end of a dart; can also be used to indicate stitching lines for seams, darts, tucks, or pleats
5. fold line for center of dart—it is easier to fold and stitch an accurate dart if this line is indicated
6. stitching line for seam
7. cutting line—an allowance usually ½" to ⅝" which is added to the stitching line in the finished pattern piece

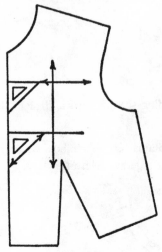

Fig. 13

How to draw the grain line parallel to the center front or back

1. Place the largest angle (the right angle—90°) of your triangle against the center front line with the leg of the triangle directly over the center front line. Lightly draw a line several inches in length. This is called "squaring a line" and is a term frequently used in pattern making. (Fig. 13)
2. Now move the triangle down several inches and repeat.
3. Measure over an equal distance from the center front line on both horizontal lines.
4. Connect these two points with a straight line.
5. Add small arrowheads at each end. This is the lengthwise grain of the fabric.
6. The horizontal line, at right angles to the center front, is the horizontal grain of the fabric.
7. The diagonal line of the equilateral triangle, which connects the horizontal with the vertical grain, is the true bias of your material.

Table of lengths for darts

All slashing, shifting, and division of darts are worked from the dart point. A finished dart, however, is usually shortened from this point. This produces a softer effect. Here is a guide for the length of darts. The finished lengths below are for size 14, so be guided accordingly.

Waistline dart—front—shortened ½″ to 1″ depending on the effect you like on yourself.

    Back—generally shortened to 6″.

Underarm dart—this is *always* found at bust-point height, that is, a line leading to the bust point but entering the side seam from any point from 2″ below the armhole to 2″ above the waistline. It is generally shortened to 3″, but in fuller figures it may be somewhat longer to give more shape. Even in this event it should end no closer than 2″ from the bust point.

Shoulder dart—front—from any point on the shoulder seam to any point about 2″ above the bust point.

Back—usually 3″ in length.

French underarm dart—this dart is an exception. It is stitched to the dart point except in larger figures where it is shortened ½″ to 1″.

Elbow dart—generally 2½″ to 3″.

Skirt front dart—shortened to 5″.

Skirt back dart—shortened to 6″.

The above lengths are standard lengths. In fitting your own clothes, be guided by what looks best on you even if it departs from the "standard."

HOW TO DIVIDE THE DART CONTROL

In the preceding lesson we shifted the dart control from one position to another. The entire amount of control was shifted. In an actual garment this is rarely so. (The French underarm dart is the exception.) More often the dart control is divided between waistline and underarm or waistline and shoulder. Any amount of the original dart control can be thrown into another position in the pattern as long as it starts on a seam line and extends to the high point. In doing this, the amount of dart control still remains constant but the shape of the pattern piece is changed, thus changing the style of the garment.

Divide the control between the waistline dart and the underarm dart
Study the sketch and diagrams in Fig. 14, p. 32.
Directions for constructing the pattern:
1. Trace the front-bodice sloper.
2. Cut out the tracing and the dart.
3. Locate the position of the new dart—2½″ below the armhole on the side seam (Fig. 14a).
4. Slash on the new dart line (Fig. 14a).
5. Close PART of the original dart; the remaining control is automatically shifted to the new dart (Fig. 14b).
6. Shorten the darts as previously directed (Fig. 14c).

7. Trace the new pattern.

*8. Fold the darts closed in the position in which they are pressed—*down* for the underarm dart, *toward the center* for the waistline dart. Using your tracing wheel, trace the seam line. This will give you the seam line shape for the dart.

9. Complete the pattern (Fig. 14d).

add ½″ seam allowance on all edges but the fold of fabric

indicate the fold of the material

indicate the grain of the material

mark all notches that can be matched to corresponding seam of back

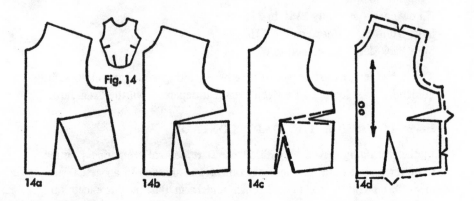

Fig. 14

14a   14b   14c   14d

Divide the control between the waistline dart and the shoulder dart

Study the following sketch and diagrams.

Directions for constructing the pattern:

1. Trace the front-bodice sloper.
2. Cut out the front-bodice sloper.
3. Locate the position of the new dart—midway on the shoulder (Fig. 15a).
4. Connect this point with the bust point (Fig. 15a).
5. Slash on this line.
6. Shift part of this control to the shoulder dart (Fig. 15b).
7. Trace the new pattern.
8. Shorten the darts (Fig. 15c).

---

*Have you noticed the little pointed shape at the seam line of a dart in the final pattern? This indicates the amount of material necessary to catch the dart in the seam. Construct as directed in step 8. The rule for folding the dart is toward the waistline for horizontal darts and toward the center for vertical darts.

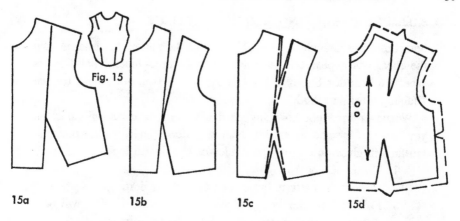

Fig. 15

15a   15b   15c   15d

9. Fold the darts into position and trace the seam, using the tracing wheel.

10. Complete the pattern (Fig. 15d).
    add ½″ seam allowance
    indicate fold of material
    add notches
    indicate grain line

Consider your fabric, too

From the standpoint of fit, almost any combination of darts is better than a single dart. The more darts, the more opportunity for gradual ease because there are more places for fitting.

When you are using a material of solid color, your chief concerns in deciding which darts to use are which look best on you and which best carry out your design idea. When you are using a figured material—a spaced print of either large or small units, a stripe, a check, a plaid, a vertical, horizontal, or diagonal weave—then the choice of darts becomes more complex. Any dart will interrupt the continuity of the fabric design. Therefore, you must choose darts which will do so with the least disturbing effect.

For this reason, too, almost any combination of darts is better than a single dart because the break in the design is minimized.

The combination of underarm and waistline darts is particularly good since the underarm dart is partly hidden by the position of the arm and the waistline dart is so reduced in size that the break in the fabric design is not too objectionable.

Always consider your fabric as well as fit in deciding which dart or darts to use.

S.O.S.—THE "BULGING BLOCK" PATTERN

Sometimes it is difficult when working with a flat pattern to visualize how the effect will appear on the body, which is three-dimensional. This is especially true for beginners. If this applies to you, you might try the "bulging block" method.

Whenever in doubt how any particular dart or darts will look on you, try this method in muslin. Half a pattern (really your sloper) in muslin will give you a pretty good idea of how it will look.

1. Trace the sloper full size.
2. Cut out the pattern, but do *not* cut out the dart.
3. Fold and pin the dart as if you were stitching it. This will produce a bulging pattern. Try it on before a mirror.
4. Locate the new dart in any place or at any angle you think will be becoming to you. You may have to experiment with this a bit.
5. Draw the new line for the dart. Remove the pattern. Cut on the dart line. When the pattern is flattened out, you will have a dart in the new position.
6. If you wish to divide the control, cut out the waistline dart and follow the procedure outlined in the preceding exercises.

THE MORE, THE MERRIER

Multiple darts

While darts are essentially a matter of structure, they are at the same time an element of design. From the design point of view, several darts may be more interesting than one, or even two. There are some considerations. Which dart or darts are more flattering to the individual figure? Which dart or darts utilize the patterned or textured surface of the material to the best advantage? Is there too much dart control for just one or two darts?

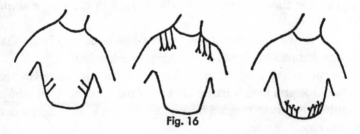

Fig. 16

In the next few exercises you will learn how to convert the dart control into multiple darts or dart tucks as in the designs in Fig. 16.

Multiple French darts   *(2 parallel darts)*

1. Trace the front-bodice sloper.
2. Draw the line for the French underarm dart (see Figs. 7 and 17a).
3. Draw a line on either side of this, parallel and ½" away (Fig. 17b).
4. These two new lines end about 1" below the bust point. This will shorten the darts to these points. Label the points D and C. Connect D and C with the bust point (Fig. 17b).

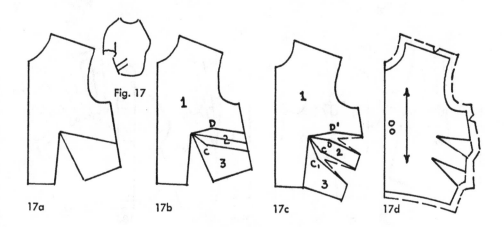

Fig. 17

17a   17b   17c   17d

5. Label sections 1, 2, and 3 (Fig. 17b).
6. Cut out the waistline dart and section 2.
7. Close the waistline dart—sections 1 and 3 (Fig. 17c).
8. Place section 2 in the new dart opening with the point touching the bust point; make it lie halfway between sections 1 and 3 (Fig. 17c).
9. Label C–1 and D–1 (Fig. 17c).
10. Find the center of the space between C and C–1 and between D and D–1.
    Connect these points to the dart ends (Fig. 17c).
11. Trace the new pattern (Fig. 17d).
12. Fold the darts toward the waistline and trace the side seam with a tracing wheel.
13. Complete the pattern (Fig. 17d) as in previous exercises.

The next two exercises feature dart tucks. These are darts that are stitched only part way. The released fullness tends to give a bloused look. Since dart tucks are really part of a dart, they will taper somewhat as a dart does when stitched.

How to make multiple dart tucks at the shoulder
Study the sketch and diagrams below.

1. Trace the front-bodice sloper and cut out the tracing.
2. Connect the dart point (DP) to the center of the shoulder—line A–DP (Fig. 18a).
3. On line A–DP measure down 4″ from the shoulder and mark this point B. This will give you the length of the dart tuck. The 4″ measurement is arbitrary. It may be any length you wish (Fig. 18a).

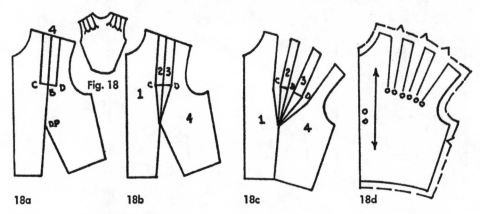

18a   18b   18c   18d

4. From B square a line 1″ in each direction. Mark points C and D (Fig. 18a).
5. From C and D draw lines to the shoulder, parallel to line A–DP (Fig. 18a).
6. From C and D draw lines to the dart point (Fig. 18b).
7. Label sections 1, 2, 3, and 4 as illustrated (Fig. 18b).
8. Cut out the dart and cut apart sections 1, 2, 3, and 4.
9. Place sections 1 and 4 on paper so that the waistline dart is closed (Fig. 18c).
   Pin or tape securely in place (Fig. 18c).
10. Place sections 2 and 3 so that there are three equal openings at the shoulder and the points touch the dart point. Pin or tape in place (Fig. 18c).
11. Trace the new pattern. The dart tucks will be stitched to points B, C, and D. Trace this far and mark with small circles to show where the stitching ends (Fig. 18d).

12. Fold the darts toward the center and trace the seam line with the tracing wheel.

13. Complete the pattern by adding seam allowances, notches, fold indicator, and grain of fabric (Fig. 18d).

Shoulder tucks can be as long as desired but should not come closer than 2″ above the bust point. They are usually 1″ apart when two or three are used. If more than this, they must be closer together. It is well to keep them 1″ from shoulder and 1″ from neckline so that they don't interfere with the fitting of these parts.

How to make three multiple darts at the waistline

Figures 19a and 19b show the waistline dart shifted temporarily to the shoulder. This will give you the line necessary for locating the dart tucks at the waistline. More important, this gives you a convenient surface, uninterrupted by a dart, in which to locate your new darts.

Figures 19c, d, and e show the development of this pattern.

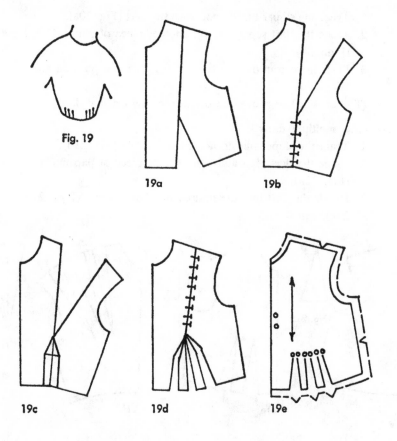

Fig. 19

19a   19b

19c   19d   19e

TRY THIS SHORT CUT

Here is another and quite simple method for relocating your dart or dividing it into several darts. This method can be used only for darts on the same seam line. It will not work any other way.

To relocate a dart

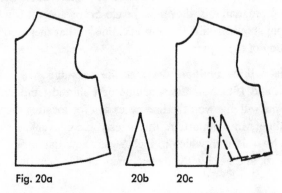

Fig. 20a   20b   20c

1. Trace the sloper but do not trace the dart (Fig. 20a).
2. Trace the dart separately on another piece of paper. Cut it out (Fig. 20b).
3. Place the cutout dart on the sloper in the new position and trace (Fig. 20c).

(The broken line shows the position of the original dart.)

To make multiple darts

1. Trace the sloper but do not trace the dart (Fig. 21d).
2. Trace the dart separately on another piece of paper. Cut it out (Fig. 21a).
3. Divide the dart into the desired number of darts (Figs. 21b and 21c). Cut them out.

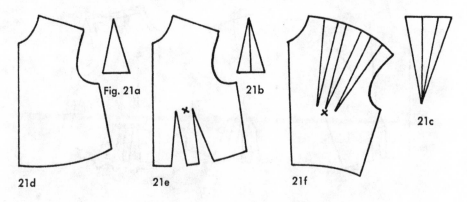

Fig. 21a   21b   21c

21d   21e   21f

4. Set the dart sections into position either side of the bust point (X) and about 1″ apart at the seam. Allow for correction of the length of the dart legs since they must be equal (Figs. 21e and 21f).

5. Trace the darts on the sloper. Correct the dart legs for length (Figs. 21e and 21f).

6. Shorten the darts.

7. Complete the pattern.

Darts may be divided into any number of sections, but be very sure that you make the dart legs equal in length. They are not equal in length as you cut them out.

Feel proud? You now have at your command three different methods for working out your pattern. The first is the flat pattern arrived at by drafting. This classic method is the one used by professional pattern drafters. The other two methods—the paper dart or the bulging block pattern—may be easier for you, as a non-professional, to experiment with. Use your judgment as to which method suits a particular problem better than the others.

See if you can work out the pattern for these sketches by any of the methods suggested. You're on your own.

darts equal in length   *graduated darts*   *center front seam*

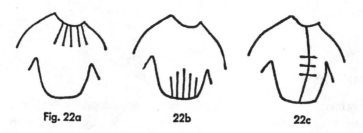

Fig. 22a   22b   22c

The cluster of darts in Fig. 22b may be located more easily if the waistline dart is temporarily shifted to the shoulder (Fig. 6).

In working out the pattern for Fig. 22c, note that the center front becomes a curved seam line. Sketch this curved line freehand, then true up the line with one of your curved instruments. The grain line in this case is the original center front line, that is, a straight line from the neck to the waistline.

LOOK, MA, NO DARTS

You have learned how to shift the dart control, how to divide it, how to make multiple darts and multiple dart tucks. You can further vary your design by replacing your dart control with gathers, shirring, or decorative smocking.

Study the sketch and diagrams in Fig. 23.

Keep lines 1″ from the neckline and 1″ from the armscye (armhole) for smoother fit at neck and armhole. Slash three or four times and spread so the spaces between are equal. This will give you a guide line for the new extended shoulder seam. Connect A and B with a freehand curved line, then true up the line with your instruments. In this design the area from A to B is gathered or shirred. Note that the only fullness here is that of the shifted basic dart. There is no additional fullness. Directions for added fullness will be given you in a later lesson.

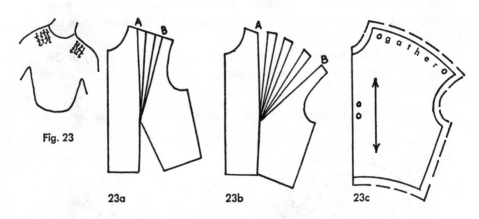

Fig. 23

23a   23b   23c

SAME PRINCIPLE—SKIRTS AND SLEEVES

The principles used in bodice styling are also used in skirt styling or sleeve styling. Dart control may be shifted or divided; it may be used as darts, dart tucks, or pleats; it may be taken out in gathers, shirring, or smocking. Following are three skirts which illustrate this.

The four-gored skirt

The four-gored skirt has seams at sides, center front and back. It is constructed simply through the shifting of the dart control and the addition of a slight amount of flare.

Constructing the skirt pattern

1. Trace the front- and back-skirt slopers.

2. Locate notches at the hip—7″ down on the side seam. The zipper is set in on the left side to this notch.
3. Draw slash lines from the dart point to the hem line, parallel to center front and back (Fig. 24a).
4. Cut out the front and back patterns; cut out the darts.
5. Slash on the slash lines.
6. Close the waistline darts, thereby shifting the control to the hem line (Fig. 24b).

Note in your pattern that the side seam has more flare than the center front or center back. This is because some flare was added to the side seam of the basic sloper. To equalize this, some flare must be added to the center front and the center back in order to get a nicely balanced gore. This is done in either of two ways. In Fig. 24c the flare breaks from the hip line, assuring a smooth fit over the hips. If you're inclined to be hippy, this is a good plan for you. In Fig. 24d the flare breaks from the waistline, giving a little more fullness over the hips. Either way is correct; choose what, for you, is the most flattering.

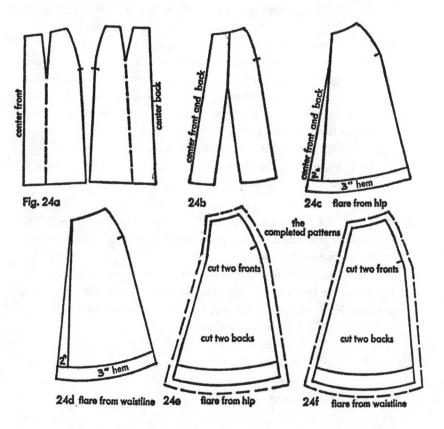

Fig. 24a   24b   24c   flare from hip

24d flare from waistline   24e   flare from hip   24f   flare from waistline

the completed patterns
cut two fronts
cut two backs

7. Add flare: extend the hem line 2″ at the center front and center back. Connect these points with the hip (Fig. 24c) or with the waist (Fig. 24d). Correct the line where necessary for a smooth continuous line.

8. Add seam allowance and notches (Figs. 24e and 24f).

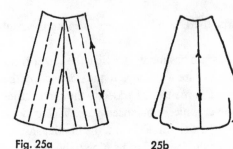 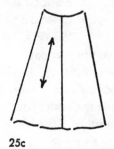

Fig. 25a   25b   25c

9. Mark the grain line. Where you place the grain line depends on the effect you would like in your design and/or the material you are using. Just remember that the grain line will always hang straight. If you wish a straight side with front and back ripple (Fig. 25a), place the grain line parallel to the side seam or make the side seam the straight of goods. If you are using a plaid or a striped material and wish a straight look to the side seam, use this placing of the grain (Fig. 25a). If you wish the center front and center back to hang straight with flare at the sides, place the grain line parallel to the center front and center back or use the center front and back as the straight of goods (Fig. 25b). If you wish some flare both at the front and side or back and side, then fold the gore of the skirt in half. The fold line becomes the straight of goods (Fig. 25c).

A note on waistbands

Waistbands 1″ to 1½″ wide are satisfactory for fit. The 1″ will hug the waist better. If waistbands are wider than this, some shaping is necessary to fit the curve of the waist.

The length of the waistband is equal to the waist measurement *plus* ½″ for ease, *plus* 1½″ for the underlay, *plus* seam allowance (Fig. 26).

For example: the *length* of the waistband for a 26″ waist will be

26″—the waist measurement
½″—for ease
1½″—for underlay
1″—two seam allowances (½″ each)
_____
29″—total

The width will be

> 2"—folded 1" width
> 1"—two seam allowances (½" each)
> ———
> 3"—total

and will look like this:

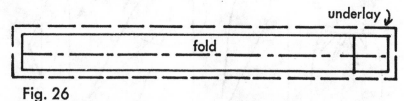

underlay

fold

Fig. 26

A wider waistband would have to be drafted from the hip-length sloper with side seams to take care of the curve. (Directions for hip-length sloper will be given later.)

How to make a straight skirt with two darts or dart tucks in front

1. Trace the skirt-back sloper.
2. Shorten the back dart to 6" and set the skirt back aside.
3. Trace the skirt-front sloper, but do not trace the dart (Fig. 27a).
4. Trace the skirt-front dart on another piece of paper. Cut it out (Fig. 27b).
5. Divide the cutout dart in half (Fig. 27b).

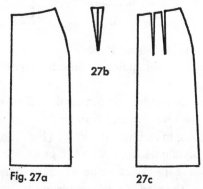

Fig. 27a   27b   27c

6. Place the darts in the new position on the skirt front and trace (Fig. 27c).
7. If darts are desired, shorten to 5" and stitch.
   If dart tucks are desired, stitch to the chosen length.
8. Complete the pattern—notches, grain, hem allowance, seam allowance.
9. Construct the waistband.

Getting at the bottom of the peg-top skirt

There are several interesting problems involved in the construction of this skirt. Let us do it first and then analyze what we have done.

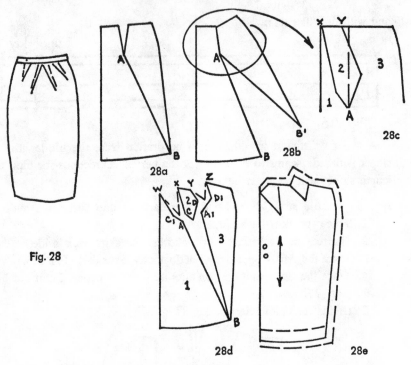

Fig. 28

1. Trace the skirt-front sloper.
2. Connect the dart point to the side seam at the hem line—A to B (Fig. 28a).
3. Cut out the pattern; cut out the dart. Slash on line A–B.
4. Close the waistline dart with Scotch tape. The dart control will be thrown to B. Label B and B1 (Fig. 28b).
5. Draw style lines from X and Y in the approximate length and position in the sketch. (You will have to train your eye to judge lengths, direction of line, proportion.)
6. Connect the ends of these lines with A (Fig. 28c).
7. Label sections 1, 2, and 3 (Fig. 28c). Cut these three sections apart.
8. Place sections 1 and 3 so that they touch at B and are 2″ apart at A–A1. Place section 2 between 1 and 3 so that darts are equal at the waistline and the point midway between A and A1. Mark points C1 and D1, W and Z (Fig. 28d).

9. Locate points midway between C and C1 and D and D1. Connect these points to the dart ends W–X and Y–Z.
10. Each pair of dart legs should be equal in length, that is, WC equals XC and YD equals ZD.
11. Fold darts toward the center and trace the waistline seam.
12. Trace the new front pattern (Fig. 28e).
13. Trace the back-skirt sloper. Shorten the dart to 6″.
14. Complete front and back skirt patterns as previously directed.

The peg-top skirt has more ease in the hip line, but the waistline and the sweep of the hem line remain the same. The pegging was added in the open area in step 8. More ease can be added if a more pegged effect is desired. In order to be able to locate the ease at the proper place, the waistline dart had to be relocated at the hem line temporarily and then shifted back to the hip—a sort of pass, waistline to hem line to hip. In order to get the new style line* which our darts have now become, we had to have an area uninterrupted by the waistline dart (Fig. 28d). This is a procedure to which you have already been introduced and which you will use many times.

---

*This is the first time you have encountered the term "style line." It is one you will hear often from now on. A style line is a seam line within the confines of the pattern.

CHAPTER 2

The case of the disappearing dart

HIDDEN DARTS

The preceding chapter has described the simplest way in which dart control can be utilized in pattern making. If this were all there were to it, the fashion game would be a pleasing but not very challenging one. The real fun in this, as in any other art or craft, is to use simple and fundamental information to develop more intricate and more complex patterns.

Let us go back a bit. We have learned that all pattern variations are built on the fundamental principle that basic patterns have a constant amount of dart control. This can be shifted or divided into two or more parts as long as the control starts on some seam and extends to the high point or heads in that direction. We know this dart control need not appear as a dart; it may appear as gathers, shirring, smocking, tucks, pleats, or folds. Many simple patterns remain on this level. And many beautiful garments are made in just this manner, depending for their effect on beautiful fabric and perfect fit.

It is possible (and fun!) to use this very simple information ingeniously to create more intricate designs. Study the sketches in Fig. 29. There are no visible darts (or their equivalent), yet we know the dart control must be there. What have these designs in common? Simply this, that the dart control has been concealed in a seam which is used as a decorative feature of the design.

Where a seam is used as a substitute for the control dart it generally falls across the high point of the body. Control in this manner will produce the French-dart bodice, the yoke, and the yoke panel. It may be used as a basis for a French bodice or basque, for the princess dress, or for a suit jacket. It is a graceful line, lends itself to endless variations, and is beautiful in fit.

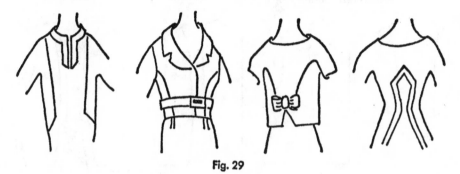

Fig. 29

How to produce the French-dart bodice

1. Trace the bodice-front sloper.
2. Cut out the tracing and the dart.
3. Shift part (less than half) of the dart control to the shoulder (Figs. 30a and 30b).

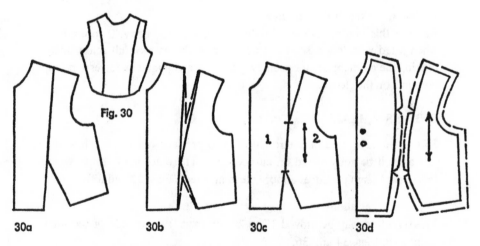

Fig. 30

30a   30b   30c   30d

4. Shorten both darts. See p. 30 for lengths (Fig. 30b).
5. Connect both new dart points with a straight line (Fig. 30c).
6. Label sections 1 and 2.
7. Locate the grain line in section 2 parallel to the center front.
8. Make notches at the points of the darts.
9. Cut sections 1 and 2 apart (Fig. 30d).

10. Correct the angular line in section 2 with a smooth curve. Use the French curve for this.

11. Indicate the fold of material and add seam allowance (Fig. 30d).

The French-dart bodice back

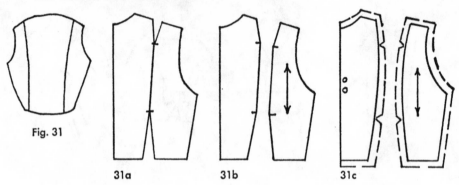

Fig. 31

31a   31b   31c

This is constructed in the same way as the front. You already have a dart at the shoulder so that it is not necessary to divide the waistline dart control. Connect the shoulder dart (which is already shortened) and the shortened waistline dart with a straight line. Proceed as for front bodice (Fig. 31).

Fitting the French-dart bodice

Because this bodice follows closely the lines of the body, it looks best when fitted with less ease. Take up some of the ease on all seam lines, making the garment fit more snugly. Make sure you take in corresponding amounts on the sleeve.

CURVES AHEAD

So far, we have used only straight lines to produce our darts. They can just as well be constructed on curved lines. There are many times when this curved seam produces a more pleasing effect (Figs. 32 and 33).

Try some variations

The style line may be moved 1″ to 2″ (no more!) either side of the high point as in Figs. 34 and 36.

For Fig. 34 the directions are as follows:

1. Draw the style line and slash line (Fig. 35a).

2. Relocate part of the waistline dart control at the new style line. Divide this between waistline and shoulder. Some of the waistline dart control of the side section will automatically be shifted to the style line (Fig. 35b).

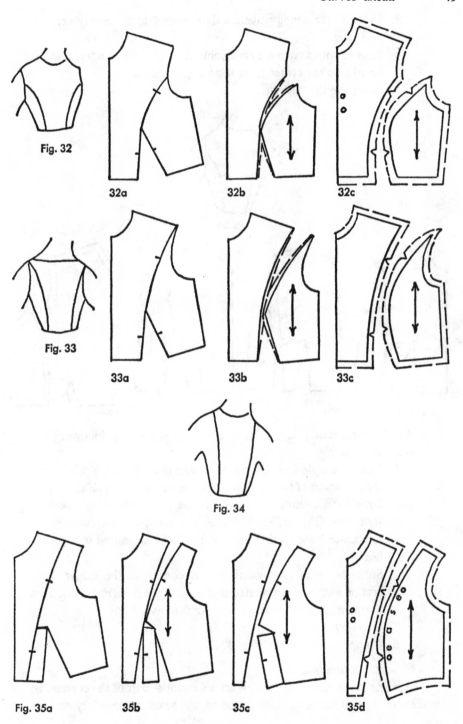

Fig. 32

32a 32b 32c

Fig. 33

33a 33b 33c

Fig. 34

Fig. 35a 35b 35c 35d

3. Shift the remaining waistline dart control to the newly created dart (Fig. 35c).
4. Smooth with a rounded continuous line. This dart control may be eased into the center front section (Fig. 35d).
5. Complete the pattern.

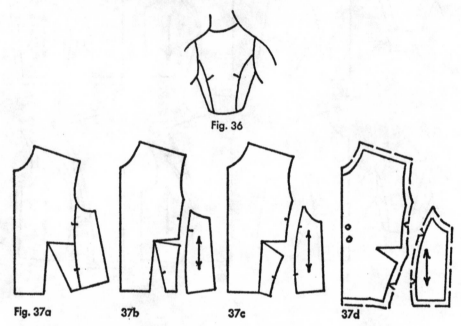

Fig. 36

Fig. 37a   37b   37c   37d

Another variation (Fig. 36) may be accomplished by following the instructions below.

1. Draw the style line and the slash line (Fig. 37a).
2. Relocate part of the dart control at the new style line (Fig. 37b).
3. Divide the control between waistline and armhole on the new style line (Fig. 37b). Some of the waistline dart control of the center front section will automatically be shifted to the style line.
4. Shift the remaining waistline dart control in the center front section to the newly created dart at the style line (Fig. 37c). This dart control may be eased in or stitched as a dart.
5. Correct the seam line (Fig. 37d).
6. Complete the pattern (Fig. 37d).

Add some decorations

The seams in the preceding designs are an essential part of the control. In sketches 38 and 39, in addition to the control seam, a secondary seam is

added which repeats the line for emphasis. This is purely decorative and
without any control.

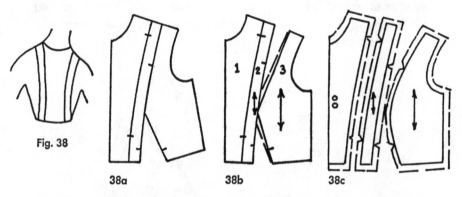

Fig. 38

38a   38b   38c

NOTE FOR FIG. 38:   This might be quite pretty if section 2 were a contrasting color or a print-and-plain combination. It would be very interesting in a three-way color scheme.

The following design (Fig. 39) illustrates the same principle used
horizontally. The dart control is divided and hidden on either side of the
center band. The other two bands repeat the design line for emphasis.

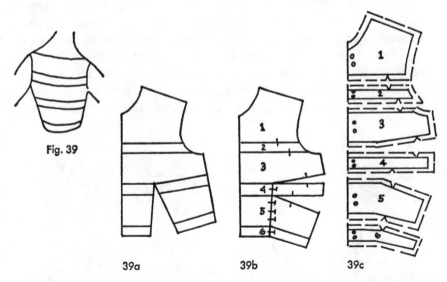

Fig. 39

39a   39b   39c

Often, decorative bands (Fig. 39) are applied to the construction
seams, giving much the same effect. These bands may be of contrasting
color or texture (linen and satin or wool and satin), braid, eyelet, beading,
ribbon, embroidery. Here is a good chance to haul out those charming

bits of apparently useless stuff which you simply could not bypass. Insertions of lace, ruffles, piping, edgings, ric-rac, and as many variations as your unleashed fancy can devise—all have a place here. Figure 40 offers two suggestions. You doubtless have dozens of your own inventions as good or better.

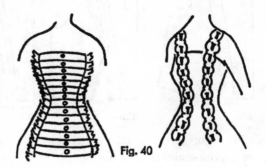

Fig. 40

THE VERSATILE YOKE

It appears in many forms

Here again is an example of structural detail—the dart concealed in a seam—which is turned to design use in the yoke (Fig. 41). The yoke serves many purposes. It may conceal the dart control in its seam. It may divide the bodice or skirt into interesting areas. It may provide a smooth, trim look in the yoke area in contrast to fullness above or below. It may separate a highly decorative area from a simple area. The yoke may appear in the upper bodice, as in many blouses, or the lower bodice as the torso yoke. It may appear in the upper area of the skirt. Here in its narrowest

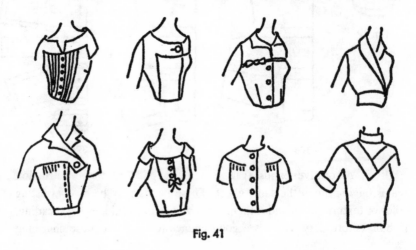

Fig. 41

form it becomes the contour belt. There are simulated yokes, yokes in one with a panel, yokes in one with a sleeve. The yoke has enormous versatility and wonderful possibilities.

Put the control in the yoke seam
1. Trace the front-bodice sloper.
2. Cut out the tracing and the waistline dart.
3. Draw the style line, that is, the line from the center front to the bust point and the line from the shoulder to the bust point (Fig. 42a).
4. Label sections 1, 2, and 3 (Fig. 42a).

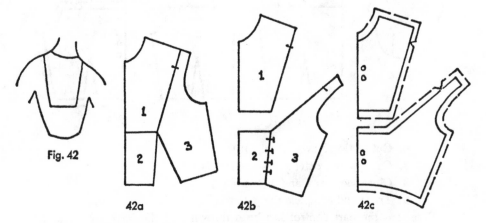

Fig. 42

42a   42b   42c

5. Cut section 1 away from the rest. This is the yoke (Fig. 42b).
6. Close the waistline dart. What has happened to the dart control? Actually it has been thrown into a shoulder dart. But since one side of that dart (the side which is yoke) has been cut away, the control really lands in a seam instead of a dart. Add section 1 to section 2 if you have trouble seeing this (Fig. 42b).
7. Complete the pattern in the usual manner (Fig. 42c).

Try to figure out the construction of these yokes in Fig. 43.

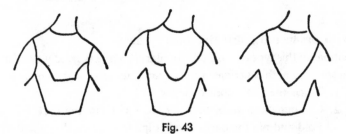

Fig. 43

Put the control in the back-yoke seam
1. Trace the back sloper (Fig. 44a).
2. Cut out the sloper and the dart.
3. Locate the style line (Fig. 44a).
4. Extend the shoulder dart to the yoke line (Fig. 44a).
5. Label sections 1, 2, 3. Mark notches (Fig. 44a).

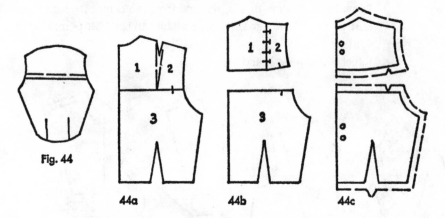

Fig. 44

44a   44b   44c

6. Cut section 3 away (Fig. 44b).
7. Cut out the extended shoulder dart.
8. Close sections 1 and 2 (Fig. 44b).
9. Trace and complete the pattern (Fig. 44c).

Note that the dart control has been thrown into the back-yoke seam. Try the simple variations in Fig. 45.

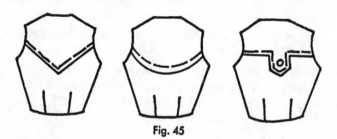

Fig. 45

How to produce the flattering torso yoke
Variations of this type of yoke are popular. It is a very good way to emphasize a small smooth waistline and yet retain fullness for the bust.
1. Trace the front-bodice sloper.
2. Cut out the bodice, but DO NOT cut out the dart.
3. Fold and pin the dart closed (Fig. 46a).

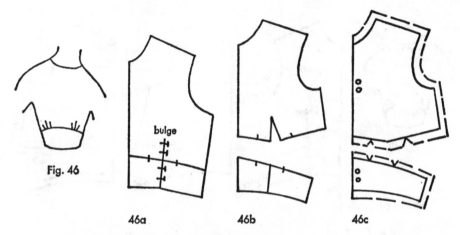

Fig. 46

46a   46b   46c

*4. Draw the style line for the yoke (Fig. 46a).
5. Cut away the yoke and trace (Fig. 46b).
6. Unpin the remaining dart control on the upper bodice and trace. This may be used as one dart, multiple darts, or gathers (Fig. 46b). (Instructions for adding more fullness will be given you in the next chapter.)
7. Complete the pattern (Fig. 46c).

A yoke that doesn't quite make it—the simulated yoke

Here the yoke is not cut away entirely from the rest of the bodice, only part way, making the pattern all one piece (Figs. 47 and 48). This presents certain difficulties in sewing since there is very little seam allowance at the point where the yoke is cut away. Reinforce this point and sew carefully.

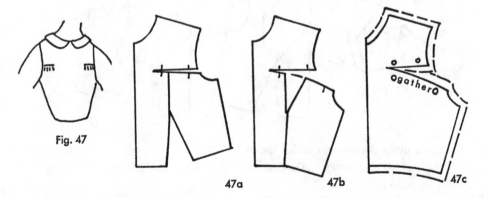

Fig. 47

47a   47b   47c

*Square a line about ⅛" in length at the center front and then proceed to draw your curve. This will avoid a point at center front when your material is unfolded.

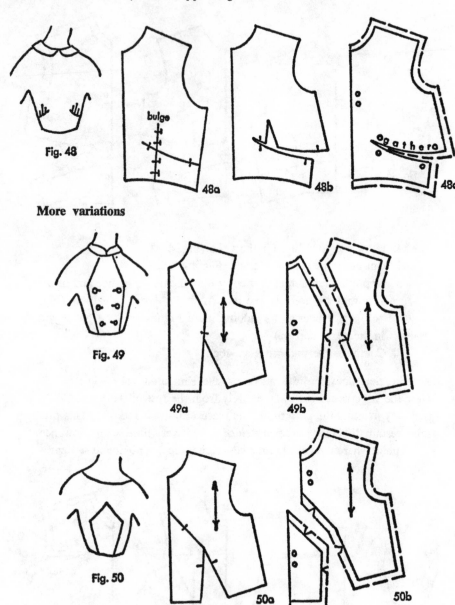

Fig. 48   48a   48b   48c

More variations

Fig. 49   49a   49b

Fig. 50   50a   50b

Let's place the control under the yoke

Refresh your memory on the construction of multiple darts and dart tucks (see p. 34).

In this exercise we are going to combine the construction of a yoke and multiple dart tucks.

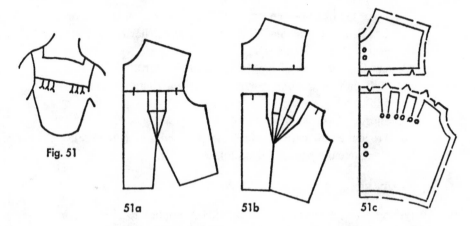

Fig. 51

51a   51b   51c

1. Trace the front-bodice sloper; cut out the tracing and the dart.
2. Establish the style line of the yoke and determine the position of the dart tucks (Fig. 51a). Locate notches on the yoke seam line.
3. Cut the yoke from the rest of the bodice (Fig. 51b).
4. Slash on the dart-tuck lines.
5. Close the waistline dart and space the dart tucks (Fig. 51b).
6. Trace the new pattern. Mark punch holes for the stitching line of the dart tucks (Fig. 51c).
7. Complete the pattern (Fig. 51c).

In the preceding pattern all of the dart control was shifted to the dart tucks. In this pattern only part of the control will be shifted. Instead of darts or dart tucks, the area will be gathered.

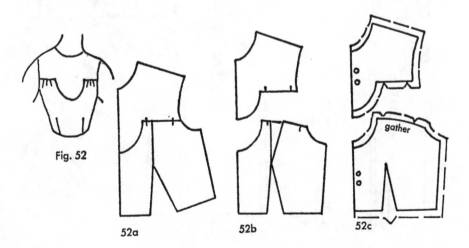

Fig. 52

52a   52b   52c

gather

1. Trace the front-bodice sloper. Cut out the tracing and the dart.
2. Establish the style line. Mark notches on the horizontal style line near each end (Fig. 52a).
3. Cut the yoke away from the bodice (Fig. 52b).
4. Shift part of the dart control to the horizontal style line (Fig. 52b).
5. Shorten the waistline dart.
6. Trace the new pattern. Mark the gathered area (Fig. 52c).
7. Complete the pattern (Fig. 52c).

. . . AND SKIRTS, TOO

Everything you have learned about bodices applies to skirts as well.

The control may appear in a seam or a yoke. The two exercises in Figs. 53 and 54 illustrate dart control in a seam and yoke panel.

The six-gored skirt—*three gores front, three gores back*

1. Trace the skirt front and back, side seams and hips touching (Fig. 53a).

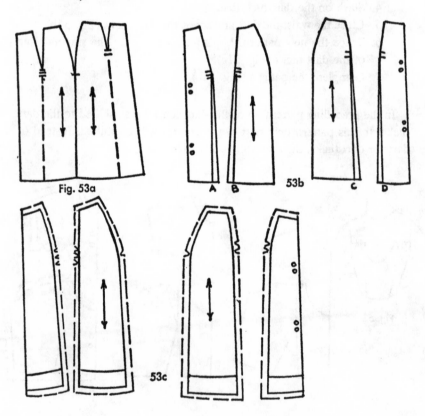

Fig. 53a   A   B   53b   C   D

53c

2. Draw slash lines from the dart points to the hem line, parallel to the center front and back (Fig. 53a).
3. Locate notches at the hips and at the points of the darts. Locate the grain lines near the side seams and parallel to the center front and center back (Fig. 53a).
4. Cut out the pattern; cut out the darts; slash on the slash lines.
5. Pin to a new piece of paper, separating the gores as in the diagram (Fig. 53b).
6. Add 1″ flare at A, B, C, and D by extending the hem line and connecting with the hip (Fig. 53b).
7. Trace the new pattern and complete in the usual manner. Don't forget the hem (Fig. 53c).

The eight-gored skirt—*four gores front, four gores back*
This is made in the same manner. Instead of a center fold at front and back, these lines become seam lines. Add 1″ flare to center front and center back to balance the other side of the gore (Fig. 54).

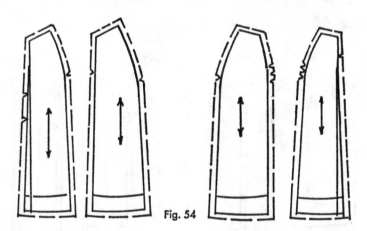

Fig. 54

NOTE: If additional flare is desired, more than 1″ may be added at each of specified places.

How the skirt with the yoke panel is made
In this design (Fig. 55), the dart control is shifted to a yoke panel. It is a fine illustration of how the construction seams are used for a decorative effect, especially if the seams are topstitched.

1. Trace the front- and back-skirt slopers, side seams touching at the hip (Fig. 55a).
2. Draw the style line—the broken line in the diagram—parallel to

the center front and back, the curve touching at the dart point (Fig. 55a).

Remember that darts may be lengthened to the style line (as in previous exercises).

3. Indicate notches (Fig. 55a).
4. Label sections 1, 2, 3, and 4 (Fig. 55a). Cut them apart.

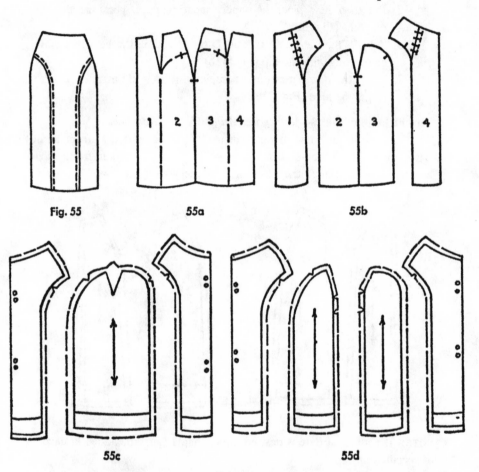

Fig. 55   55a   55b

55c   55d

5. Close the darts in sections 1 and 4. These sections become yoke panels. The dart control has been shifted to the curved seam (Fig. 55b).
6. Sections 2 and 3 may be used as one or two pieces.

   If made in one piece: match notches at the hip and join the side seam; trace the one-piece pattern; the original side seams become the grain line and the remaining portion of the hip dart control is used as a dart (see completed pattern, Fig. 55c).

If made in two pieces: trace sections 2 and 3 separately; the side seams become the grain lines (Fig. 55d).

The contour belt is easy to make

The contour belt could be considered a very narrow skirt yoke.

1. Trace the upper part of the skirt-front and -back slopers (Fig. 56a).
2. Pin the darts closed; pin the side seams closed (Fig. 56b).
3. Sketch in the design line of the contour belt. Usually this is narrower in front (Fig. 56b).
4. Cut away the yoke from the rest of the skirt.
5. Allow for the overlap on the right front, usually 3″ in addition to the waist measurement, curved to match the left side (Fig. 56c).
6. Complete the pattern.

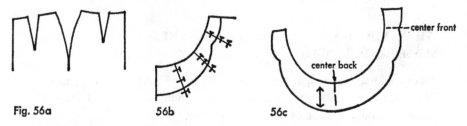

Fig. 56a   56b   56c

Double-contour belt (*girdle, or basque type*)

This would be composed of two contour belts, one made for the bodice, one for the skirt, and joined at the waistline. Use the directions above for the skirt part; use the directions for making the torso yoke for the bodice part (see p. 54). Close in any manner desired at center front, but be sure to make due allowances for closing.

CHAPTER *3*

Slash, spread and twirl

WHEN YOU WANT ADDITIONAL FULLNESS— SLASH AND SPREAD

All of the foregoing designs have been variations of the basic dart control. There are many times, however, when more fullness is desired than is possible through the use of dart control alone.

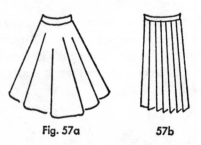

Fig. 57a   **57b**

Here are two ways by which this fullness is achieved. In the first instance, the fullness appears in the sweep of the hem line, while the waistline retains its original measurement (as in the semicircle or circle skirts, Fig. 57a). In the second, the fullness appears in equal amounts both at the waistline and the hem line (as in the knife-pleated skirt, Fig. 57b). These two types of fullness may be found in bodices, skirts, sleeves, collars, cuffs, peplums, capes, jabots, etc. Wherever found, the principles of construction remain the same.

Type 1—The semicircle or circle skirt (Figs. 58–62)
(The measurements in this exercise are arbitrary; the exercise merely
illustrates a point.)

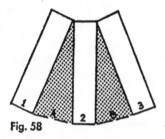

Fig. 58

1. Draw a rectangle 1½″ by 2½″.
2. Divide it lengthwise into three equal parts.
3. Slash on these lines.
4. While maintaining the 1½″ measurement at the top, spread
   the bottom to any desired fullness, making sure to leave an equal
   amount between sections. (A and B are equal. They represent
   flare which has been added.)

A fold will appear in the material where the pattern has been slashed
and spread. The pattern may be slashed into as many sections as you desire
folds in the finished garment.

If slashed sufficiently, the spread can be continued until a complete
circle is obtained (Fig. 59).

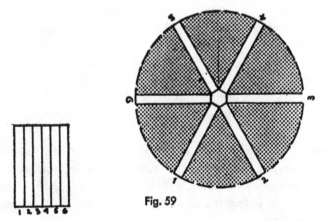

Fig. 59

One edge will always maintain one original measurement (in this
case the inner circle).

FASHION IN THE ROUND

The semicircle and circle skirt

The foundation for this pattern is the four-gored skirt. Any amount of fullness may be added from just more flare to the amount necessary for the semicircle and the circle skirt.

The semicircle skirt

1. Proceed as for the four-gored skirt through step 7, p. 40.
2. Correct the side seam by drawing a straight line from the hem to the waistline (Fig. 60).

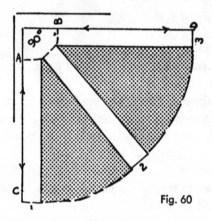

Fig. 60

3. Divide each skirt section, front and back, into three equal parts.
4. Slash the slash lines.
5. Spread the hem of the skirt while maintaining the original waistline, placing sections 1 and 3 against the square (the 90° angle of your triangle). This will place the straight grain at the side seams A–C and B–D; the center front and center back will be on the bias.
6. Correct the waistline with a curved line.
7. Complete the pattern.

The circle skirt

The circle skirt is produced in the same way, except that the waistline A–B represents one half the waistline measurement for front, or one half the back waistline measurement; A–C is placed on a fold of the material (Fig. 61). This will place the straight grain at center front, center back, and the side seams.

NOTE: All bias areas will stretch. In a circle skirt there is the additional pull on the waistline of the weight of the material. Therefore, it is best to make the waistline measurement of the skirt between 1" to 2" less than the actual measurement. The new measurement also tends to make the skirt fit more smoothly over the hips and lowers the point at which the folds or ripples start. This new waistline is then eased into the waistband whose measurements are in *no way changed*.

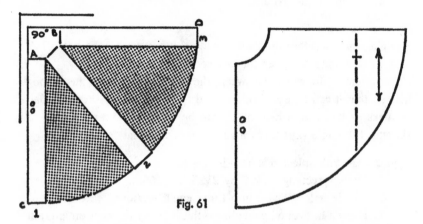

Fig. 61

If piecing of material is necessary, it should be done with the grain of the fabric as if to widen the fabric and in such position that it will be lost in the folds of the skirt. Note the dotted line in the diagram.

For the circle skirt use material that will drape easily and fall gracefully.

Another short cut
With the foregoing principles in mind, it should be possible for you to make a circle skirt merely by knowing the waist measurement and the length of the skirt.

   1. Draw the necessary square with your tailor's square or triangle and yardstick (Fig. 62a).

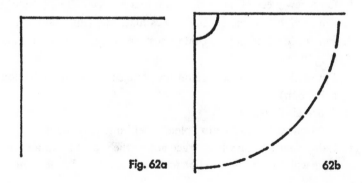

Fig. 62a   62b

2. Establish the waistline—waist measurement less 2″ (Fig. 62b). The front waistline is generally 1″ larger than the back waistline.
3. Starting from the waistline, measure down the length of the skirt in a sufficient number of places to produce the curve at the sweep of the skirt (Fig. 62b).
4. Complete the pattern.

A note on hems

Straight hems, whether on slim or wide skirts, usually take hems 1½″ to 3″. (They may be wider for any special reasons.)

Curved hems—the wider the sweep, the narrower the hem; just enough hem so that it can be eased or steamed to fit without resorting to darts or tucks or bunches; a hem of 1″ can be eased so, except in very full skirts; a full circle skirt takes a rolled hem or a bias facing.

Type 2—the knife-pleated skirt (Fig. 63–65)

1. Draw a rectangle 1½″ by 2½″ (Fig. 63a).
2. Divide it lengthwise into three equal sections.
3. Draw a horizontal guide line—this is really the horizontal grain line at right angles to the first line.
4. Slash on slash lines.

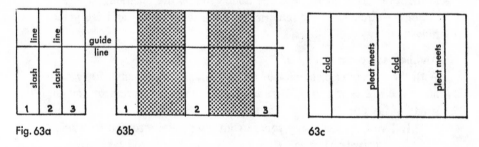

Fig. 63a   63b   63c

5. On a new piece of paper draw a horizontal guide line (Fig. 63b).
6. Pin section 1 to paper, guide lines matching (Fig. 63b).
7. Pin section 2 to paper, guide lines matching, 1″ from section 1 (Fig. 63b).
8. Pin section 3 to paper, guide lines matching, 1″ from section 2 (Fig. 63b).
9. Trace all lines.
10. Fold on each fold line to "pleat meet" line (Fig. 63c).
11. Using your tracing wheel, trace across the top and bottom lines. This will give the proper line for the underpleat. While it makes

very little difference in this particular exercise, it is well to get into the habit. It will make a very big difference where a shaped area is involved.

For gathers or shirring in place of pleats, follow steps 1 to 9.

There are many types of pleats. The most common are:

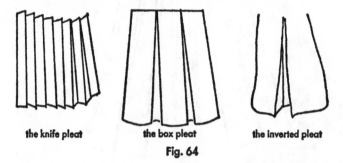

the knife pleat   the box pleat   the inverted pleat

Fig. 64

The pattern will depend on how the pleat is folded and the depth of the pleat. In each case there will be a fold line and a "meet pleat" line. In general, pleats in heavier materials should be deep, or the effect of the pleat is lost. Lightweight materials may have shallow pleats. When using heavy materials, try not to overlap or lay pleat on pleat; this will result in too much bulk. But with lightweight materials this may be done with fine effect for extra fullness. Normally each pleat takes three times its own width.

Fullness may be added vertically (lengthwise) as well as horizontally. You will learn how to do this in a later exercise.

A curve that comes to you straight

A straight length of material, if sufficiently darted (Fig. 65a), will produce a curved effect (Fig. 65b).

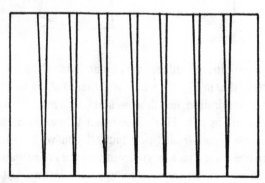

Fig. 65a

Darts may be stitched inside or outside. A series of outside darts can be very effective.

Actually this is the reverse of the slash and spread.

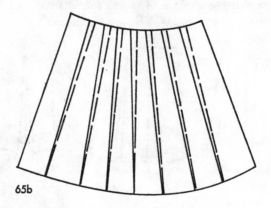

65b

"MORE" MAY BE BETTER

Unstitched dart control

A certain amount of fullness can be gotten just by using the *dart control unstitched*. The dart area may be gathered, as in Fig. 66a, or just left hanging, as in the box jacket (Fig. 66b). Add the necessary length at side front.

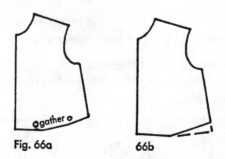

Fig. 66a   66b

Bloused effect—additional fullness may be added to the above pattern for the effect in the bodice in Fig. 67, which is gathered at the waistline.

If a bloused effect is desired, length as well as width must be added. Notice the deeper curve in Fig. 67b. This added length allows for the bust contour while keeping the center front fairly taut. If you wish more blousiness over the entire area, add extra length evenly to the entire waistline of Fig. 67c. Now look back at the torso yoke on p. 54. Extra width and length can be added to the upper bodice in the same way.

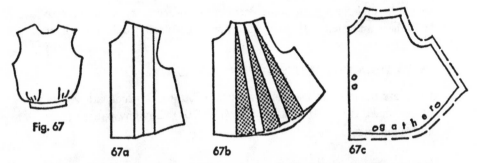

Fig. 67   67a   67b   67c

Here are a few effects which can be achieved in bodices using the principle of slash and spread (Figs. 68–79).

Bodice with gathers at shoulders
Correct the shoulder line with a smooth continuous curve coming midway between high and low points at shoulder sections.

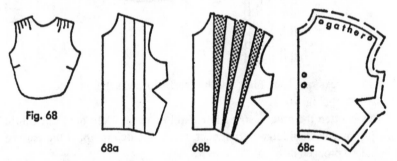

Fig. 68   68a   68b   68c

In slashing it is easier if you slash *to* the edge but not through. Spread to any fullness you wish. You may have to experiment to determine just how much fullness you want. Remember to keep fullness 1″ from the neckline and armhole for a smoother fit.

Bodice with gathers or pleats at shoulder and waistline
Correct the shoulder line and the waistline.

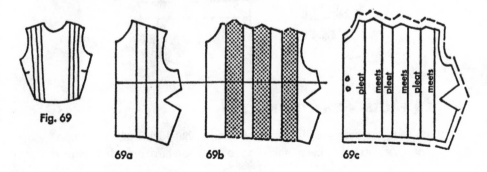

Fig. 69   69a   69b   69c

Notice the underarm dart. Some dart control is necessary in addition to the gathers and pleats. If there were none, the pleats would open over the bust.

AN ALTERNATE METHOD FOR TUCKS OR PLEATS

If you are planning to use narrow tucks or pin tucks which are ⅛" or smaller, make these in the fabric first (Fig. 70a). Lay any pattern piece on this and cut as usual.

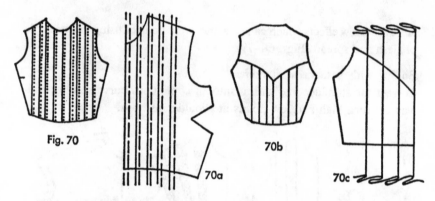

Fig. 70   70a   70b   70c

Wider tucks or pleats may also be worked out in this manner for any special effect (Fig. 70c).

This is often the case in striped or plaid material. Fold out your fabric first just as you would like it to appear, pin it or stitch it, apply the pattern piece, and proceed as usual.

This can be done horizontally as well as vertically (Fig. 71).

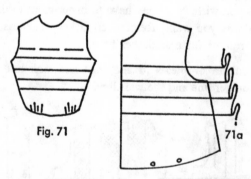

Fig. 71   71a

OLD FACTS—NEW POSSIBILITIES

This book has been growing like the "House that Jack Built." Each new bit of information has been tacked on to what you have already mastered.

As you go on you will find more and more that *several* features or principles are combined in each pattern design. While more complex, the patterns become more interesting, more appealing, and more wearable. The patterns which follow in this chapter are all actually variations and combinations of what you have learned thus far.

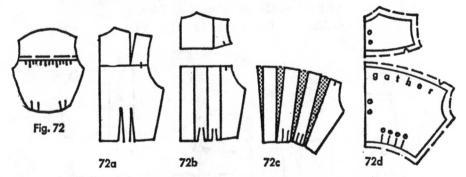

Fig. 72

72a   72b   72c   72d

Here is a back bodice with a yoke which has gathers below it for extra fullness (Fig. 72). The dart control is retained at the waistline in two dart tucks. Note that half the amount of spread is added to the center back so fullness is continuous.

The back bodice in Fig. 73 has a yoke and a box pleat at the center back. In this design the dart control appears as gathers at the waistline.

If you can follow these diagrams without directions, you are well on your way to successful pattern making.

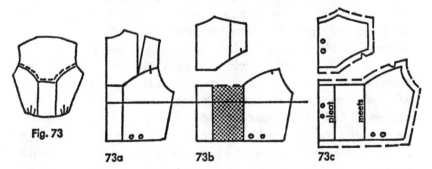

Fig. 73

73a   73b   73c

Some useful tips

The box pleat in a skirt is produced in this same way.

Pleats that are to be pressed are designed on the straight of the fabric; you can see what a pressing problem they would be otherwise.

Allow twice the desired depth of the pleat. In Fig. 73b, the 4″ depth makes a 2″ pleat. Unless the material is very sheer, when designing a series of pleats, see that they don't overlap. Overlapping causes bulk.

Make this blouse with an inverted pleat and yoke; *the dart appears as gathers*

In this pleat the folds of the pleat appear on the surface while the pleat itself is on the underside.

Trace the back-bodice sloper.

Locate the yoke line and the pleat line (Fig. 74a).

Extend the shoulder dart to the yoke line (Fig. 74a).

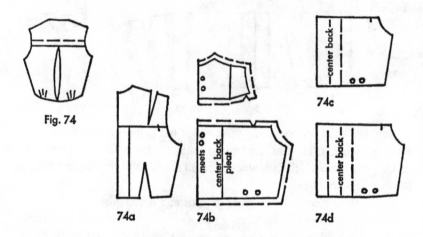

Fig. 74

74a   **74b**   **74c**   **74d**

In the previous exercise you learned that a 2″ pleat requires a 4″ depth. This is true whether the pleat is box or inverted. It would be quite easy in this design merely to extend the center back by 4″ as in the accompanying Fig. 74b. If the yoke, however, is shaped instead of straight, as this one is, you would run into difficulty. Better learn how it is constructed. Fold on center back and trace (with tracing wheel) the pleat line. Unfold the pattern top and bottom; this will give you the part of the pleat which folds back against the bodice (Fig. 74c). You need another piece to bring the pleat back to the center back. Fold on the new edge and trace once more as indicated. Open pattern (Fig. 74d). Complete the pattern.

You try it!

Now see if you can make the pattern for this blouse with its shaped yoke. In Fig. 75 you will find the sketch and the completed pattern.

You work out the construction pattern.

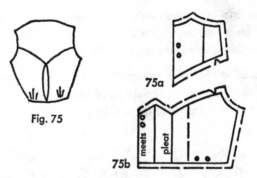

Fig. 75

75a

75b

Anywhere you wish it

Additional fullness may appear anywhere you want it. Try this bodice variation.

1. Locate the style line of the front panel (Fig. 76a).
2. Indicate the new position to which dart control will be shifted (Fig. 76a).
3. Cut away the center front panel; shift the dart control in the side section as indicated. This will produce some fullness but not enough to be interesting or pleasing (Fig. 76b).

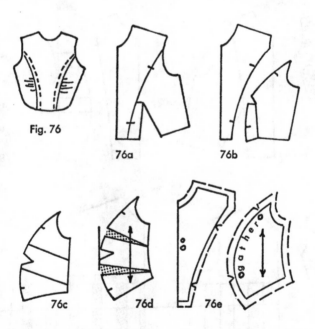

Fig. 76

76a

76b

76c

76d

76e

4. Draw two slash lines above and below the dart (Fig. 76c).
5. Slash on these lines and spread for desired fullness (Fig. 76d).

6. Grain line—draw a straight line connecting the small dart points. The grain line is parallel to this line (Fig. 76d).
7. Trace the pattern and complete (Fig. 76e).

NOTE: "o-gather-o" includes newly added fullness (Fig. 76e).
Here is a group of interesting variations of fullness. The diagrams tell the story. Can you follow them? (Figs. 77–79).

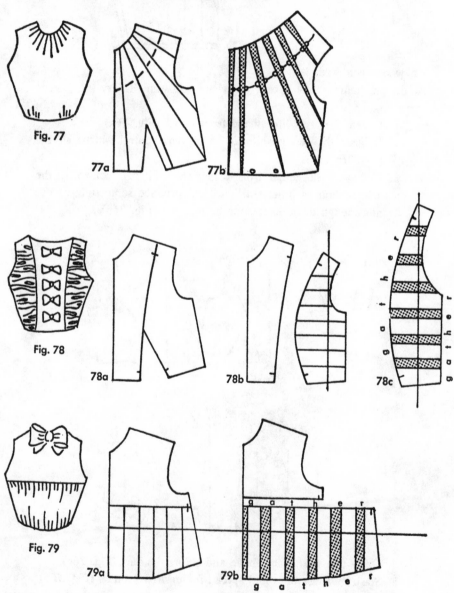

Fig. 77   77a   77b

Fig. 78   78a   78b   78c

Fig. 79   79a   79b

SKIRTS GET IN THE ACT

The principles you have learned in the preceding exercises apply to skirts as well as bodices. Work out the patterns for these two skirts.

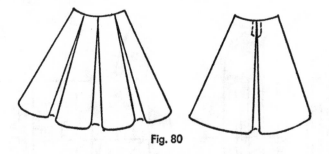

Fig. 80

Following are a few skirts using the very same ideas as the bodices (Figs. 81–90). Here is a skirt with a yoke and flared section below.

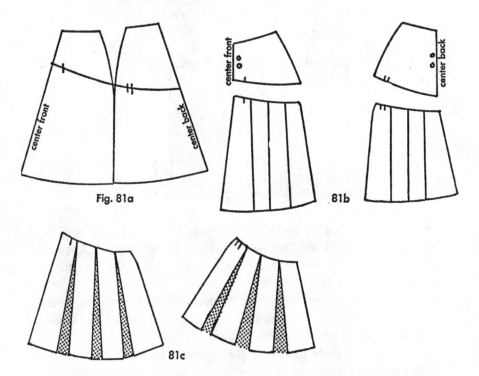

Fig. 81a   81b

81c

1. Proceed as for the four-gored skirt through step 7 (see p. 40).
2. Locate the style line for the yoke. This is best done with the side seams and hip touching to ensure a continuous line (Fig. 81a).

3. Locate notches.
4. Cut the yokes away.
5. Draw slash lines parallel to the grain line (Fig. 81b).
6. Slash and spread for desired fullness (Fig. 81c).

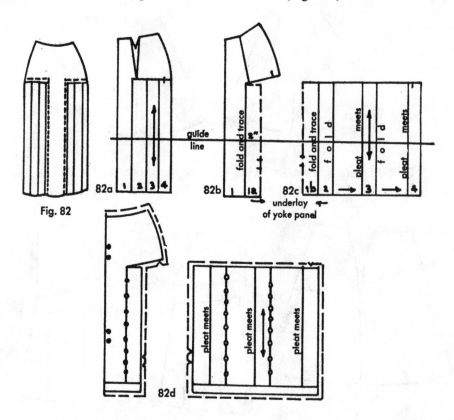

Fig. 82

This is an interesting skirt with a yoke panel and released pleats.

Fig. 82a. Locate the design lines for the yoke panel and the pleats. Locate notches; locate the grain line on section 3. Draw a guide line. Lengthen the dart to the yoke line.

Fig. 82b. Cut the pattern apart. Close the dart. Section 1a is 2″ over and represents the underlay of the first pleat. A seam will occur here, as no seam should be visible at the folded edge.

Fig. 82c. Draw a guide line on another piece of paper. Lay section 2 on it, guide lines matching. Place sections 3 and 4 in like manner 4″ away from each other.

So far we have added only 2″ for the underlay for the first pleat. We need 2″ more. This is added to section 2 so that it will meet the seam of the front section. Fold and trace section 2; open. Fold the pleats in the manner indicated—toward the center or toward the side seam as desired. Trace with tracing wheel. This gives the proper shape to the underlay. With the pleats folded, check to see if this has the same style line as in the original design.

Fig. 82d. Trace the final pattern, being sure to trace the notches, the fold lines, the pleat lines, and the grain lines. Add the hem and seam allowance.

The design in Fig. 83 is similar to the preceding one except for the shaped yoke panel. It is constructed in the same way.

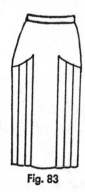

Fig. 83

Always a favorite—the skirt with a kick pleat (*a kick pleat is an inverted pleat*)

In the foregoing exercises, pleats appeared all in one with the bodice or skirt. Often, however, pleats are used on a seam line. When this is done, the underlay is designed as a separate piece.

There are certain advantages to this. The pleat may be located only in that area where it is needed or wanted; it is not necessary to carry the extra bulk of material up to the waist. (Most women are padded enough in this area already.) The pleat may be added to a shaped piece—as in a four-gored skirt. The underlay may be so shaped that it is larger at the hem line than at the start of the pleat.

All of these factors make for a more graceful skirt. The following exercise demonstrates this method.

1. Trace the front-skirt sloper. (The back is done in the same way.)
2. Locate the pleat as indicated; A–B is squared off the center front (Fig. 84a).
3. Fold the pattern on the center front and trace A–D and D–C and the hem line (Fig. 84b).

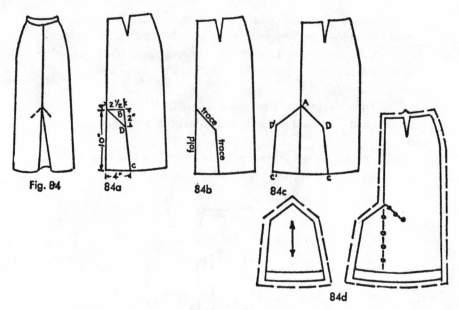

Fig. 84   84a   84b   84c

84d

4. Open the pattern and mark D^1 and C^1 (Fig. 84c). The underlay is $A–D–C–C^1–D^1–A$.

5. Lay a new piece of paper beneath the underlay and trace it. Trace the original center front line, which will become the grain of the underlay section (Fig. 84d).

6. Complete the pattern. Be sure to mark the fold line for the pleat and the stitching line (Fig. 84d).

For a pleat in a gored skirt the same procedure is followed (Fig. 85).

Fig. 85

Understand a diagram?

On the following pages are a number of sketches and construction patterns (Figs. 86–90). You may feel justifiably proud if you can read and understand the diagrams. Make one up just to see if it really does work.

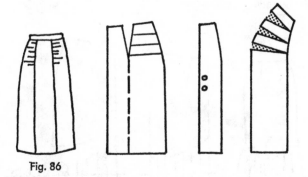

Fig. 86

Remember that the dart may be moved 1″ to 2″ in either direction.

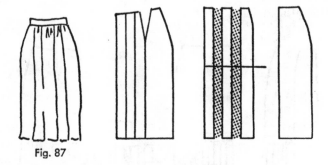

Fig. 87

The dart has been moved 1″ to the side seam.

Trumpet skirt

Fig. 88

The trumpet skirt is based on the gored skirt. The treatment for each gore is illustrated.

Skirt with flounce

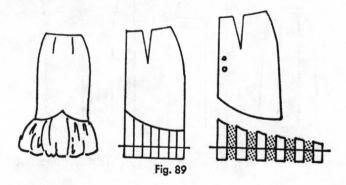

Fig. 89

Skirt with pleated inset

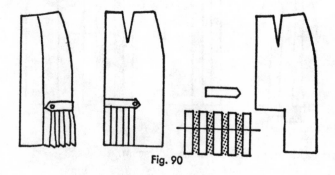

Fig. 90

CHAPTER 4

A basic pattern of your own

If you run true to form, you are chafing at the bit by now. How eager you are to try out these pattern principles on a real life-size pattern of your very own instead of playing around with scale models! This chapter tells you how to make the basic pattern you will need for creating your own designs.

WHAT IS A BASIC PATTERN?

All new patterns are variations of a basic pattern or sloper. Sometimes this pattern is called the foundation pattern, the master pattern, or the block pattern.

Standard-size patterns start with standard-size slopers made from tables of standard measurements to fit standard figures (as rare as the proverbial hen's teeth). Custom-made patterns are variations of personal slopers made from personal measurements to fit individual figures. Since most of you will be creating patterns for yourselves, you will need to know how to make the basic pattern with which to start your designing.

A few suggestions before you begin

Read the chapter through first so you may have some idea of its scope. Don't get excited about ¼″ personal measurements; generally the muslin fitting will take care of such small changes. Lay out your basic pattern with sufficient room for alteration around it. Keep your measurement chart before you as you work. Perhaps it would be easier to handle if you made a simplified form and put it on a separate sheet of paper.

A note of warning. You will find that the most controversial subject in the world is the subject of your personal measurements. A tape measure in the hand can be a dangerous weapon. Remember that you really are sweet-tempered. Keep calm.

What pieces are necessary for this pattern?

There are five pieces necessary for this pattern—the bodice front, the bodice back, the skirt front, the skirt back, and a sleeve. The professional pattern maker will draft this from a set of measurements. The actual drafting is somewhat complicated and unnecessary for the home sewer.

A basic pattern should contain certain basic information as to:

size—the length, width, and proportions which correspond to body measurements

ease—an amount added to the body measurements in length and width to allow for body movements and comfort in wearing

dart control—the proper amount and the proper placement of the darts in each pattern piece

contour—the outline, or silhouette of the piece which follows the proper fit of the body at neck, shoulders, armhole, side seams, waistline, and hem line

Each pattern piece should be one piece. It should have no seam allowance. It should look like this:

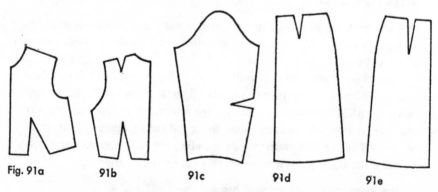

Fig. 91a   91b   91c   91d   91e

The bodice front (Fig. 91a) has a high, round neck, an armhole for a set-in sleeve, and a dart at the waistline. In a figure with a large bust measurement where the dart control is too much to place in one dart, the dart control may be divided. Sometimes it is divided between a waistline and an underarm dart; or it may be divided between a waistline and shoulder dart. Remember that all darts are worked from bust-point height and they must be placed in this position on your pattern.

The bodice back (Fig. 91b) has a high, round neck, an armhole for a set-in sleeve, a shoulder dart, and a waistline dart which extends to the fleshy part of the lower shoulder blade.

The skirt front (Fig. 91d) has one dart placed over the high point of the front hip. The waistline matches the bodice-front waistline.

The skirt back (Fig. 91e) has one dart placed over the high point of the buttock. The waistline matches the bodice-back waistline.

The long sleeve (Fig. 91c) fits the armhole of the bodice front and back plus a little ease. It has one dart at the elbow.

Where can I get these pattern pieces?
Since the sloper is not being drafted from scratch, it will be necessary to start with standard-size pieces and alter them to the required measurements. Almost all of the big pattern companies offer basic patterns in standard sizes, which are excellent for this purpose. There are also several commercial basic patterns on the market which cost a little more. If none of these is available, a good basic pattern can be made by piecing one together from any old patterns in your collection or any suitable new patterns which contain the features we want.

What size pattern shall I get?
The answer to this question requires some honest measurement-taking and some thought. You cannot go by the size you wear in ready-to-wear clothing. Designers and manufacturers do not adhere to a uniform, standard set of measurements. Most pattern companies, however, have accepted a standard set of body measurements as a basis for their patterns, based on statistics issued by the U. S. Government. You will find this table of measurements in all pattern books and on pp. 287 and 288.

If your body measurements correspond to a given set of measurements listed in this chart, choosing your pattern is simple. But alas! This is rarely true. So many of us find that our tops don't match our bottoms. When the bust measurement corresponds, the waist and hips do not. If the hip measurement is correct, the bust and waist don't match. And as if that weren't trouble enough, there is the problem of shoulders broad and narrow. What size to choose?

Choose that size standard pattern which most *nearly* meets your measurements. Since the bodice is the most difficult to fit, let that determine the size. For average figures the bust measurement is a good guide. But consider also the build of neck, shoulders, and chest. These can be difficult to fit. It is ofttimes better to choose a smaller pattern which fits these areas and adjust the rest. It is comparatively simple to let out a pattern at bust, waist, or hips.

If the discrepancy between bodice and skirt is very great—say, a difference of more than one size—buy two patterns, the correct size for the bodice and the correct size for the skirt. Alter both so they join accurately at the waistline.

—— AND A YARD WIDE!

How to take your body measurements

You will need help on this since there are certain important measurements which you cannot possibly take for yourself. It is a good plan to get several sewers together who will take measurements and who will fit the muslins for each other. It is really more fun this way, too. It takes some of the sting out of this painful procedure to discover that the rest of the girls are in the same sorry predicament. Swear each other to eternal secrecy and begin!

WHO . . . ME?

The best measurements are taken in a slip over your best bra and girdle (if you wear one). Wear shoes with the heel height you generally favor. Figure 92 will illustrate where these measurements are taken. Figure 93 will show the corresponding measurements on the pattern. Make a chart for yourself like the one below.

item	me	plus ease	total	pattern
1. *bust*—taken over the high point of the bust and across the shoulder blades in back		plus 3″ 2″ in front 1″ in back		
2. *waistline*—taken snugly in the hollow of the waist or where you would like your waistline to be		plus ½″ to 1″ half in front half in back		
3. *hips*—taken generally about 7″ below the waist or around the fullest part of the hips; if lower or higher than 7″, note this on the chart		plus 2″ half in front half in back		

The bodice

Now, take a piece of string and tie it snugly around your waistline. Push the string into the position you want for a waistline. This will give you a fixed point from which and to which you may measure.

item	me	plus ease	total	pattern
4. *center front*—from the hollow between the collarbones to the string		no ease		
5. *center back*—bend head forward and locate the bone at which the head bends; straighten and measure from this bone at the neckline to the string		no ease		
6. *over bust length*—from the middle of the shoulder seam over the bust to the string		no ease		
7. *over shoulder blades*—from the middle of the shoulder seam over the shoulder blades to the string		no ease		
8. *bust-point height*—from the highest point of the bust to the string		no ease		
9. *bust-point width*—from bust point to bust point		no ease		
10. *shoulder-blade height*—from the prominent part of the shoulder blade to the string		no ease		
11. *shoulder-blade width*—from the prominent or fleshy part of one shoulder blade to the other		no ease		
12. *across-the-chest width*—from the crease where arm meets body to the opposite crease		¼″ to ½″		
13. *across-the-shoulder-blades width*—from the crease where arm meets the body to the opposite crease		¼″ to ½″		

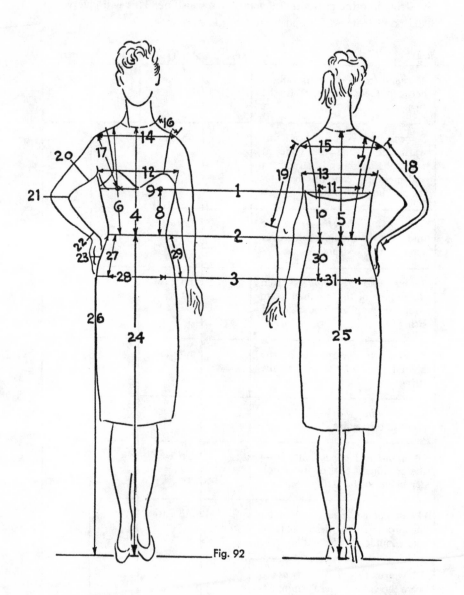

Fig. 92

Where to take the measurements

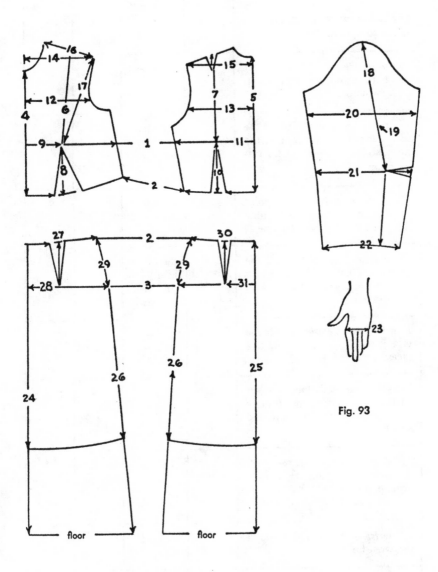

Fig. 93

Corresponding positions of measurements on the pattern

item	me	plus ease	total	pattern
14. *upper-front width*—shoulder point to shoulder point; this is the prominent bone where the arm is hinged; the measurement is taken straight across		no ease		
15. *upper-back width*—shoulder point to shoulder point taken straight across		no ease		
16. *shoulder seam*—from the shoulder point to the base of the neck, slightly forward of the trapezius muscle		no ease		
17. *shoulder-point-to-bust-point height*—this will help determine the slope of the shoulder line		no ease		
18. *overarm length*—from the shoulder point to the elbow to the wrist at the little finger, with the arm bent		the bent arm provides the ease		
19. *shoulder to elbow*—while the tape is still in position, note this measurement				
20. *girth*—around the heaviest part of the upper arm; usually about midway between elbow and shoulder		2″		
21. *elbow circumference*—with the arm bent, measure loosely around the elbow		the bent arm provides the ease		
22. *wrist*—taken loosely around the wrist bone		½″ to 1″		
23. *knuckle circumference*—around the fullest part of the hand as you would slip the hand through a sleeve		½″		

The skirt

Tie a second string around your hips (or fullest part).

item	me	plus ease	total	pattern
24. *center-front length*—from waistline string to floor; subtract the number of inches the skirt is worn from the floor		no ease		
25. *center-back length*—from waistline string to the floor; subtract the number of inches the skirt is worn from the floor		no ease		
26. *side length*—from waistline string to the floor on the side seam; subtract the number of inches the skirt is worn from the floor		no ease		
27. *front-hip depth*—from the waistline string to the hip string over the front hipbone		no ease		
28. *front-hip width*—from one front hipbone to the other		no ease		
29. *side-hip depth*—from waistline string to the hip string on the side seam		no ease		
30. *back-hip depth*—from the waistline string to the hip string over the high point of the buttock		no ease		
31. *back-hip width*—from the high point of one buttock to the other		no ease		

This lengthy list of measurements by no means exhausts the list of possible body measurements, but it is comprehensive enough to enable you to alter your standard-size pattern so that it will come close to your own measurements. At the same time it is not too difficult for an amateur.

EASY DOES IT!

Ease in addition to body measurements

If you were to construct your clothes merely on body measurements, you might look very glamorous but you would not be able to wash dishes, make beds, drive the car, battle the subway crowds, or keep up with your active children.

Body measurements are not enough. Clothes must have room for body movement, room to make them comfortable to wear, room to conceal certain figure defects. This additional room is called *ease*.

All garments have ease in varying amounts. An evening dress has less ease than a shirtwaist dress for golfing. Some women like to wear their clothes a little more snugly than others. The amount of ease is a matter of personal preference as well as function. Column 3 in your chart indicates an average amount. You may add a little if you like to wear your clothes somewhat looser or subtract a little if you like them tighter. Pattern companies all allow more ease than is indicated here. But they vary in the amount of ease which they add to the standard measurements. Each has its own policy in this regard. This accounts for the differences in the fit of patterns produced by the various pattern companies, though most of them start with the same set of body measurements.

In making your basic pattern, you must work with the *total amount of your measurements plus ease*. For example, if your bust measures 34" and you add 3" for ease, then 37" is the amount you need in your pattern. If your waistline measures 26" and you add ½" for ease, then 26½" is the amount you will work with. If your hip measures 36" plus 2" for ease, then 38" is the amount to consider.

MAKE THE PATTERN

Prepare your pattern pieces

Lay out the five pieces which you need for your basic pattern—bodice front, bodice back, skirt front, skirt back, and sleeve. Cut off all seam allowances; they will only confuse you. Press the pieces flat with a warm iron. Work with these tissue pattern pieces if you have to make only simple changes. For more extensive alterations trace them on blank paper (shelf paper will do fine) and leave plenty of room around each piece for changes.

Measure your pattern pieces

Now measure your standard-size pattern for each item listed in your chart. Write down the measurement in the proper column.

Remember:
1. The standard pattern already has had ease added to it so you do not need to do so.
2. The standard pattern is half a pattern so you will need to halve all your width measurements.

Compare:

Compare your measurements plus ease with the pattern measurements. Decide where and how much the pattern needs to be altered. Note these changes right on your pattern or tracing. You may have to do a little arithmetic at this point. Don't bother about very small changes of ¼″ or less. These tiny adjustments can be made at the seams.

MAKE IT FIT

How to alter the standard-size sloper to fit your personal measurements

A few reminders

Any changes you make in a standard sloper are, in effect, designing, since you are altering the shape of the original pattern piece. Think of your pattern alteration in this way and go about it as if you were creating a new design. You are, really. You are creating a pattern that will fit your contours.

These few reminders will serve as a review of principles developed in the preceding chapters:
1. The larger the dart, the greater the resulting bulge.
2. The smaller the bulge, the less dart control you will need.
3. Flat figures, whether heavy or slight, have less dart control because of the smaller difference between measurements at high point and measurement of adjoining area.
4. You may add or subtract in the dart area.
5. Too much dart control in one dart throws the grain off; it is better to divide the control in two darts.
6. In large-bosomed figures, darts in several positions will give a better fit—more darts, more fit.
7. Darts can be relocated to positions where they really belong and where they will do most good.
8. Changes are very specific; make them only where indicated by your figure.
9. Make each change, or alteration separately, one at a time, as you would go about creating a new design.

10. In making a pattern larger, use the slash-and-spread principle. Slash and open evenly for balanced changes; slash and spread as for circularity where fullness is required in one place.

11. In making a pattern smaller, tuck or overlap to the required measurement.

12. Add in length as well as in width to accommodate heavy bulges such as a large bust, a large abdomen, round shoulders or back, a prominent seat.

13. Correct jagged lines resulting from overlapping or spreading.

14. Use all your tools—the armscye and French curve for armholes and necklines, the curved stick or ruler on the side seam of the skirt or any other place where the curve is similar.

15. All slashes in patterns should be at right angles to the grain, either vertical or horizontal.

A little arithmetic

If, in doing your arithmetic, you discover you have to make too many changes or to make *over-all* changes amounting to 2″ or more, then you had better get the next size pattern. There is a 2″ differential between pattern sizes. This does not apply in the case where most of the pattern fits but some change has to be made that amounts to more than 2″ perhaps at the bust or waist or hips.

A little courage

Feel free to cut sections of your pattern apart and adjust for length and width just as you would work out a new pattern.

Where you slash and spread, insert paper in the opening and pin or tape into position. Don't forget to use a guide line as a help in lining up these slashed-and-spread areas.

A little judgment

Try not to change the shape of the neckline, shoulders, and armhole any more than is absolutely necessary. If changes are made in the armhole, use your armscye (✳17 curve) to correct the line or superimpose the original pattern and trace the armhole.

And once more, *make changes only where needed*.

Over-all changes in length

The simplest changes to make are those in length (Fig. 94). Decide whether the pattern is too long or too short. Decide just where it will need to be changed—above or below the bust point, above or below the hips, above or below the elbow, or perhaps in both places. Will an adjustment merely at waistline, wrist, or hem line do? Refer to your chart. Make the changes *only where needed*.

Wherever you wish to make this type of balanced change, draw a line at right angles to the grain line.

To add length, slash the pattern and spread to the desired amount. Insert paper. Fasten with pins or tape.

To shorten, overlap or tuck to the desired amount. Fasten with pins or tape.

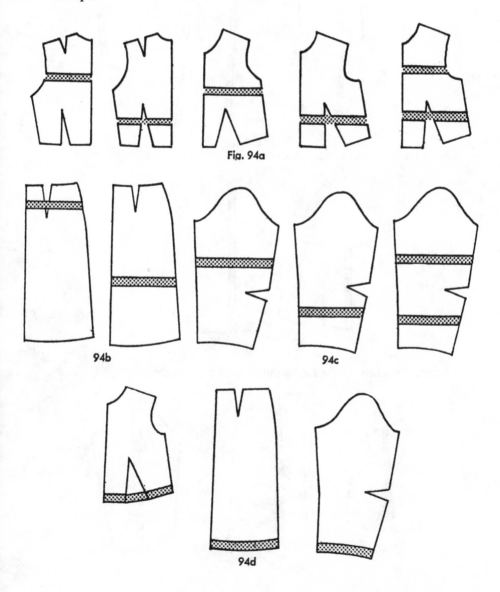

Fig. 94a

94b   94c

94d

Over-all changes in width (Fig. 95)

Study your measurements carefully. They will guide you as to where to
make your balanced changes. Your pattern may be made larger or smaller
in the following ways:

at side seams

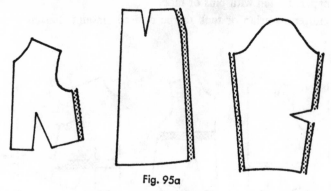

Fig. 95a

at center front and center back

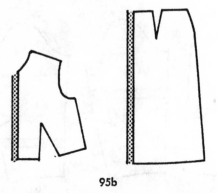

95b

through the center of the section, preferably through the dart

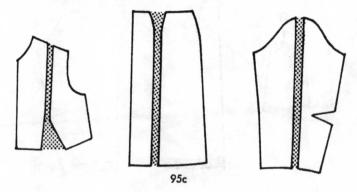

95c

small amounts in all three places

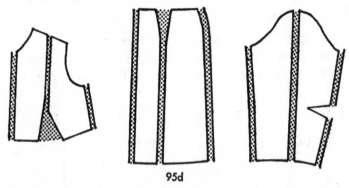

95d

CAUTION: Do not add or subtract more than ⅝" at the side seams, center front, or center back, otherwise you will distort the shape of the neckline or armhole. For changes over ⅝" make your changes in several places as in Fig. 95d. This will change the entire pattern piece proportionately.

How to lengthen center front or center back only
The foregoing were over-all changes. Sometimes only the center front or center back needs lengthening or shortening while the side seam remains the same (Fig. 96). In this case we use the principle of slash and spread or slash and overlap, as for circularity.

1. Where the bodice needs change below the armhole—as for a large bosom:
   Slash and spread. Extend the center front or center back line. Take off the side seam at the waistline an amount equal to that added to the center (Fig. 96a).

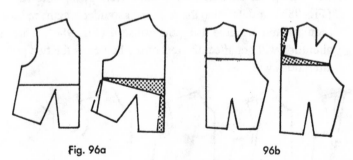

Fig. 96a   96b

2. Where the bodice needs change above the armhole—as for round-shouldered or fleshy back:
   Slash and spread. Extend the center front or center back line.

This adds an extra amount to the upper portion of front or back.
On the back add a dart to the back neckline to take out an amount
equal to that added at the center (Fig. 96b).

How to shorten center front or center back only

Decide whether the upper or lower part of the bodice needs change (Figs.
97a and 97c). This process is the reverse of the previous one.

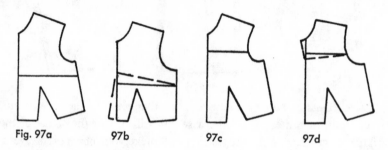

Fig. 97a   97b   97c   97d

1. Slash and overlap the required amount (Figs. 97b and 97d).
2. Taper to nothing at the side seam (Fig. 97b) or the armhole
   (Fig. 97d).
3. Correct the jog at the waistline (Fig. 97b) or the neckline (Fig.
   97d).
4. Make any necessary adjustment at the side seam or dart to make
   the waistline measurement match the body measurement.
5. The back is worked in the same way.

How to make shoulder changes

1. To widen the shoulders, slash and spread; taper to the waist (Fig.
   98a).
2. To shorten the shoulders, slash and overlap; taper to the waist
   (Fig. 98b) or determine the required shoulder length; redraw the
   shoulder and armhole using the armscye (Fig. 98c). This latter
   alteration will not affect the rest of the bodice as the two previous
   alterations will.

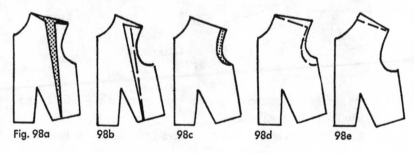

Fig. 98a   98b   98c   98d   98e

3. For square shoulders, raise the shoulder and raise the armhole a corresponding amount (Fig. 98d). Redraw, using the armscye, or trace from the original pattern armhole.
4. For sloping shoulders, raise at the neckline, slope to the shoulder point (Fig. 98e).

How to change the neckline

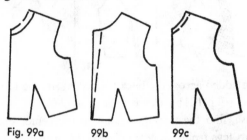

Fig. 99a   99b   99c

If the neckline is too small, lower the neckline slightly (Fig. 99a), or add the necessary amount at the neckline, taper to the waist (Fig. 99b). The new line becomes the new center front. This is a good change where the garment pulls across the chest.

If the neckline is too large, insert paper at the neck. Draw a new line where it will fit (Fig. 99c).

How to change the armhole

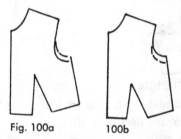

Fig. 100a   100b

If the armhole needs changing, be sure to change both front and back; be sure the side seams match. The notch is placed at the point where the armscye swings into the lower curve. Changes are made from this point.

To lower the armhole, use the armscye and draw a curve below the notch (Fig. 100a).

To raise the armhole, draw curves below the notch, using the armscye (Fig. 100b).

More ease

Sometimes a little more ease across the bust or across the back will make a garment more comfortable.

Ease may be added across the bust in the following manner. Cut out the dart. Slash from the dart point to the shoulder. Spread at the dart point (Fig. 101a).

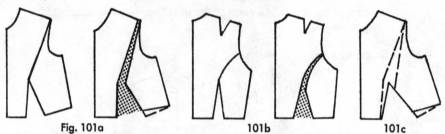

Fig. 101a   101b   101c

Ease may be added across the back from the armhole to the dart point in the same way (Fig. 101b). Correct the armhole.

In either case, find the new dart point in the center of the opening. Redraw the dart legs from the new point to the original dart ends. Make them equal in length. Trim off the jog (Fig. 101c).

Darts in position

Locate the darts in their proper places and draw them in position.

1. Bodice

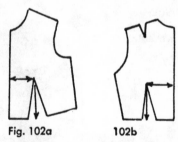

Fig. 102a   102b

Starting at bodice center front, measure half of the bust-point width at bust-point height. Relocate dart (Fig. 102a).

Starting at bodice center back, measure half of the shoulder-blade width at shoulder-blade height. Relocate dart (Fig. 102b).

2. Skirt

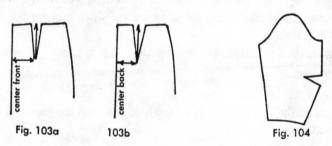

Fig. 103a   103b   Fig. 104

Starting at skirt center front, measure half of the front-hip width. Relocate dart (Fig. 103a).

Starting at skirt center back, measure half of the back-hip width at back-hip depth. Relocate dart (Fig. 103b).

3. Sleeve

In the sleeve, place the sleeve dart at the elbow (Fig. 104).

Waistline changes in bodice and skirt

1. Bodice

More waistline needed in bodice? Reduce the size of the dart or add to the side seam at the waistline; taper to the armhole. Or do both (Fig. 105a).

Less waistline desirable? Make a larger dart or take some off the waistline at the side seam; taper to the armhole. Or do both (Fig. 105b).

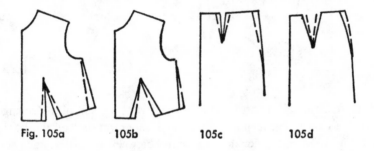

Fig. 105a   105b   105c   105d

2. Skirt

For more waistline width in skirt, reduce the size of the dart or add to the side seam at the waistline; taper to the hip. Or do both (Fig. 105c).

For less waistline width, make a larger dart or take off some of the side seam at the waistline; taper to the hip. Or do both (Fig. 105d).

Fig. 106

Additional hip width

For more hip width, measure the needed addition to the hip line. Use the curved stick to draw a gradual curve from waist to hip. Continue the amount added to the hip in a straight line to the hem (Fig. 106).

Where length as well as width is needed

1. Bodice

Where length as well as width is needed, slash and spread vertically as well as horizontally (Figs. 107a and 107b). Relocate the dart point at the center of the dart opening. Draw new, equal dart legs; correct jog (Fig. 107c).

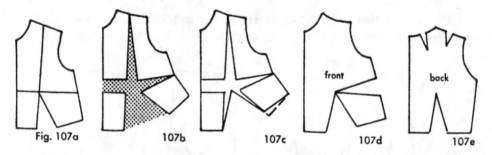

Fig. 107a   107b   107c   front 107d   back 107e

If there is too much dart control in one dart as a result of this change, divide the control between a waistline and underarm dart on the bodice front (Fig. 107d). Or divide the dart control between a waistline and neckline dart on the bodice back (Fig. 107e).

This principle works on skirts and sleeves, too.

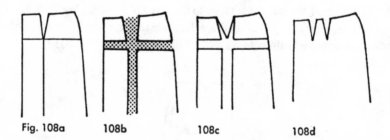

Fig. 108a   108b   108c   108d

2. Skirt

Where length as well as width is needed in the skirt, follow the same directions listed above. Slash and spread vertically as well as horizontally (Figs. 108a and 108b). Relocate dart (Fig. 108c). If the resulting dart is too large, then convert it to multiple darts as illustrated in Fig. 108d. These are the corrections for a prominent abdomen or prominent seat.

3. Sleeves

a. The entire sleeve

To make the sleeve longer and wider, slash and spread (Fig. 109a).

To make the sleeve shorter and narrower, slash and overlap or tuck; correct jog (Fig. 109b).

To widen the upper arm, slash and spread (Fig. 109c).

To reduce the upper arm, slash and overlap or tuck (Fig. 109d). Correct jog.

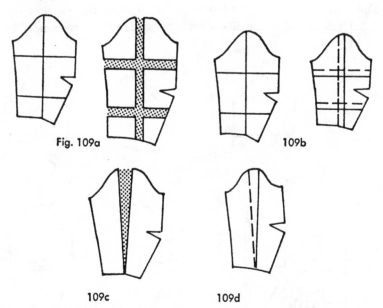

Fig. 109a   109b

109c   109d

b. The sleeve cap

To make the sleeve cap longer, rule off the cap evenly (Fig. 110a). Then slash and spread (Fig. 110b).

To make the sleeve cap shorter, overlap or tuck (Fig. 110c).

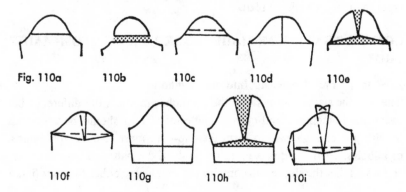

Fig. 110a   110b   110c   110d   110e

110f   110g   110h   110i

To make the sleeve cap wider, slash and spread vertically as well as horizontally (Figs. 110d and 110e).

To make the sleeve cap narrower, slash and overlap (Fig. 110f).

For a fuller sleeve cap with more width and more length in the upper arm, slash and spread vertically and horizontally (Fig. 110h).

For a narrower sleeve cap that is shorter and has less width in the upper arm, slash and overlap (Fig. 110i). Correct jog.

c. The elbow

For more elbow room, slash and spread, making a larger dart (Fig. 111a). Or slash below the elbow dart and spread to create a new dart (Fig. 111b).

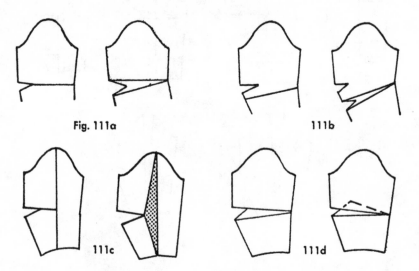

Fig. 111a   111b

111c   111d

For more elbow room and more width, slash and spread vertically and horizontally (Fig. 111c).

If less dart is desired at elbow, cut out dart; slash sleeve; close dart; taper to other side (Fig. 111d).

CHANGE THAT "HOMEMADE" LOOK TO A "CUSTOM-MADE" LOOK

How to fit the sleeve cap into the armhole

The way the sleeve cap fits into the armhole can affect the difference between the homemade and custom-made look. This should be a smooth fit with just enough ease to form the cap—no more. No bumps, lumps, or bubbles. Ofttimes this is more the fault of the pattern than the sewer. It is a sign that the sleeve cap contains too much ease either for your figure or for your fabric. Here is your big chance to get just the right amount for an easy fit.

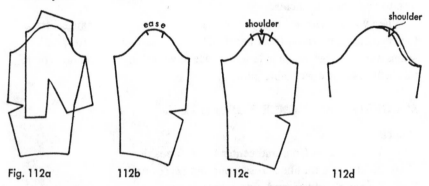

Fig. 112a   112b   112c   112d

The cap of the sleeve from underarm seam to underarm seam should fit the armhole of the bodice with about 1″ to 1½″ left over for ease. This can be tested by matching the sleeve cap to the armhole (Fig. 112a). Start at the underarm seam and pivot a tiny section, about ¼″ at a time, from the seam to the shoulder. Mark the place where the shoulder of the bodice appears on the sleeve cap, both front and back. You will find a space between these two points. This leftover area is the ease and should measure between 1″ to 1½″ (Fig. 112b). The shoulder notch of the sleeve cap is placed in the center of this area, thus dividing the ease equally between front and back (Fig. 112c). It should be at the crest of the curve. If it isn't, redraw the curve so that it will be (Fig. 112d).

If your comparison of sleeve cap and bodice armhole reveals too much ease, lower or narrow the sleeve cap, depending on your build. This can be done by the method illustrated in Fig. 110 or simply by redrawing the curve with your armscye. You will have to test this to see if you have the right amount.

If you have not enough ease, raise or widen the sleeve cap as illustrated in Fig. 110 or redraw the curve, using your armscye. Once more, the only way to tell if you have the right amount is by testing the sleeve cap in the armhole.

Figures are no more alike than thumbprints
There are an infinite variety and complexity of figure problems. It would be quite impossible to anticipate every possible contingency. But the foregoing principles should provide you with a method of working out a solution to your individual figure problem.

Study your measurement chart carefully and honestly. Analyze your figure problems, that is, how your measurements deviate from the standard measurements on which all commercial patterns are constructed. Select the appropriate alteration as outlined in this chapter. Adjust the standard pattern to your measurements.

When you are satisfied that you have made the necessary changes, trace the corrected pattern on fresh paper. Check to see that all corresponding seams and dart legs match in length. Place any markings or notations on it that will make it a workable pattern.

SUGGESTED SEQUENCE FOR FITTING

Bodice

1. pin center front and center back in position
2. check grain line across front and across back
3. pin shoulders and side seams tentatively
4. fit bust; check dart control
5. fit back; check dart control
6. pin corrected shoulder seam
7. pin corrected side seam
8. mark waistline
9. mark neckline
10. mark armhole

Skirt

1. pin center front and center back at waistline to bodice
2. pin hips at side seams, checking grain lines
3. fit area between hips and waist; check dart control
4. pin side seams, continuing line of bodice
5. mark waistline
6. mark hem line

Sleeves

1. pin seam
2. gather and shrink out fullness in sleeve cap
3. turn under seam allowance of sleeve cap
4. set top of cap at shoulder seam, matching notch to seam
5. pin in cap at upper armhole
6. check grain of sleeve cap and smoothness of fit
7. pin in underarm where it falls on bodice
8. check elbow dart
9. mark wrist length
10. mark armhole on bodice and place notches at cap and bodice front and back

NOW FOR THE TEST!

Make the muslin foundation pattern

Measurements alone, no matter how accurate or how extensive, cannot guarantee the proper fit of a garment. For a shoulder measurement 5" tells you nothing except that the shoulder is 5" long. But the 5" can be slanted, straight, or a concave curve, as in Fig. 113.

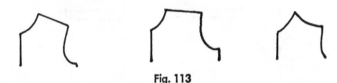

Fig. 113

It is necessary to test your pattern in actual material to make sure that not only lengths and widths and proportions are considered but curves and posture, also. A trial fitting in fabric may also show the advisability of departing somewhat from the actual measurements to create an illusion of a more beautifully proportioned figure. Your basic pattern should not only fit you, it should enhance you.

This test pattern is generally made of unbleached muslin of a medium weight. Sometimes it is made of checked gingham or percale. Old sheeting can be used if it is not too tough for pin fitting. Whatever you make it of, treat it as you would the finest satin or brocade. The proper care and preparation of your muslin will help determine the fit.

All materials are woven with lengthwise and crosswise threads. There are many variations in the design of the weave but all are woven in this way. This thread, whether lengthwise or crosswise, is the grain of the fabric. It is often called the straight of goods.

All materials, and therefore all garments, hang with the grain of the fabric. For this reason it is most important that all material be cut with a proper respect for the grain. It can make all the difference in the world between a garment that hangs right and one that does not. Every pattern piece, from the smallest stay or welt to the largest skirt or sleeve, has the grain marked on it. Generally the pattern is laid in such a way on the fabric that the straight of goods is parallel to the selvage, which is the vertical grain. (Sometimes, for effect, the pattern may be laid with the straight of goods parallel to the horizontal grain, or on the bias.)

Prepare the fabric

In order to make sure that these grain lines are in the proper position, you must prepare your fabric. If you can, tear your fabric horizontally. Fabric tears with the grain. Or pull a horizontal thread and cut on the line created by the pulled thread, a little at a time, until you have established the horizontal grain.

Pin the torn edges together. Pin the selvages together (Fig. 114). If the material does not lie smoothly in this position, dampen it and press it into position.

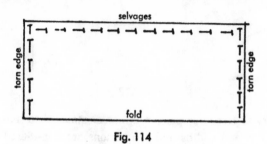

Fig. 114

Now lay on your pattern pieces with the grain lines parallel to the selvage (Fig. 115).

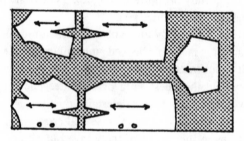

Fig. 115

Trace all the seam lines and darts on your muslin. This may be done by slipping your carbon paper between the pattern and the muslin and against the underside of your material. Trace with the tracing wheel or a pencil. This will mark both sides at once. Don't try this on your dining room table unless you like the decorative effect of the tracing wheel. Use a surface you don't mind marking. A magazine or a piece of board will do. Hard or metal surfaces do not work as well.

Leave 1" seam allowance on all edges but the neck edge. Leave ½" seam allowance on the neck edge.

Cut out the pattern

Cut out the pattern and clip all curved edges at neck, armhole, and under-arm of sleeve. Mark very clearly with heavy or colored pencil or with basting thread *all* horizontal and vertical grain lines (Fig. 116). These lines will be a guide to the proper fit. On checked gingham the grain will be indicated by the line of the checks.

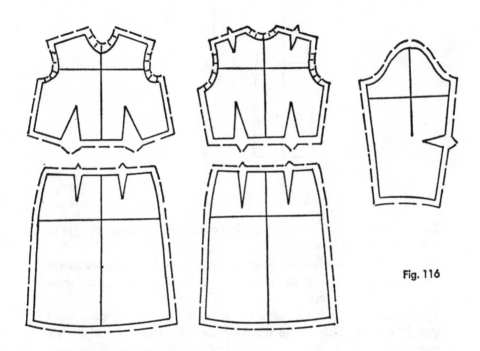

Fig. 116

Pin it together
Pin very closely and very carefully on the right side all darts and seam lines of the bodice, skirt, and sleeve. Do not join these three parts yet. Be sure to leave yourself an opening so that you can get into them.

Fit your muslin
Your best sewing friends and a full-length mirror are necessary for the next operation—fitting your muslin. There are five points to be considered for each section—bodice, skirt, sleeve:

    1. the grain lines
    2. the darts
    3. the seam lines
    4. ease
    5. what looks best on you

We will deal with each point separately.

The grain line

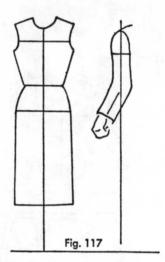

Fig. 117

The center front and center back grain (vertical grain) hangs straight at right angles to the floor.

The horizontal grain should be checked at several places—across the chest, across the hips. It should be at right angles to the vertical grain and parallel to the floor.

The upper sleeve only is considered for grain. The vertical grain hangs straight and perpendicular to the floor; the horizontal grain is at right angles to the vertical grain and parallel to floor; the grain line of the lower arm will continue to the little finger. Wherever the grain departs from this position, release the seam involved and repin with the grain in the proper position. Your pencil marking or basting will guide you here. Actually the fitting is as simple as that.

For instance,

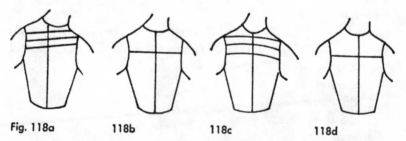

Fig. 118a   118b   118c   118d

if the crosswise grain slants out of its horizontal position as in Fig. 118a, release the left shoulder seam and repin correctly as in Fig. 118b.

if the grain droops, Fig. 118c, release the shoulder seam and repin in the proper position (Fig. 118d).

The trick is to mark the grain line clearly, train your eye to see it true, and pin it in proper position.

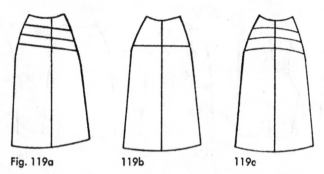

Fig. 119a   119b   119c

The same is true of the skirt. Release the side seams (Figs. 119a and 119c) and repin with the grain in the proper position (Fig. 119b). It is helpful in doing this first to pin the side seams at the hip with front and back grain in proper position. Then proceed with the rest of the seam.

In setting the sleeve, place the sleeve cap in such position that the horizontal and vertical grains form a cross. The vertical grain is perpendicular to the floor, the horizontal grain is parallel to the floor (Fig. 120a). In Fig. 120b, the sleeve cap should be moved back until the sleeve hangs with the proper grain. In Fig. 120c, the sleeve cap should be moved forward to bring it into the proper position.

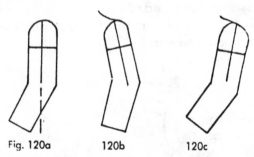

Fig. 120a   120b   120c

If you follow this simple rule for the position of the grain, your clothes will hang correctly.

Fitting the darts

You have carefully established the amount of dart control you need. Your muslin fitting will reveal where this dart control will be most effective for your figure. In the bodice it may be advisable for you to shift some of the waistline dart control to the underarm or to the shoulder (Figs. 121a and 121b). Fitting your muslin may reveal the need for more dart control, less dart control, no dart control, or dart control in different positions. Remember that the larger the dart, the greater the bulge.

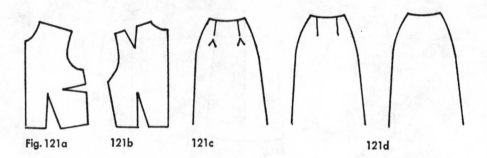

Fig. 121a   121b   121c   121d

A skirt that bulges at the dart point means you have too much dart control (Fig. 121c). Eliminate some or all of it as necessary by shifting the control to the side seam (Fig. 121d). In an actual garment, multiple darts may be more flattering than a single dart, but for pattern-design purposes a single dart is more convenient.

Wrinkles which appear in either skirt or bodice indicate one of two things—either the grain is not right or more dart control is needed. First check the grain. Release the seam involved, smooth out the wrinkles, and repin. If the grain is correct and wrinkles still persist, then more dart control is necessary because a wrinkle or bulge is really an uncontrolled dart. Smooth and push excess material into any existing dart or make a new dart where it seems necessary.

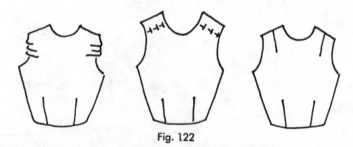

Fig. 122

If wrinkling appears at the upper armhole (Fig. 122), smooth the material and raise the shoulder or create a shoulder dart.

Fig. 123

If wrinkling appears at the lower armhole (Fig. 123), push the excess material into an underarm dart or shoulder dart.

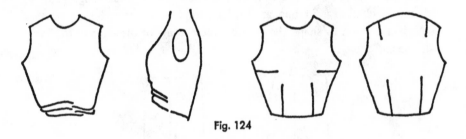

Fig. 124

Excess material at the waistline, either front or back (Fig. 124), usually hikes up, calling for a larger waistline dart; if this is true of the bodice front, create an underarm dart; if true of the bodice back, make a larger shoulder dart.

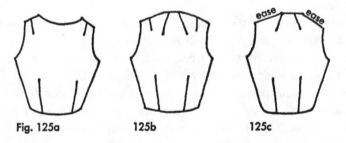

Fig. 125a   125b   125c

If the back neckline stands away from the neck (Fig. 125a), the excess material may be pushed into a dart at the back of the neck, in addition to the shoulder dart. This new dart accommodates the dowager's hump (Fig. 125b). It is found in individuals who are round-shouldered or have fleshiness in this area. When sewing, stitch the dowager's-hump dart as a dart and ease in the dart control on the shoulder seam (Fig. 125c).

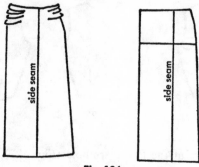

Fig. 126

If the skirt wrinkles at the waistline, either front or back (Fig. 126), unpin, check the grain line at the hips, repin the darts, taking in a sufficient amount to shape the area or throw some of the control to the side seam.

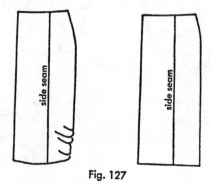

Fig. 127

If there are wrinkles in the lower skirt (Fig. 127), unpin and establish the proper grain line at the hips. Repin, fitting the hips with the proper amount of dart control at the front, back, and side seams. Let the side seam below the hips fall naturally. Pin the side seam into position.

Where there is any pulling, drawing, or binding (Figs. 128a,b,c), slash the muslin, spread the necessary amount, and pin in an insert of muslin. Check the grain line, ease of fit, proper dart control. Repin seams.

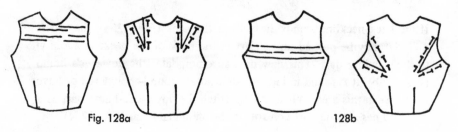

Fig. 128a　　　　　　　　　　　　**128b**

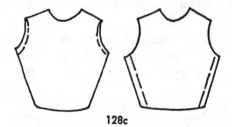

128c

If you have removed the excess fullness from your sleeve cap and set your sleeve with the proper regard for the grain line, your sleeve should fit into the armhole without difficulty.

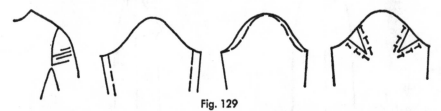

Fig. 129

If the sleeve cap pulls or draws or wrinkles, it is too narrow. Add extra width at the underarm seam, or extra width at each side of the sleeve cap, or slash and insert muslin (Fig. 129).

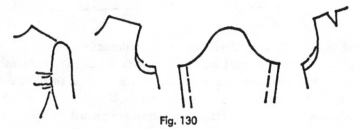

Fig. 130

If it is too tight at the armhole, lower the armscye and add to the underarm sleeve seam (Fig. 130).

Where the seam lines belong

Neck—around the base of the neck where comfortable or where desirable (Fig. 131a).

Shoulders—along the top of the shoulder, slightly forward of the trapezius muscle from the hollow at the base of the neck to the shoulder point. This brings the shoulder seam slightly forward and is visible from the front (Fig. 131b).

Armhole—curves over the top of the shoulder, appears as a straight line from the shoulder point to the crease where the arm and body join, then swings into the underarm curve about 1″ to 1½″ below the armpit (Fig. 131c).

Sides—on the bodice the seam is directly under the arm, about ½″ back of the middle of the armhole. On the skirt it continues from the bodice underarm seam in a straight line to the floor (Fig. 131c).

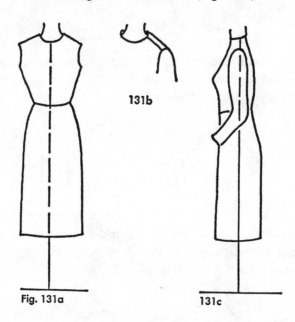

Fig. 131a   131b   131c

Waistline—at the natural waistline or where desired for effect.

Hem line—the number of inches from the floor currently fashionable.

Sleeve—underarm seam meets bodice underarm seam, shoulder notch matches shoulder seam, hem at desired length.

The shoulder seam, side seam, and sleeve are pinned into place correctly and marked with colored pencil. The neck, waistline, and hem line are drawn in as follows:

Neck—with a colored or heavy pencil or ball-point pen, draw a line around the base of the neck where it feels comfortable or where you would like it to be for a round-neck dress or blouse. A close fitting string will help locate this line.

Waistline—tie a piece of heavy string around the bodice and skirt separately. Mark where the string indicates. The waistline generally dips in front slightly. In sway-backed individuals the waistline dips in back. Join the bodice and the skirt on the waistline marked for each.

Hem line—mark the number of inches from the floor with a skirt marker or yardstick. Allow a 2″ hem for a straight skirt.

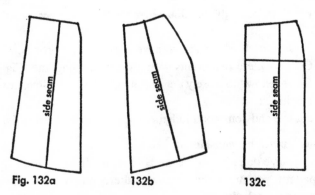

Fig. 132a   132b   132c

If the side seam of the skirt swings forward or backward (Figs. 132a and 132b), release the side seam. Establish the proper grain line at the hips (Fig. 132c). Check the dart control. Fit the skirt above the hips. Allow the rest of the skirt to hang naturally from the hips. Repin the side seams, noting the proper position for the seam. Take off or add to front or back in order to bring the seam into position (Fig. 132c).

Side seams adjusted to fit your contour
The front of your skirt is always somewhat larger than the back at waistline and hips. In an average figure this is generally about 1″. This would bring your skirt side seam in position to continue the bodice side seam straight to the floor. This works fine for the average figure. But consider the startling result you might get if you followed this rule for the woman with a heavy figure and prominent seat (Fig. 133a).

Obviously an adjustment is needed. The skirt front must be larger than the skirt back at hips as well as at waistline to create a line that is more flattering.

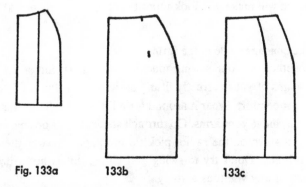

Fig. 133a   133b   133c

1. Find a point on the waistline where the front is larger than the back (Fig. 133b).

2. Find a point on the hip line where the front is larger than the back (Fig. 133b).
3. Be sure both of the above have pleasing proportions.
4. Connect these two points with a gently curving line (Fig. 133c). Don't follow too closely the contour of a bad back line, or you will emphasize it.

Use your eye and your good judgment in creating a pleasing line.

The "look" must be considered, too

Well now, you've done just what the book said. You chose the right size for the pattern, you made the necessary alterations, you cut the pattern with care, you checked the grain, the darts, and the seams. This should be perfection. March over to the mirror and see. Happy? Not so happy? Downright sad? Sometimes, following the rules isn't quite enough. You have to use your artistry to bring out all your good features and hide all your bad ones.

Would your basic pattern be more flattering IF

the shoulders were wider? the shoulders were narrower?

the shoulder seams were moved forward or moved backward?

there was a little more ease across the chest, across the back, across the bust?

the waistline and hip line were not quite so loose or so tight?

the sleeve were wider? or perhaps narrower?

there was more dart control? or less dart control?

the darts were moved a bit? or divided?

the waistline were raised or lowered?

the side seams were moved forward? moved backward?

All of these are possibilities. And you should feel free to make those changes which will make you look more beautiful.

The final test

Mark all the changes made in the fitting.

Stitch together on your sewing machine with a basting stitch all the darts and seams of your correctly fitting basic pattern. Put a zipper in it. Now test it for comfort. Wear it around for a little while. Sit in it, stand in it, walk about, move your arms. Go through some of your ordinary household motions—turn on the radio, pick up the paper, answer the phone, sit down to lunch. Don't try to swing golf clubs; this is not a dress for sports action or any vigorous activity.

Take it in a little if it is too loose. Let it out a bit where it feels too snug. It is yours. Make it comfortable.

THE COMPLETED PATTERN

Line up the pattern

When you have made all the refinements you wish in your muslin, remove it and mark all the corrections clearly. Take your muslin apart and press each section flat. Trace the corrected section to paper.

Check to see that all corresponding seams match in length—side seams, shoulder seams, the bodice front and the skirt front, the bodice back and the skirt back. All dart legs should be equal in length. The sleeve cap should fit easily into the armhole with the proper amount of ease. Using your ruler, your curved stick, your yardstick, your armscye, true up all lines.

Trace to heavy paper or tag

When you examine your corrected pattern, you may find that your right side and left side are different. This is true of everyone to some extent. However it is not practical to make two basic patterns, a right side and a left side. You can see how this would complicate your designing and your cutting of a garment. Nor is it desirable. If you overfit, you may look lop-sided. (All rules are made to be broken. If you have some unusual requirement, if your sides vary greatly, then *do* make two patterns—one for the right side and one for the left side.)

For most it is better to settle on one side—the larger one—so that your pattern will always be large enough. You may mark (or keep a record of) your smaller side and use it when actually fitting.

Make your pattern look symmetrical. Make your darts the same height and equally distant from the center. The amount of dart control may vary, since no one will ever know how much is stitched into the dart. Make the shoulders equal in width, though they may be fitted differently for slope. (You may build them up to look equal with shoulder padding.) Make your armholes and sleeves the same size, though one may fit a higher shoulder than the other. In other words, keep a balanced look to your basic pattern where it will show. Fit out those deviations from standard where they won't show or attract attention or distort the balanced look of your garment. Best of all, design your clothes in such a way as to disguise your defects and enhance your good features.

Trace the chosen half of your pattern to heavy Kraft paper or wrapping paper or several sheets of Manila tag. If you have place to store a flat pattern, the Manila tag holds up better and is easier to use. If your storage space is limited to a drawer, then obviously you will choose the heavy paper which can be rolled up.

The finished sloper

Mark on your pattern the grain line for each piece, the fold line, notches, notations which are helpful, such as: no seam allowance, no shoulder-pad allowance, ease included, and perhaps the date of the fitting.

A FEW EXTRAS

How to add shoulder-pad allowance

Our pattern was made without shoulder-pad allowance. If you wear shoulder pads, make your basic pattern with shoulder-pad allowance. If not, you will want to know how to add this feature for reference or possible future use.

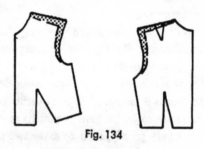

Fig. 134

Raise and *extend* the shoulder half the thickness of the shoulder pad, both front and back (Fig. 134). The new line meets the armhole at the notch and meets the shoulder at the neckline. Use the armscye and ruler.

If your shoulder pad is ½″ thick, then raise and extend the shoulder ¼″ in front and ¼″ in back. If your shoulder pad is 1″ thick, then raise and extend both front and back shoulders ½″. The sleeve needs a corresponding adjustment.

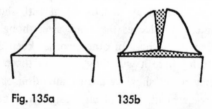

Fig. 135a   **135b**

Draw a line across the cap from underarm to underarm. Draw a line at right angles to this line and to the shoulder notch (Fig. 135a). Slash on these lines. Raise the cap to the amount of the thickness of the pad, keeping points together (Fig. 135b). This spreads the top of the cap automatically to the right amount. Locate a new shoulder notch at the center of the opening.

How to make the hip-length sloper

This sloper is used as the basis for constructing patterns for a blouse, a chemise dress, a sheath dress, a long torso dress, a princess dress, and, with some modifications, becomes the basis for the suit sloper and the coat sloper.

The back hip-length sloper

1. Trace the bodice-back sloper.
2. Extend the center back line to hip depth (Fig. 136a).
3. Lay the skirt pattern on in such a way that the center back lies on the newly drawn line and the side seam touches at the waistline (Fig. 136b).
4. Trace the side seam to the side hip depth (Fig. 136b).

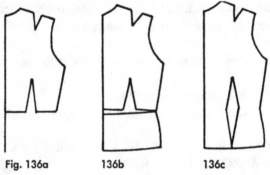

Fig. 136a   136b   136c

5. Connect the center back and the side seam with a slightly curved line (Fig. 136b).
6. Measure over, on the hip line, an amount equal to the distance from the center back to the dart point—half the shoulder-blade width (Fig. 136c).
7. Connect the dart on the back bodice to the new point on the hips (Fig. 136c).

The front hip-length sloper

1. Trace the bodice-front sloper.
2. Extend the center front line to hip depth (Fig. 137a).
3. Divide the dart control into waistline and underarm darts in such amount that the side seam of the bodice follows the contour of the body (Fig. 137b).
4. Lay the skirt front on in such a way that the center front is parallel to the newly drawn line and it touches the waistline at the side seam (Fig. 137b).
5. Trace the side seam to side hip depth (Fig. 137b).

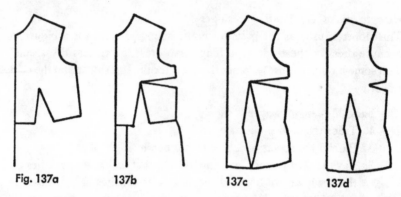

Fig. 137a   137b   137c   137d

6. Connect the center front and the side seam with a slightly curved line (Fig. 137c).
7. Measure an amount on the hip line equal to the distance from the center front to the dart point—half the bust point width (Fig. 137c).
8. Connect the waistline dart on the bodice to the new point on the hips.
9. Shorten the underarm dart (Fig. 137d).

NOTE: If your sloper already contains the underarm dart, skip step ✄3.

SUGGESTIONS ON THE USE OF YOUR BASIC PATTERN WITH COMMERCIAL PATTERNS

This basic pattern (sloper) is not only the basis for future original designs but a wonderful guide for altering commercial patterns. For it has built into it all the many little ways in which your own requirements differ from the standard. Instead of guessing or measuring for each new pattern, use this basic pattern for making adjustments.

Your basic pattern can also help you determine the size commercial pattern which best fits you. If you are in doubt about size, it is worth the time and expense to buy several patterns and see which size requires least alteration. It is generally easier to start with a smaller size and adjust to fit than to use a larger one and grade it down. Many women err in choosing pattern sizes that are too big for them. Spend a little time experimenting for size. It is worth the effort.

When you select a commercial pattern from the hundreds which are offered you, you do so because you like its *style*. Your basic pattern is used to make it *fit* properly. Don't eliminate the style in an effort to ensure the fit. If you remove the style features, you will return your pattern to the original sloper. Use your basic pattern merely as a guide to the proper length, width, proportion, contour, amount and placement of dart control.

Lay the bodice of the commercial tissue pattern over your basic pattern, matching center front (or back) at the waistline. Compare these for length and width. Make the adjustments necessary to bring the bodice in such position that you can compare the neck, shoulder, and armscye. Trace the contour of this area from your sloper. Check the position and amount of the dart control. Alter accordingly. Trace your waistline from your pattern.

Lay the tissue skirt pattern on your skirt sloper, matching the center back or center front waistline. Compare length and width. Check the position and the amount of the dart. Make any necessary changes. Trace your waistline and the contour of your hip at the side seam.

Lay the commercial sleeve pattern on your sleeve sloper, matching the grain. Match the sleeve caps, starting at the underarm seams. Make adjustments in length and width. Trace the cap of your sleeve sloper as this will have the proper shape and ease to fit your armscye.

Where the bodice, skirt, or sleeve of your pattern is composed of several sections, pin the sections together, then compare them with your sloper.

Where the style depends on extra fullness for its effect, fold and pin out pleats, tucks, gathers, drapery, etc., and then compare with your basic pattern.

All corresponding pieces must be adjusted to fit, i.e., collar to neck, facings to garment, cuffs to sleeves, etc.

Use your hip-length sloper when comparing patterns for blouses, sheaths, chemise dresses, long torso or middy lines, and princess dresses.

Remember that your basic pattern does not have seam allowance on it, while the commercial pattern does.

You will find your basic pattern an invaluable help in pattern adjustment and in fitting.

As you have seen in the preceding chapters, all new designs are really variations of a basic pattern. Now, using your own basic pattern, you will be able to make full-scale patterns designed especially to fit your figure.

CHAPTER 5

A frame for your face—the neckline

YOUR FACE IS YOU

Sitting or standing, moving or at rest, your face is the center of interest. Its attractiveness can be greatly enhanced by an appropriate frame. In a large measure the neckline provides that frame.

Designing for this area, therefore, calls for a careful study and analysis of type, shape of head, style of hairdo, characteristics of neck and shoulders. Past experience, some study, and a little experimentation should help you decide which style lines and which proportions are most pleasing and most suitable for you.

HIGH—LOW NECKLINE

Any neckline which drops below the neckline of your sloper, however little, is called a dropped neckline. Any neckline which rises above that of your sloper, however little, is called a raised neckline. There are endless variations of both types.

In making the pattern for a neckline, both front and back must be considered. In general, when the front neckline is low, the back neckline should be high; where the front neckline is high, the back neckline may be low. A deep décolletage, both front and back, presents the problem of keeping your garment on your shoulders. Such a neckline requires construction similar to the strapless dress.

SOME LIKE THEM LOW—THE DROPPED NECKLINES

How to make the oval neckline

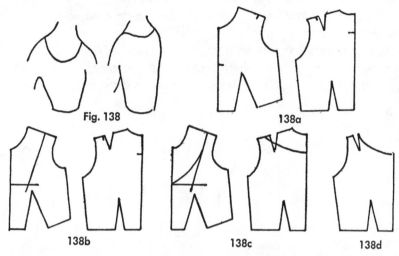

Fig. 138   138a

138b   138c   138d

1. Trace the front- and back-bodice slopers.
2. Decide the amount of the drop at the center front and the center back (Fig. 138a).
3. Decide where the style line will appear on the front shoulder (Fig. 138a).
4. Measure a similar distance from the armhole on the back shoulder (Fig. 138a).
5. On the front bodice, square lines at the shoulder and center front from the point of each drop. Allow these lines to cross. These are the guide lines for your curve (Fig. 138b).
6. Square a ¼″ line from the center back at the point of the drop (Fig. 138b).
7. Draw the curve of your new style line. Use any instrument which will give you the curve you want. Or draw a freehand curve; then use your instrument to true it (Fig. 138c).
8. Cut out the new pattern.
9. Add seam allowance, fold indicator, grain, and notches.

NOTE: Sometimes the style line of the back neckline will eliminate completely the back shoulder dart. In that case you obviously don't need it. At times it may slice off part of it. If this makes the dart appear awkwardly placed, move it to the point at which shoulder and neckline meet (Fig. 137d). Or you could shift what little is left of the dart to the new back shoulder seam and ease it into the front shoulder seam.

The square neckline is constructed in the same way, omitting step 7. The slight incline of the style line from the shoulder to the horizontal style line produces a better fit for the square neckline.

The scalloped neckline may be constructed in the same way, too. Instead of the curved line in step 7, trace scallops.

Any shaped style line may be substituted for step 7. Whenever drawing a curved line, square off a short distance at the center front or back to prevent a point from forming at the center of the curve when opened.

The V neckline

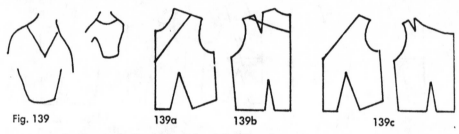

Fig. 139   139a   139b   139c

1. Trace the front- and back-bodice slopers.
2. Decide the amount of the drop at the center front and the center back.
3. Decide where the style line will appear on the front shoulder.
4. Measure a similar distance from the armhole on the back shoulder.
5. Draw a straight line from the dropped center front to the point of drop on the shoulder (Fig. 139a).
6. Draw the back style line (Fig. 139b).
7. Adjust the back shoulder dart as previously directed (Fig. 139c).

FIRST AID FOR GAPPING NECKLINES

The dropped neckline should lie flat against the body without any rippling or gapping. This can be accomplished in part by the pattern design and in part by careful cutting, handling, and sewing.

Why your neckline gaps

Your sloper has a straight vertical line for its center front (Fig. 140a). Your body, however, does not. In profile, your body silhouette is more like Fig. 140b. The vertical center front line really stands away from your body contour (Fig. 140c).

The lower portion below the bust point is controlled by your darts. The upper portion above the bust point remains as ease in your garment. In most cases this is desirable. But in the dropped neckline this is the area which will gap (Fig. 140d).

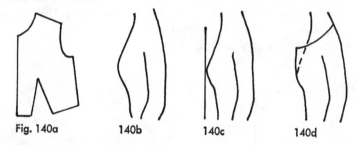

Fig. 140a   140b   140c   140d

Eliminate the ease at the neckline area

The length of the style line should correspond to the measurement of the area *without ease*. This means designing the pattern on a sloper without ease in the shoulder-chest area. On p. 130 of this chapter you will find directions for constructing such a sloper.

Gapping can also be corrected when fitting. Lift the bodice-front neckline at the shoulder as much as is needed for a flat fit; then taper to the normal shoulder seam (Fig. 141). This will remove the ease by shifting it to the shoulder seam and then eliminating it.

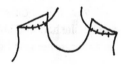

Fig. 141

Handle with care

As soon as you remove your pattern, stay-stitch all curved and bias areas so that they will not stretch or ripple in handling. (Stay-stitching is a line of machine stitching just outside the seam line.)

Face and interface your neckline

Most collarless necklines need a facing to finish the edge. (The exception to this is the collarless neckline with fullness. This may be finished with bias binding, cording, or casing for elastic or ribbon.) A firm interfacing applied to the neckline will also help it lie flat against the body. There are a variety of interfacings on the market. Use that which seems suitable in weight for the fabric of your garment.

How to make the pattern for the facing and the interfacing

These are both cut from the same pattern and are made as follows:

1. From the new neckline on both the front and the back, measure down in a number of places the width of the facing. This is usually about 1½″ to 2″ (Fig. 142a).
2. Connect these points (Fig. 142b).

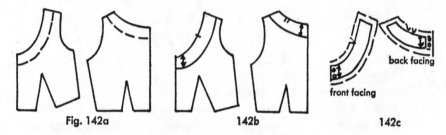

Fig. 142a   142b   142c

3. Locate the grain line. This is in the same position as in the bodice. Mark notches on the neckline (Fig. 142b).
4. Trace the facing to another piece of paper. Use this same pattern for the interfacing (Fig. 142c).
5. Add seam allowance and fold indicators (Fig. 142c).

NOTE: Any shaped area needs a shaped facing. It cannot simply be extended and turned up for a facing or hem. Nor can it be folded and traced. Try folding a curved hem and you will soon see the impossibility. The facing (or hem) would have to be slashed and spread to fit, in which case you would have a fringe rather than a hem or facing.

A ONE-SIDED AFFAIR—THE ASYMMETRIC NECKLINE

All of the foregoing necklines were exactly the same on both sides. This is termed formal balance. The asymmetric neckline is different on each side. Its beauty is its informal balance. Its exaggerated and free form style lines can be quite interesting and rather sophisticated. Here are a few asymmetric necklines (Fig. 143).

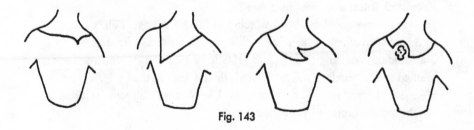

Fig. 143

In order to design this neckline you will need to use a sloper for the entire front or back. Place the center front or back on a fold of paper and trace the bodice pattern (Fig. 144a).

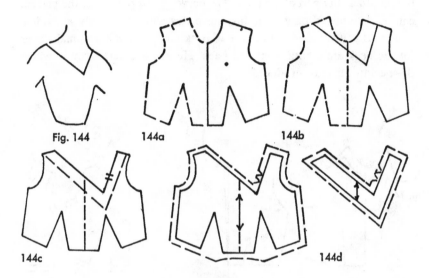

Fig. 144   144a   144b

144c   144d

1. Trace the entire bodice front (Fig. 144a).
2. Decide the drop on the shoulders. This is generally the same on both sides (Fig. 144a).
3. Decide the position and the amount of the drop of the style line (Fig. 144a).
4. Draw the style line (Fig. 144b).
5. Cut out the new pattern (Fig. 144c).
6. Draw the facing (Fig. 144c).
7. Trace the facing (Fig. 144d).
8. Complete the pattern. Add the seam allowance, grain, and notches on the bodice and facing (Fig. 144d).

Now try to make the patterns for all the necklines illustrated in Fig. 143.

PLAIN AND FANCY

As with all simple things, the beauty of a collarless neckline depends on the beauty of its proportion and the simplicity and grace of its style line. However, there may be occasions when, in addition to the facing, the edge may be finished effectively with braid, fringe, ruffles, pleating, lace, ribbon, etc. Unadorned, the very simplicity of this type of neckline calls for a good neck and shoulders.

SOME LIKE THEM HIGH—THE RAISED NECKLINE

The raised neckline looks best on a slim, youthful neck. It will make a short, thick neck look shorter and thicker. This neckline must fit not only the shoulders but part of the neck. The curve of this portion of the pattern can be determined only by fitting, since this will be a highly individual matter. If you are fond of this type of neckline, prepare a personal sloper for the neck area, both front and back. Here is a general way in which this neckline may be produced.

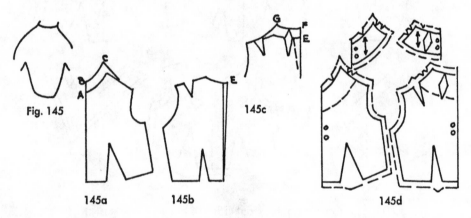

Fig. 145   145c   145a   145b   145d

1. Trace the front- and back-bodice slopers.
2. Extend the center front line 1″ from A. Label point B (Fig. 145a).
3. Draw a line parallel to the curved neckline and equal to it in length. Label the end of it C (Fig. 145a).
4. Draw a curved line from C to the shoulder, easing it into the shoulder line (Fig. 145a). This line needs careful fitting.
5. On the back sloper, measure over ¼″ beyond the center back at the neckline. Label this point E (Fig. 145b).
6. Connect E with the waistline. This will become the new center back line (Fig. 145b).
7. Extend the new center back line 1″ at the neckline. Label point F (Fig. 145c).
8. From point F draw a line parallel to the back neckline and equal to it. Label the end of the line G (Fig. 145c).
9. From G draw a curved line to the shoulder. This curve should match the corresponding front curve (Fig. 145c).
10. Locate a neck dart 1½″ from the center back. Make this dart ¼″ at the original neckline (this takes off the ¼″ added to the

center back in step 7), taper to nothing at the new raised neck-line, and taper to nothing 3″ below on the back bodice. This back neckline dart is necessary for a smooth fit in a bodice with a raised neckline (Fig. 145c).

11. For both front and back facings measure down from the new neckline, in a number of places, the depth of the facing. Con-nect these points with a curved line. Mark notches and back neckline dart (Fig. 145d). Trace.

12. Complete the pattern. On both bodice and facing add seam allowance, grain, fold of material, notches at neckline and shoulder.

A raised neckline with a dropped, shaped center front or center back

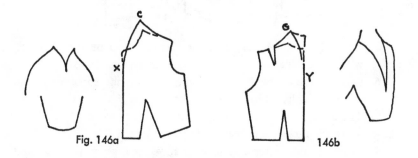

Fig. 146a   146b

For the dropped-front neckline (Fig. 146a), insert these steps between steps 4 and 5:

a. Determine the drop at the center front. Label point X.

b. Connect X and C with a curved style line.

For the dropped-back neckline (Fig. 146b):

a. Omit steps 5, 6, and 10.

b. Substitute for 10 the following: determine the drop at the center back. Label point Y.

c. Insert between the new step (10) and 11 the following: Connect Y and G with a curved style line.

The bateau, or boat neckline may be a raised neckline

1. Trace the front- and back-bodice slopers.

2. Raise the front neckline about an inch (Fig. 147a).

3. Drop the neckline at the shoulder to any desired point (Fig. 147a).

4. Measure the same distance from the armhole on the back shoul-der. Adjust the dart as necessary (Fig. 147b).

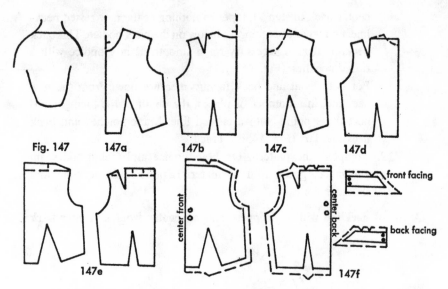

Fig. 147   147a   147b   147c   147d

147e   147f

5. Connect the raised center front and the drop on the shoulder with a straight (or slightly curved) line (Fig. 147c).
6. Connect the center back with the drop on the shoulder in the same way (Fig. 147d).
7. Trace the new pattern (Fig. 147e).
8. Mark the facing (Fig. 147e). Trace.
9. Complete the pattern. Add seam allowance, grain, notches, and fold indicators. (Fig. 147f).

CAUTION—SOFT SHOULDERS

Décolleté and strapless dresses

This is the glamour department in your closet. These dresses are worn to show you off at your prettiest and shapeliest. They are cut and fitted accordingly.

Décolleté dresses may have deep plunges in front, in back, or both. They may or may not have sleeves. They obviously need a little assistance to stay where they belong. The strapless gown needs more than a little assistance. It needs downright support.

Both types fit snugly; therefore, they must be designed on a somewhat altered bodice sloper, using very little or no ease.

To get this sloper you may do one of the following things, depending on your need:

1. Construct another basic bodice pattern, using your body measurements, with no ease or very little ease.

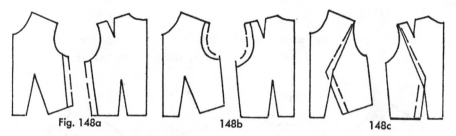

Fig. 148a   148b   148c

2. Reduce or remove the ease in your bodice sloper by taking some off at the side seams (Fig. 148a).

3. Reduce or remove the ease across the chest and back by taking some off at the armscye (Fig. 148b).

4. Slash the bodice front and back from the shoulder point to the point of the waistline dart. Overlap the necessary amount at the dart point. This is the reverse of the procedure described in Chapter 4, p. 98 (Fig. 148c).

Design your décolleté or strapless pattern on this new sloper. Larger darts, curved darts, and darts in more places will help you shape your bodice front over the bust. For a snug midriff section eliminate the darts altogether on both front and back.

"Will it ever stay in place?"
Yes, if you secure it adequately.

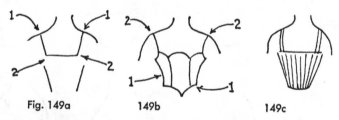

Fig. 149a   149b   149c

A broad, deep décolletage (Fig. 149a) may be held in place in the following manner:

1. Place lingerie straps at the shoulder seams.

2. Fasten elastic to a corner of the front or back neckline; bring it around the body so it fits snugly; fasten to the opposite corner.

For off-the-shoulder or near off-the-shoulder dresses (Fig. 149b):

1. Place boning in the seams.

2. Sew elastic to the neckline over the shoulders.

Evening dresses may be designed with straps which help support them (Fig. 149c). Strapless evening dresses must be supported upward from the waistline by placing boning in the seams and darts.

FUN TO TRY

Here are some necklines it might be fun for you to try. Make the patterns. Choose one and make a blouse, using the neckline pattern.

Fig. 150

DRAPERY SOFTENS THE NECKLINE—THE COWL

Long before the era of fitted clothing, all clothing was draped. This drapery reached a high degree of beauty with the Greeks, as is evidenced by their sculpture, ceramics, and painting. This classic drapery, with its fluid, stately lines, has inspired designers through the centuries to the present day. There is a certain dignity and statuesque quality to drapery that makes a distinguished evening dress or late-day dress.

The cowl neckline is derived from this early drapery. It comes to us more directly from the medieval monk's hood. The cowl is a softly flattering neckline. A blouse with a high cowl is a perfect fill-in for a suit. It should be made of fabric that will fall in soft folds, like velvet, chiffon, jersey, crepe, and satin. This style is best cut on the bias because bias material drapes better.

The shape of the cowl pattern

The cowl neckline can be constructed on the usual bodice-front sloper or on a sloper with some of the dart control shifted to the center front. The latter adds a little extra fullness for the drape (Fig. 151a). A very simple cowl can be designed by extending the center front from C to A and squaring a line from A to the shoulder at B (Fig. 151b).

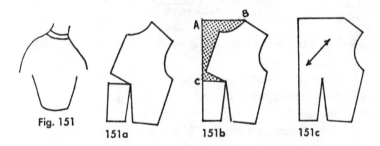

Fig. 151   151a   151b   151c

AB represents the depth of the new neckline. AC adds the amount of fabric needed for this simple drape. This squared shape at the center front is the characteristic shape of the cowl (Fig. 151c).

The cowl may be designed on the standard-sloper neckline and have either a raised or dropped neckline. It may have one, two, three, or as many drapes as you want. The drapes may be as deep as you would like them; they may appear from the shoulder or the armhole. Before the drapes are designed, however, the neckline must be determined.

Here is a *cowl with one drape* drafted from your standard bodice-front sloper.

1. Trace the front-bodice sloper. Cut out the tracing (Fig. 152a).
2. Measure down 1″ on the shoulder from the neckline. Label point A (Fig. 152a).
3. Draw a deeply curved line from the center front neckline, B, to A (Fig. 152a).

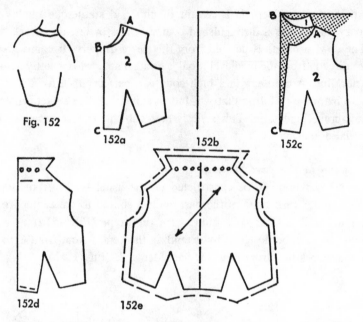

Fig. 152

152a   152b   152c

152d   152e

4. Label the center front at the waistline C. Mark sections 1 and 2 (Fig. 152a).

5. Draw a squared line on new paper (Fig. 152b).

6. Slash on the drape line AB. (It is best if you slash *to* but not through A.)

7. Spread sections 1 and 2 as illustrated in Fig. 152c.
   the shoulder remains closed at A
   B is placed at the 90° angle of the squared line
   C touches the vertical line
   the slash-and-spread principle is used to create the extra fullness needed for the drape. There will be a drape where each slashed line is spread.

8. Trace the new pattern. The squared lines become the new center front and neckline. Correct the angular shoulder line with a curved line (Fig. 152d).

9. Measure down 1″ from the new neckline for the facing (the broken line in the diagram), (Fig. 152d).

10. Fold the neckline. Trace the facing line and the necessary section of the center front and shoulder seam (Fig. 152d).

11. Fold the center front and trace the entire front pattern. Correct the center front waistline (Fig. 152e). This pattern is used on the bias for better drape. When fabric is so used, it is easier to lay

out, cut, and handle if the entire pattern section is used. A fold
or seam at the center tends to ripple in working and wearing.

12. Mark the grain line, seam allowance, notches, and the fold line
for the facing (Fig. 152e).

The cowl on a raised neckline

The cowl neckline illustrated in Fig. 151 is in reality a cowl on a raised
neckline. Note how the squared area rises above the normal neckline.

The cowl on a lowered neckline

This is a three-drape cowl designed on a V neckline.

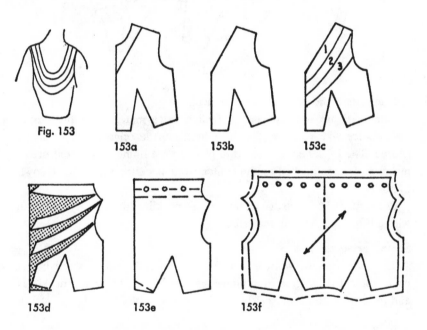

Fig. 153

153a   153b   153c

153d   153e   153f

1. Trace the front-bodice sloper. Cut out the tracing.
2. Draw the V neckline (Fig. 153a).
3. Cut the pattern to the new neckline (Fig. 153b).
4. Locate the drape lines where desired (Fig. 153c). Mark the
   sections 1, 2, 3.
5. Draw a squared line on new paper.
6. Slash the drape lines and spread as illustrated (Fig. 153d).
   Note the position of the bottom points of sections 2 and 3 against
   the vertical line of the square (Fig. 153d).
7. Trace the pattern. Correct the shoulder line and waistline.
   Draw the facing (Fig. 153e).

8. Fold the neckline and trace the facing (Fig. 153e).
9. Fold the center front and trace the entire pattern (Fig. 153f).
10. Complete the pattern. Add the seam allowance, grain, notches, and the fold line for the facing (Fig. 153f).

A very deep cowl may be made very simply by the following short cut.

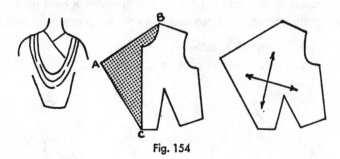

Fig. 154

AB represents the depth of the new neckline.

CA and AB are squared lines providing extra material for the drape. This bodice will fit better if a sheer lining in the original bodice shape is used. The folds may be tacked in place to the lining. A covered dressmaker's weight attached to the center front neckline will hold it down in position.

Suggestion: The deep décolletage of this neckline looks pretty if filled in with a bib of contrasting material.

Some variations

A low cowl may be worn in a variety of ways. It can be worn in the usual manner (Fig. 155a). Its fullness can be arranged into new necklines and fastened with decorative pins, clips, bows, buttons, etc. (Fig. 155b).

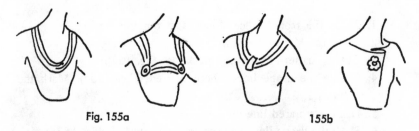

Fig. 155a   **155b**

The cowl in a yoke has the advantage of being cut separately from the bodice. While the cowl is cut on the bias, the rest of the bodice can be cut on the straight of the goods. This produces a fitted bodice with drapes only in the yoke area.

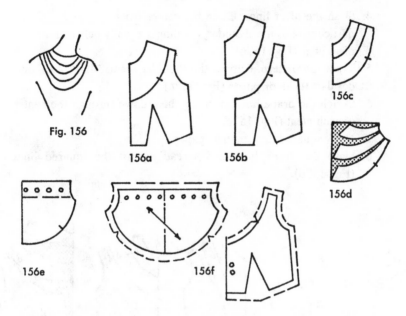

Fig. 156
156a
156b
156c
156d
156e
156f

1. Trace the front-bodice sloper.
2. Draw the style line for the yoke. Locate notches on the yoke line (Fig. 156a).
3. Cut out the tracing.
4. Cut the yoke from the rest of the bodice, which can be used as it is (Fig. 156b).
5. Locate the drape lines on the yoke (Fig. 156c).
6. Draw squared lines on new paper.
7. Slash the drape lines and spread (Fig. 156d).
8. Trace the pattern. Correct the shoulder line. Draw the facing (Fig. 156e).
9. Fold the neckline and trace the facing (Fig. 156e).
10. Fold the center front and trace the entire yoke (Fig. 156f).
11. On yoke and bodice, add the seam allowance, grain, notches, and the fold line for the yoke facing and the center front of the bodice (Fig. 156f).

A pleated cowl will provide a deeper and fuller draped effect.

1. Trace the front-bodice sloper which has part of the dart control shifted to the center front (Fig. 157a).
2. Mark the position for the pleats or dart tucks from the center front dart to the shoulder (Fig. 157a).
3. Cut out the tracing.

4. Slash the pleat lines. Close the center front dart and shift the dart control to the shoulder, dividing it equally between the two pleat lines (Fig. 157b).
5. Trace the pattern. Correct the shoulder seam. Mark the shoulder dart tucks or pleats (Fig. 157c).
6. Sketch the drape lines, bringing them down through the center of each pleat (Fig. 157c).
7. Draw squared lines on new paper.
8. Slash the drape lines and spread against the squared lines (Fig. 157d).

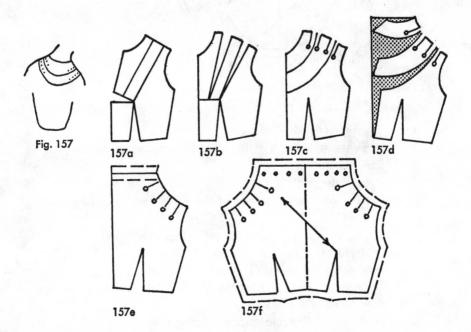

Fig. 157

157a   157b   157c   157d

157e   157f

9. Trace the pattern and the pleats. Draw the facing (Fig. 157e).
10. Fold the neckline and trace the facing. Fold the center front and trace the entire pattern. Correct the waistline at center front with a curved line (Fig. 157f).
11. Mark the grain line, pleats, seam allowance, notches, and the fold line for the facing (Fig. 157f).

NOTE: The pleats or dart tucks may be stitched for a short distance either on the underside or topstitched. Or they may be folded into position as unpressed pleats and stitched into the shoulder seam.

Here is an *alternate way to make the pleated cowl*. There are times when this method may be preferable. This would be true in those instances when the dart control cannot be utilized for pleats or when the dart control produces pleats which are not deep enough for the design.

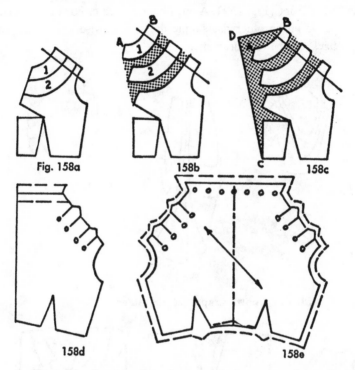

1. Trace the front-bodice sloper with the center front dart.
2. Draw drape lines. Mark sections 1 and 2 (Fig. 158a).
3. Draw a guide line parallel to the shoulder seam (Fig. 158a).
4. Draw a guide line on new paper.
5. Cut out the tracing.
6. Slash the drape lines and spread as for pleats, matching the guide line of the pattern to the guide line on the paper (Fig. 158b).
7. Measure the neckline length AB.
8. Draw squared lines. Make DB equal the neckline length. Draw DC to the center front waistline (Fig. 158c).
9. Trace the pattern and the pleats (Fig. 158d).
10. Draw the facing and trace it (Fig. 158d).
11. Fold the center front and trace the entire front pattern. Correct the waistline with a curved line (Fig. 158e).

12. Complete the pattern. Add seam allowance, grain, notches, and fold indicator for the facing. Mark the pleats (Fig. 158e).

More cowls

Bodice backs, skirts, and sleeves, too, can have the same cowl treatment as the bodice front (Fig. 159). A cowl bodice back or cowl sleeve can be very effective on an otherwise simple dress. A cowl-draped skirt front, side, or back, can be very dramatic.

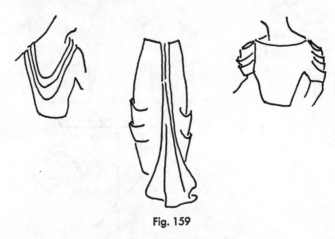

Fig. 159

The skirt with deep cowl drapes at the sides

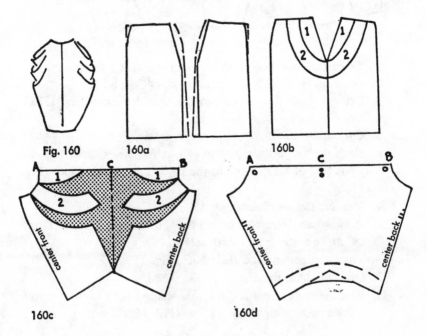

Fig. 160   160a   160b

160c   160d

1. Trace the skirt slopers, front and back.
2. Eliminate the darts by shifting part of the dart control to the center front and center back and the rest to the side seams at the waistline. Use straight lines from the waist to the hip instead of the normal curve (Fig. 160a).
3. Eliminate the flare, if any, at the side seams (Fig. 160a).
4. Cut out the new skirt pattern.
5. Sketch in the drape lines on the skirt front and skirt back, matching them at the side seams (Fig. 160b).
6. Draw a horizontal line on paper large enough for the skirt, as it will be spread.
7. Slash the drape lines and spread sections 1 and 2 as illustrated (Fig. 160c).
   the waistline of the skirt remains closed
   the skirt front and skirt back touch at the side hem line
   section 1 lies against the straight line
   section 2 is placed between section 1 and the rest of the skirt
8. Trace the entire outside line of the pattern. Correct the hem line and the waistline with curved lines (Fig. 160d).
9. Draw the facing for the hem (Fig. 160d).

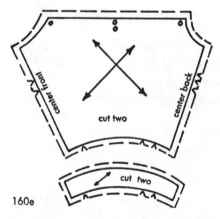

10. Trace the pattern of the skirt and the facing. Mark the grain, seam allowance, notches, fold. Cut two skirt patterns and two facing patterns (Fig. 160e).
11. A sheer skirt lining in the original shape of the skirt, used as a stay, will improve the hang and fit of this skirt.

NOTE: The side section of this skirt is cut on the bias for better drape. The grain of the facing is the same as that of the skirt.

There will be seams at the center front and center back but none at the sides as this would interfere with the drape. There will be a seam at the new hip line AB. Fold the center of this line, C; bring B to meet A; stitch. A covered dressmaker's weight may be attached to C to hold the drape in place.

A very simple skirt cowl may be made in the following manner:

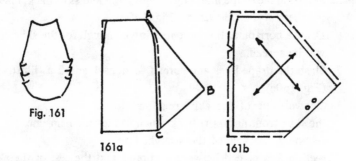

Fig. 161   161a   161b

Front and back are treated in the same way. Use a dartless sloper as in the previous exercise.

AB represents the depth of the drape (Fig. 161a).

AB and BC are squared lines—the amount needed for the drape (Fig. 161a).

BC is on a fold of the fabric; there will be seams at the center front, center back, and new hip AB (Fig. 161b).

Weight B with a covered dressmaker's weight.

Use a sheer lining in the original shape of the skirt as a stay for the fullness.

For an evening skirt, additional fullness can be added to the back of this pattern while the side drapes in a cowl (Fig. 162).

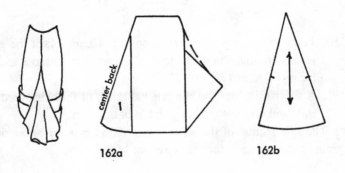

162a   162b

Either extend the center back as illustrated in Fig. 162a or design section 1 as a godet* to be stitched into the center back seam.

The cowl on the sleeve is constructed in the same manner as the skirt.

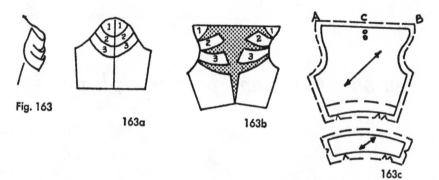

Fig. 163

163a   163b

163c

1. Trace the sleeve pattern. Cut out the tracing.
2. Draw a line through the center of the sleeve (Fig. 163a).
3. Sketch in drape lines (Fig. 163a). Label sections 1, 2, 3.
4. Draw a horizontal straight line on paper large enough for the pattern.
5. Slash the center line and the drape lines.
6. Spread sections 1, 2, and 3 as illustrated (Fig. 163b).
   the hem of the sleeve remains closed at the center
   section 1 lies against the straight line
   sections 2 and 3 are spaced between section 1 and the lower portion of the sleeve
7. Trace the outside line of the pattern (Fig. 163c). Correct the hem line with a curved line.
8. Draw the facing for the hem (Fig. 163c). Trace the facing.
9. Mark the grain, seam allowance, notches, and fold indicator at point C. (Fold C, bring B to meet A, and stitch.)

In testing any of the cowl drapes, use a test material which will drape. Use batiste rather than the muslin suggested for the previous patterns. A little experimentation will undoubtedly be needed to achieve the effect you have in mind, but the result is so immediate and so beautiful that your new clothes will probably burgeon with cowl drapes.

---

*A godet (Fig. 162b) is a triangular section of material inserted into seams or slashes of fabric for extra fullness.

CHAPTER 6

Buttons, bows, and pockets a'plenty

NO EXIT

We have worked out some very good designs to this point, but they all have one unfortunate feature in common—no opening which would permit you to get into them. It's somewhat like designing a house without doors or a two-story building without a stairway. It is true that some of the designs could be slipped over the head and tied in the middle, but that would be hardly appealing and rather monotonous for all of your dresses. Most clothing requires some means of opening and closing plus a fastening to make it easy to get into and out of the garment, especially if it is a fitted one.

AN OPEN-AND-SHUT CASE

We have seen before how designers make decorative use of a structural necessity. This is particularly true of closings. If a closing there must be, it may as well be beautiful. Here your imagination and creativity can have full sway.

As you study fashions, you will become aware of an endless array of ingenious closings and fastenings. Your garment may be single-breasted, surplice, or double-breasted; it may be fastened with interesting or rare buttons; it may sport beautiful or unusual buttonholes; it may be fastened with braid or frogs, ribbon or bows, oversize hooks and eyes, tiny studs, or just plain zippers. It may have a straight vertical closing, a diagonal closing, or a shaped closing. It can be very simple or it may be very intricate. But whatever the closing may be, it is so essential and so prominent a part of the design that it requires some special thought in planning. Often the closing and its method of fastening can "make" the design feature of your dress.

Start with a plan

In planning the closing, it is helpful to make a preliminary sketch showing the center front or center back line, the type of closing, and the kind of fastening you intend to use. If you are going to use buttons, show where they will be placed and what size they will be (Fig. 164a). If you are going to use a zippered closing, show how it will be used (Fig. 164b). It is important to decide these things in advance. They will determine the amount of material to be added for the opening extension.

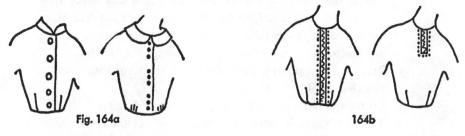

Fig. 164a   164b

How to make the single-breasted opening extension

Your dresses, blouses, jackets, and coats usually open with a single-breasted opening extension. This is how to make it.

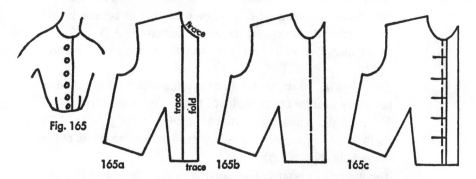

Fig. 165   165a   165b   165c

1. Trace the bodice-front sloper, allowing space for the extension.
2. Locate a line on the bodice front, inward from the center line, that will be equal to the amount desired for the front extension. The amount of the opening extension is determined by the size of the button. When the garment is buttoned, the button should sit ex-

actly on the center line. This will permit half the button to extend inward from the center line and the other half toward the outer edge. There should be at least half a button's width from the rim of the button to the edge of the garment. All of this adds up to the fact that the opening extension is placed a button's width from the center line (Fig. 165a).

When very large buttons are used, the line of the opening may be half a button's width plus ½". This will prevent an unreasonably wide extension while assuring a safe margin from button's rim to outer edge.

3. Fold on the center front (Fig. 165a).

4. Trace the opening extension line, the neckline, and the waistline from the center front to the extension line (Fig. 165a).

5. Unfold the pattern and draw the lines just traced which form the opening extension. Note the shape of the neckline. This shaping is necessary so that the necklines will fit when the center fronts are placed over each other for the closing (Fig. 165b).

6. Trace this new pattern. Trace the center front line with a broken line (Fig. 165b).

7. Locate the buttons and buttonholes (Fig. 165c).

The first button is placed a button's width below the neckline. When buttons extend below the waistline, one button should appear at the waistline to prevent gapping. If a belt is used at the waistline, place the buttons sufficiently above and below so they don't interfere with the belt. Space or group the rest of the buttons between. (Designwise, an uneven number of buttons is said to be more interesting than an even number—1, 3, 5, 7, 9, etc. rather than 2, 4, 6, 8, 10.) The buttonholes are placed accordingly.

To ensure an exact center front closing when buttoned, it is necessary to allow for the width of the button shank. Draw a line ⅛" from the center front toward the edge of the garment. The buttonholes begin on this line and extend inward the length of the buttonhole (Fig. 165c).

The buttonhole is made long enough to slide the button through easily. Usually this is a length equal to the button's width plus ⅛". For a thick or bumpy button, the length of the buttonhole is equal to the button's width plus its thickness. When in doubt as to the proper length for the buttonhole, make a test slash and see if the button slides through easily. It is a tragic discovery to find that a long row of painstakingly made buttonholes are too small for your buttons.

8. Add the seam allowance, grain, notches, center front line, and markings for placement of buttonholes and buttons.

An opening extension needs a facing

The facing for your opening extension may be done in two ways—either all in one with the front bodice or seamed at the extension line.

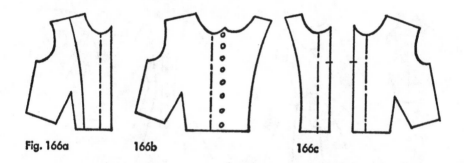

Fig. 166a   166b   166c

1. On the pattern with the opening extension, measure 1½″ down on the shoulder from the neckline.
2. Measure over 2½″ on the waistline inward from the extension line.

   The above two measurements are arbitrary. You may make the facing any suitable width. Be sure to make it wide enough to cover the buttonholes completely, plus a little over (Fig. 166a).
3. Connect these points with a straight or curved line (Fig. 166a).

For a facing all in one with the bodice

4a. Fold on the extension line and trace neckline, shoulder line, facing line, and waistline. Unfold and draw the facing all in one with the bodice. This type of facing is used when the extension line is vertical and straight, the material is wide enough, and a fold of material is desired rather than a seam (Fig. 166b).

For a separate facing

4b. Place paper under the bodice pattern and trace the entire facing. This type of facing is used when the extension line is diagonal or shaped or when the material is not wide enough (Fig. 166c).

For both types

5. Complete the pattern by adding the seam allowance, grain, notches, center front line, and fold line when necessary.

A little or a lot

An opening extension may be as long or as short as you wish it (Fig. 167). It may be for a short distance below the neckline (Fig. 167a). It may stop at the waistline as illustrated in Fig. 166. It may continue a short distance below the waistline (Fig. 167b). It may continue to the bottom of the dress (Fig. 167c). Or, it may merely appear in a yoke (Fig. 167d). The method of constructing the opening extension and the facing remains the same.

Fig. 167a   167b   167c   167d

The zippered opening

Modern technology has given us that simplest of openings—the zippered one. The ordinary seam allowance is generally sufficient for setting the zipper into the center front, center back, and underarm seam (Figs. 168a and 168b). When the zipper is set into an area that has no seam and which requires a slash in the material, a facing piece is necessary (Figs. 168c and 168d).

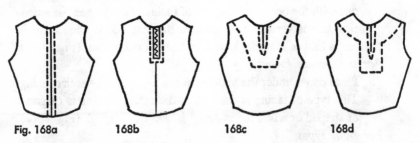

Fig. 168a   168b   168c   168d

The zipper is usually concealed by a fold of the material. But it can serve as a decorative element when the color of the metal is exposed.

Some zippers are designed for this purpose. It is most effective when the zipper is in some contrasting color.

How to make the double-breasted opening extension

1. Make a preliminary sketch showing the style line for the opening and the placement of buttons and buttonholes (Fig. 169a).
2. Trace the entire front bodice. Mark the center front line (Fig. 169b).
3. Draw the style line for the double-breasted effect (Fig. 169b).
4. Draw guide lines for the placement of buttons and buttonholes. Mark the position of buttons and buttonholes (Fig. 169c).

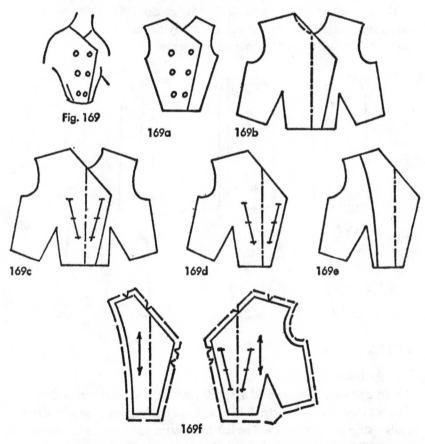

Fig. 169

169a   169b

169c   169d   169e

169f

5. Cut out the right front of the pattern. Discard what's left (Fig. 169d). Double-breasted garments fit better when right and left sides have the same extension. Therefore, cut two similar bodice-front pieces.

6. Locate the facing (Fig. 169e) and trace as previously directed. The double-breasted garment is usually too wide for the facing to be cut all in one with the front. There is this further consideration: if folded on the extension line, which is off grain, the resulting facing will be considerably off grain.

7. Complete the pattern by adding the seam allowances, notches, grain, center front line, and buttonhole markings (Fig. 169f).

Anywhere at all

In addition to the bodice front, opening extensions, either single or double-breasted, may appear anywhere at all—bodice back, skirt front, skirt back, sleeves, cuffs, pockets, bands, collars (Fig. 170). Wherever they may be, they are worked out in exactly the same way. Facings for these patterns are treated in the same manner, too.

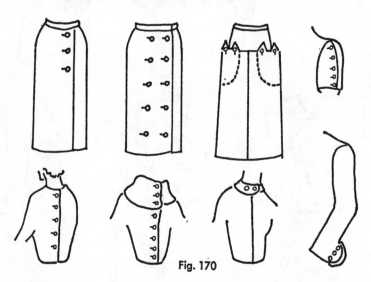

Fig. 170

ENTER—STYLE

The fly front

The fly front is frequently used in sports clothes, blouses, skirts, or dresses. This is a closing with an extra fold of material on the right front which conceals a strip of buttonholes. The left front extension is made in the usual manner. The fly front may be made in either one or two pieces. The two-piece fly front is somewhat easier to make.

The two-piece fly front

1. Make the blouse pattern with front extension.

2. Fold on the extension line an amount deep enough to cover the buttonholes plus a little over (Fig. 171a).

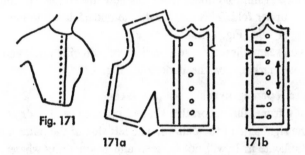

Fig. 171   171a   171b

3. Add seam allowance and notches to this new edge (Fig. 171a).
4. Make an underfold of material ⅛" narrower than the top fold. This will ensure that the understrip is covered (Fig. 171b).
5. Add seam allowance and matching notches to the underfold (Fig. 171b).
6. Mark the grain, center front, fold lines, buttonholes, and stitching line.

The one-piece fly front

1. Make the blouse pattern with front extension.
2. Fold on the extension line to an amount deep enough to cover the buttonholes plus a little over. Locate the stitching line for the upper fold at this line (Fig. 172a).

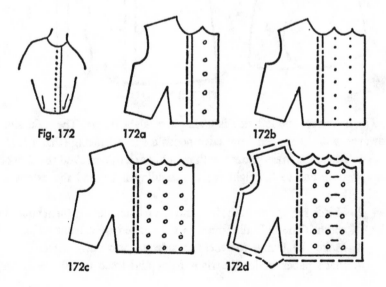

Fig. 172   172a   172b

172c   172d

3. Fold back, accordion fashion, from the stitching line to within ⅛″ of the extension fold (Fig. 172b).

4. Once again, fold under from this new line to the stitching line of the upper fold. This will create the underfold all in one with the upper fold (Fig. 172c).

5. Add seam allowance, fold indicators, stitching lines, and button-hole markings on the underfold (Fig. 172d).

The shaped opening needs a shaped facing

Like the fly front, the decorative shaped opening of this dress appears only on the right side of the pattern. The left side of the pattern does not have to duplicate it. It will not be seen and has nothing whatever to do with the fit as does the double-breasted opening extension. It would only entail a lot of unnecessary work.

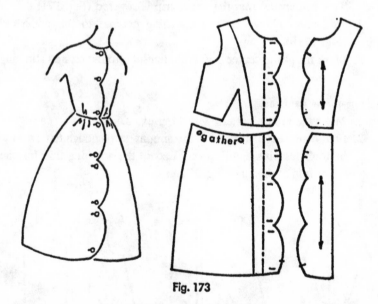

Fig. 173

The facing for the left side is a simple straight facing. The right side, however, with its shaped front edge needs a shaped facing (Fig. 173).

1. Make the dress pattern with opening extensions. Add the shaped style line to the right front, extending it beyond the extension line.

2. Sketch facings on both right and left fronts, making them equal in width. (The only difference is the shaped right front edge.)

3. Make the facing for the left side as previously directed.

4. Place paper under the right front and trace the shaped edge,

the neckline, the shoulder, the facing edge, the waistline, and the hem line. (The skirt facing is a continuation of the bodice facing, seamed at the waistline as is the dress.)

5. Add the hem, seam allowance, grain, notches, center front, fold indicators, and markings for buttons and buttonholes.

The cardigan opening

This simple opening is a great favorite because it can be worn in so many ways. It is used for formal as well as sports wear. The neckline can be worn plain or filled in with scarf, bib, gilet, collar, or necklace. The cardigan may be waist length, hip length, or dress length. It may have no buttons, few buttons, or many buttons.

You can make the usual facing for the cardigan or top-stitch the band to the right side. You may want to make it of self-fabric. Or you might try using a band of contrasting grain, color, or texture. Experiment with ribbon, embroidery, crocheted or knitted bands, beading, spangling, etc.

While the cardigan may be more fashionable some years than others, some type of cardigan seems always to be in vogue.

The directions for making the cardigan coat-dress pattern which follows will give you a chance to use your hip-length sloper for the first time.

A cardigan coat dress

1. Trace the hip-length slopers, front and back. Part of the dart control of the front sloper should be in an underarm dart (Fig. 174a).

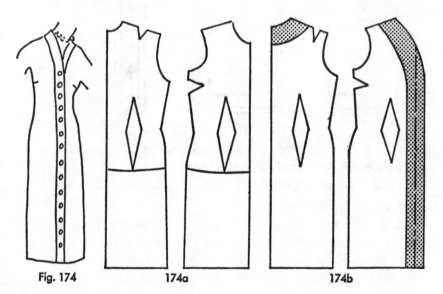

Fig. 174   174a   174b

2. Extend the slopers to dress length (Fig. 174a).

3. Determine and draw the extension necessary for the front lap (Fig. 174b).

4. Draw the neckline style line, front and back, continuing into the front extension (Fig. 174b).

5. Locate the facing band on front and back, parallel to the neckline and front edge. This is usually a narrow band about 1½″ to 2″, wide enough to cover the buttonhole made horizontally plus a little over. (On occasion, buttonholes are worked vertically in the band.)

6. Trace the front and back facing bands.

7. On both dress pattern and facing bands, add hem, seam allowance, notches, grain, center front, back fold, stitching line for band, marking for buttons and buttonholes.

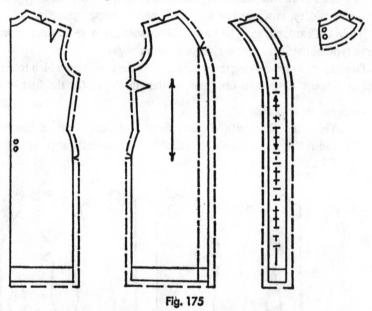

Fig. 175

NOTE: If the waistline darts are left unstitched, your dress will have a chemise effect. For a fitted dress, stitch the darts.

The completed pattern for the chemise cardigan coat dress (Fig. 175).

The asymmetric opening

Perhaps the most widely used of the asymmetric openings is the surplice style or some variation of it. Time was when only the middle aged and matronly chose this style for its slimming effect. Newer styles make the surplice or asymmetric opening young, dashing, and sophisticated.

The pattern for this opening is made in the same way as the double-breasted garment. When skirt and bodice are used together, they are treated as a design unit.

Here are a few general rules to follow in developing your pattern:

1. Sketch your design.
2. Trace the entire front or back sloper for bodice or skirt.
3. Draw the style line.
4. Cut out the pattern piece which contains the style line. Discard the unnecessary remainder.
5. Make any desired changes such as shifting darts, adding fullness.
6. Mark the facing.
7. Trace the completed pattern and the facing.
8. Add all the usual markings.

Here are several designs using the asymmetric opening (Fig. 176). Try to make the pattern for one of them. Perhaps you may even be tempted to use the pattern for a new dress.

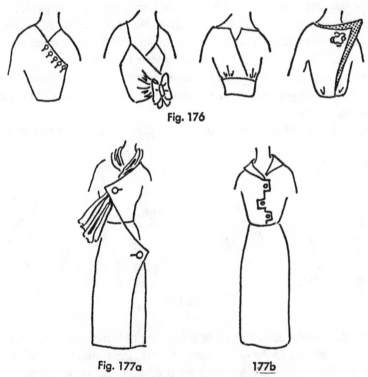

Fig. 176

Fig. 177a   1.77b

A woman's garment usually closes right over left, both front and back. A surprise design element can be introduced by lapping left over right to dramatize a style line. Or an interesting counterpoint can be achieved by lapping the bodice in one direction and the skirt in the other (Fig. 177a).

An unusual effect may be obtained with an alternate right and left lapping of shaped tab extensions (Fig. 177b).

Shaped tabs added to the opening extension can turn an ordinary opening into a distinctive one (Fig. 178).

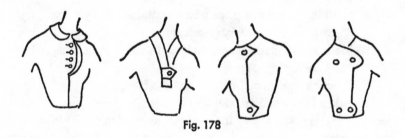

Fig. 178

How it's done:

Draw the shape you want for the tab. Cut it out and tape it or pin it to the opening extension. Or cut a freehand shape out of paper like the pin packs you used to cut out as a child. Tape it or pin it to the opening extension. Trace the entire pattern piece, including your tab.

The tab may be curved, pointed, square, round, triangular, simple, complex—anything you can invent. Of course this shaped opening will require a shaped facing.

This could be just the spot for the spectacular button or pin you've been hoarding.

More tabs! (Fig. 179).

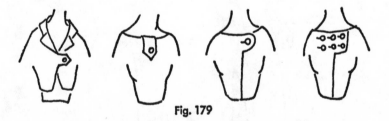

Fig. 179

And while you're at it, you might try adding or inserting a shaped tab in the same manner to the center front or back, the shoulder, the neckline, collars, sleeves, cuffs, yokes, any seam or dart, the waistline, the armhole—just about anywhere it makes sense and some places it doesn't (Fig. 180).

Fig. 180

BUTTONS AND BOWS

A closing needs a fastening

Have you ever built a dress around some very special buttons or a set of antique studs? Have you ever flirted with the idea of daringly using red piped buttonholes on a black dress? Have you ever wondered what giant-size buttonholes would be like on a simple suit? Have you ever sighed with relief at the thought that you could skip the buttonholes altogether and fasten your dress with bows? Have you ever been tempted to use that bizarre-looking chain your Aunt Hepzibah willed you? Have you ever been lured by outsize hooks and eyes, intricate frogs, fabulous buckles? Of course you have! It happens to every woman who sews! Right now you must have a collection of such choice items tucked away somewhere waiting for just the right dress to come along.

"Button, button—who's got the button?"

Your button box with its years-old collection can be a real source of inspiration. Buttons are like jewels. Old ones, new ones, novelty ones, classic ones. These are worth the time and money and love it takes to collect them. Used sparingly or profusely in interesting groupings, they can "make" a garment.

A beautiful button is worthy of a beautiful buttonhole. Learn to make good-looking ones. The narrow, self-fabric piped buttonhole is the most all-around useful. It is subdued enough not to detract from the button, which is the star. But sometimes it is fun to do the opposite. Dramatize the buttonhole by using a contrasting color—red on white—or a contrasting texture—satin on wool—or a contrasting pattern—striped on plain fabric. Sometimes it is effective to make the narrowest binding you can handle. And sometimes it is fun to make the piping giant size.

Perhaps, instead of the usual horizontal buttonhole, you might try a vertical or diagonal one or even a curved one. If you star the buttonhole, then let the button play a secondary role. Make it a button covered in the garment fabric. Buttonholes, too, can make a decorative virtue of a functional necessity (Fig. 181).

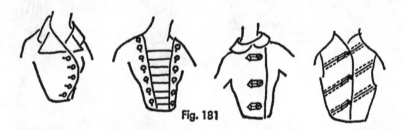

Fig. 181

Brass buckles and bands which button

Bands which button or buckle add design interest (Fig. 182). Experiment with paper cutouts for size, shape, and placement. When you find what you like, add the seam allowance, grain, button and buttonhole markings. Face. Indicate on your pattern where these bands are applied.

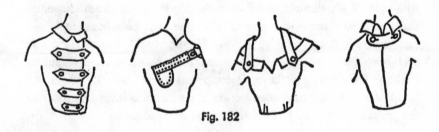

Fig. 182

Beauty and the bow

Bands which tie in bows can be a charming fastening (Fig. 183). The bows
are merely the bands extended to the necessary length. The bow ends may
be shaped.

Cut the pattern to the desired length, width, and shape. Add the seam
allowance and grain. Show where the bands are to be applied to the body
of the pattern.

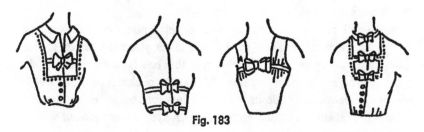

Fig. 183

Bows—little ones, big ones, stringlike ones, and sashlike ones—they're
ornamental and they're fun. They may be used as actual fastenings or
merely applied as decoration over some hidden fastening. They may be of
self-fabric or of some contrasting color or texture. Bows may be an easy
way out, but they certainly look pretty (Fig. 184).

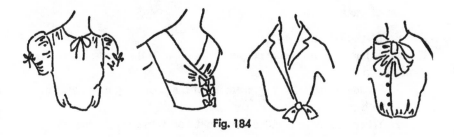

Fig. 184

POCKETS A'PLENTY

The pocket as decoration

Pockets, like fastenings, can serve a decorative as well as useful purpose.
Often they are the only decoration on a dress or jacket. Indeed, in exam-
ining contemporary fashions, it is sometimes hard to remember that they
have any use at all. They are set in the most unlikely places and appear
in the most baffling sizes. However, from a design point of view, there
are no limits. Pockets may appear in any size, any style, any place.

The pocket for use

If the pocket is really to be used, it should be so placed and so sized that you can get your hand into it. A safe rule to follow for size is to make a pocket with a horizontal or diagonal opening as wide as the fullest part of your hand plus 1″. Make a pocket which opens vertically as wide as the fullest part of your hand plus 2″. Place your pocket where you can reach it easily.

Paper pockets

It is a good plan to experiment with paper cutouts or scraps of the material to be used until you get just the effect you want for style, size, shape, and placement. For home sewers this can be done either in the designing stage or in the fitting stage. Unless the pocket is part of the style line, it can be made a little further along in your sewing. Experimenting in this latter stage has the advantage of giving you a truer idea of what is most flattering for you.

Pockets, like fastenings, can be used singly or in groups. They can be small, medium, large, or graduated in size. Whether useful or bizarre, if you are going to have pockets at all, make them an interesting and integral part of your design and not just something stuck on.

Structurally, pockets fall into two classes—those which are applied to the right side of the garment and those which are inserted into a slash or seam of the garment.

The patch pocket (Fig. 185)

The patch pocket is a completed pocket applied to the right side of the garment. To make it:

1. Decide the style, size, placement of the pocket by experimenting with paper cutouts.
2. When you have decided just what you want, sketch the pocket on your garment pattern.
3. Lay paper under the pocket area and trace the outline of the pocket with your tracing wheel.
4. Make any style changes to this piece you may wish.
   a. *For style interest,* you may do anything to the patch pocket that you have learned to do with your bodice and skirt.
      Divide the area interestingly (Fig. 185a); add fullness (Fig. 185b); add a flap or tab (Fig. 185c); button it (Fig. 185d); add a band (Fig. 185e); use the grain as part of the design (Fig. 185f); trim it (Fig. 185g).
   b. *For a straight pocket edge,* add the hem (in proportion to the

size of the pocket), seam allowance, grain, and fold indicator.

c. *For a shaped pocket edge,* add a shaped facing, seam allowance, grain, and notches.

d. *For a lined pocket* (this is sometimes desirable, depending on the weight of the fabric used), make the lining pattern ⅛″ smaller than the pocket. This will allow a little extra material on the pocket itself so that you can roll the seam under slightly. Add seam allowance, grain, notches.

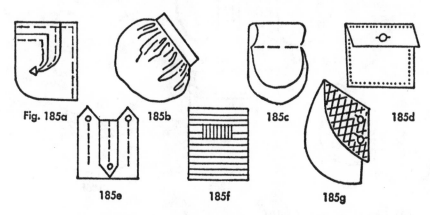

Fig. 185a   185b   185c   185d

185e   185f   185g

5. *In sewing,* make the complete patch pocket. Apply it to the garment. Usually the pocket is slip-stitched to the garment. When it is to be top-stitched, indicate the stitching line on both pocket and garment. Match these lines. If the pocket is to be top-stitched in from the edge as a line of decorative stitching, it makes a nicer finish to face the edge with the fabric of the pocket. Make this facing in the usual manner.

NOTE: Pockets of lightweight material may lie flat against the garment. Pockets of heavy or bulky materials may need a little ease when the pocket is set so that you can get your hand into it without pulling or distorting the garment. Add ¼″ ease to each side of the top edge of the pocket. Taper to the side. Set into the original marking on your garment. The top edge will stand away slightly (about ½″).

The set-in pocket (Fig. 186)

This pocket is set into a seam or a slash of the material. It may be a variation of the bound buttonhole (Fig. 186a). It may be a welt or flap pocket (Fig. 186b). It may be a pocket inserted into a seam—a style line, a side seam, a yoke seam, a panel seam (Fig. 186c). The opening for the pocket may be straight or curved (Fig. 186d). It may be horizontal, vertical, or diagonal (Fig. 186e). It may be of self-fabric or of contrasting color, texture, or grain (Fig. 186f).

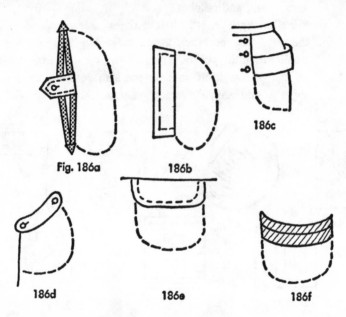

Fig. 186a   186b   186c

186d   186e   186f

The bound or welt pocket

In the bound or welt pocket, the opening of the pocket is slashed right into the garment. You must be very careful in handling and very sure the pocket is placed exactly where you want it. You can't change your mind after the opening has been cut. It is wise to experiment beforehand with paper cutouts or scraps of the material for size, style, grain and placement just as you did with the patch pocket. A little time in planning may save you a lot of heartache.

The pocket is composed of two parts. One part is seen from the outside as a binding, a piping, a welt, or a flap. The other is the pocket proper which is attached to the underside.

The pocket which is attached to the underside is a strip of fabric cut a little wider than the piping or welt to allow for the seams which join it. For a straight opening a one-piece strip can be used. It should be long enough for both upper (front) and under (back) pocket sections and proportionate in size. The two-piece pocket is used for a curved or diagonal opening. In this case the under pocket is somewhat longer than the upper pocket to compensate for the depth of the opening. The pocket sections are generally joined and stitched in a curved shape. They may be made of self-fabric if the material is light enough in weight. Should the garment fabric be heavy or bulky it is better to make the pocket of lightweight or lining material. A narrow strip of the garment fabric may be stitched over the top part of the under pocket as a facing. This ensures a continuous appearance of the garment fabric as the pocket opens. Another way to solve this problem is to use the garment fabric for the under pocket and lining material for the upper pocket.

The bound pocket (*sometimes called a slot pocket*—Fig. 187)
This is the pocket which looks and is made like a bound buttonhole.

1. Mark the position for the opening of the pocket on the pattern. This includes the slash line, the stitching line above and below the slash lines, and the ends (Figs. 187a and 187b).
2. Draw the pocket on the pattern (Figs. 187a and 187b).

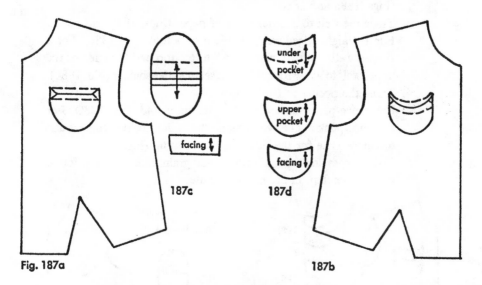

Fig. 187a   187b

3. Lay paper under the pocket area and trace the pocket (Figs. 187c and 187d). Remember either to double this for a straight pocket or cut two for a shaped pocket. Add seam allowance, grain, and notches.
4. The piping of the bound pocket is made of a strip of fabric usually four times the width of the finished binding and ½″ longer on each side. For a straight pocket it is usual to use the horizontal or vertical grain, although you may use the bias for special effect. A curved pocket must be made of a bias strip of fabric so that it can be manipulated into a curve.

NOTE: In sewing, make the bound buttonhole first in the usual manner.

Top face the under pocket with a strip of the garment fabric as suggested on p. 163. Attach the pocket sections to the seam allowance of the binding on the wrong side. Stitch the pocket sections together.

The welt pocket (Fig. 188)

For the welt pocket, a separate piece of material is inserted into a slash, forming the welt. (The flap pocket is constructed in the same way but it is inserted in a reverse position.) Remember to do a little experimenting with paper cutouts or scraps of the actual material for size, shape, placement, and grain. When you have decided on size, shape, and where you are going to place the welt:

1. Draw the welt in position on the pattern (Figs. 188a and 188d).
2. With broken lines, draw the shape of the pocket on the pattern (Figs. 188a and 188d).
3. Trace the welt to another piece of paper (Figs. 188b and 188e). For a straight-edged welt, double it on a fold (Fig. 188e). For a shaped welt, cut two, adding ⅛″ to the top and the ends of the upper welt to allow for rolling the seam under slightly (Fig. 188b).
4. Trace the pocket to fresh paper.
   For a one-piece pocket, double this on a fold (Fig. 188f). For a shaped pocket, cut two, making the under pocket long enough to compensate for the depth of the opening (Fig. 188c).
5. To all pieces add seam allowance and grain. Mark the position of the welt or flap on the garment pattern.

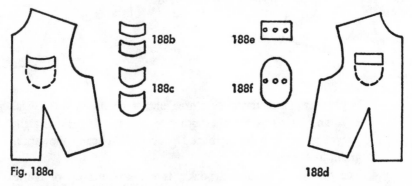

Fig. 188a   188d

Directions for sewing the welt:

1. Mark the position of the welt on the right side of the garment.
2. Make the welt. Trim and grade the seams, clip, turn, and press.
3. On the right side of the garment lay the welt in a position opposite to that of the finished pocket.
   Match the lower stitching line of the welt with the lower line of

the welt marking on the garment.

4. Stitch the welt to the garment. Trim the seam allowance close to the stitching.
5. Lay the upper and under pockets in position over the welt and baste.
6. Turn the garment to the wrong side. Stitch directly over the line of stitching which joined the welt to the garment. Make a line of stitching parallel and ¼" away. Stitch across the ends. This rectangle of stitching should be a stitch or two shorter than the welt. This will make certain that the welt will completely cover the pocket opening when it is turned to its proper position.
7. Slash between the stitching lines to within ¼" of the ends. Cut diagonally to the corners.
8. Turn the pocket to the wrong side. The welt will automatically turn up into its proper position.
9. Stitch the pockets together.
10. Fell (slip-stitch) the ends of the welt to the garment, hiding the seam and concealing the opening.

The flap pocket

The flap pocket is made in the same way as the welt pocket except that the flap is sewn to the upper side of the slash line.

When completed and pulled through to the proper position, the flap may be top-stitched ⅛" below the top seam. The rest is left open (to flap, presumably) and *not* slip-stitched to the garment as is the welt.

When a flap is stitched over a patch pocket, it should be stitched to position ½" above the pocket opening to allow the hand to get into the pocket. Trim the seam allowance and press the flap down into position. The flap may then be top-stitched ⅛" below the top seam.

The flap pocket may also be made so that the lower edge of the pocket opening is finished like the bound pocket.

To make the pocket pattern, follow the same procedure as for the welt pocket.

The pocket set in a seam (Fig. 189)

This pocket consists of two shaped pieces several inches longer than the pocket opening to allow for some depth. There are two types:

a. the pocket stitched into a seam (usually a side seam) *and* the waistline (Fig. 189a). This pocket has straight sides and a straight top.
b. the pocket stitched only into a seam (Fig. 189b).

The pocket may be made of self-fabric, lining fabric, lining fabric with facing of self-fabric, fabric for under pocket, and lining for upper pocket. To make the pattern, follow this procedure:

1. On the pattern, draw in the size, shape, and placement of the pocket.
2. Mark the point at which pocket and seam join (Figs. 189a and 189b).

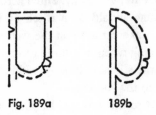

Fig. 189a   189b

3. Trace the pocket.
4. Add seam allowance, notches, grain.
5. Sewing directions:
   With right sides together, stitch the straight edges of the pockets to the seams, matching notches and the point at which the stitching ends. Turn to the inside. Stitch the pocket pieces together. Press toward the front. In type *a*, baste the top edges to the waistline and catch in the waistband or waistline seam.

The pocket set in a style line

This pocket is concealed in the joining (style line) of yoke and bodice or skirt section (Fig. 190). Indeed, any sections which need to be joined by a seam can be utilized for this purpose. In Fig. 191 the under pocket is an extension of the yoke section; the upper pocket is a facing for the lower bodice section.

The pattern for Fig. 190 illustrates the principle.

1. Trace the bodice-front sloper. Indicate gathers for the dart control (Fig. 190a).
2. Draw the yoke style line. Notch (Fig. 190a).

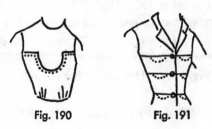

Fig. 190   Fig. 191

3. With dotted lines locate the pocket and the facing for the lower section (Fig. 190b).

4. Remember that the under pocket is an extension of the yoke. Trace the upper section of the bodice which will include the yoke, the dotted facing line, and the pocket (Fig. 190c).

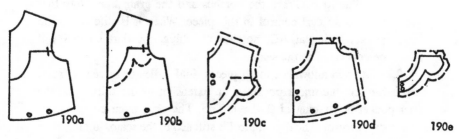

190a   190b   190c   190d   190e

5. Trace the lower section of the bodice from yoke style line down (Fig. 190d).

6. Trace the facing and pocket in one. This is the upper pocket (Fig. 190e).

7. To all pieces add seam allowance, notches, and grain.

The pocket can be made to stand away slightly by utilizing the dart control, as in the following skirt pattern.

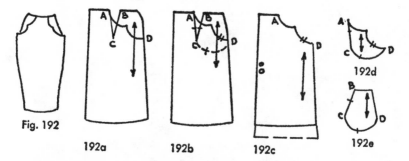

Fig. 192   192a   192b   192c   192d   192e

1. Trace the skirt-front sloper and locate the grain line near the side seam (Fig. 192a).

2. Draw the style line. Ignore the dart control (Fig. 192a).

3. Label dart points A, B, C. Label the end of the style line D (Fig. 192a).

4. Locate the shaped pocket. It has one straight side, the dart leg AC, and continues in a curve to D (Fig. 192b).

5. Locate notches on the dart, pocket, and style line (Fig. 192b).

6. Trace the skirt-front pattern—center front, waistline, style line, side seam, and hem. Note that this section contains the dart

control which remains open. Trace notches and grain. Add hem (Fig. 192c).

7. Trace the pocket facing from A to C to D and the style line back to A. Trace the notches and the grain line (Fig. 192d).

8. Trace the yoke—the dart leg BC to D, the side seam and the waistline to B. Trace the notches and the grain line. Note that there is no dart control in this piece. When it is stitched to the pocket facing at AC, notches matching, the dart control will be concealed in the seam.

9. Add seam allowance to all pieces, fold indicator to center front. As you can see, the under pocket is an extension of the skirt yoke; the upper pocket is a facing of the style line. The skirt front contains unstitched dart control. The dart control is stitched in the seam, joining yoke and facing. The effect is a smooth fit over the hips and a pocket which stands away slightly from the yoke.

CHAPTER *7*

Collars to capes

FOR THE YOUNG AND THE BEAUTIFUL ONLY

A collarless neckline, be it ever so interesting, is difficult to wear. It calls for a firm chin, a smooth and slender neck, and a good set to the shoulders—all attributes, alas, of the young and the beautiful. This leaves the majority of us out. For us, the severity of the collarless neckline needs to be softened with a gay scarf, our faithful pearls, or a pleasing collar.

FOR THE REST OF US

Fortunately there are many types of collars to choose from—little ones and big ones, tailored ones and frilly ones, dramatic ones and modest ones—something for everybody. Take your choice—but remember there are more considerations than style preference alone.

Choose a line that is flattering to the shape of your face. Preserve a nice balance between the collar and the rest of the silhouette. Consider the line of your hairdo in relation to the line of the collar. If you'll be wearing your collar under a coat, choose one that will accommodate to that.

A WORD FOR IT

Terms in collar construction
There are certain terms in collar construction with which you should be familiar since we refer to them constantly in making the collar pattern.

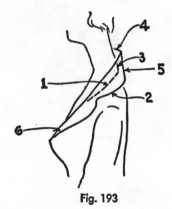

Fig. 193

1. neckline—line which is stitched to neckline of garment
2. style line—outer edge (silhouette, or circumference) of collar
3. stand—the rise of the collar from the neckline to the roll line
4. roll line—the line along which the collar turns down
5. fall—the depth of the collar from the roll line to the style line
6. break—point at which collar turns back to form lapel

Collar names

The names applied to collars frequently identify them as to type. The name of a collar may refer to the style line, as the Puritan collar, the Peter Pan collar, the Elizabethan collar. Sometimes collars are referred to by the way they fit around the neck—the flat collar, the convertible collar, the standing collar.

And sometimes they are characterized by the degree of roll, as the roll-fitted collar, the medium-roll collar, the deep-roll collar. All three characteristics are used to classify collars—the neckline shape, the degree of roll, and the style line.

COLLARS, CURVES, AND STANDS

In general

Any collar which conforms to the shape of the neck lies flat (Peter Pan collar, Fig. 194a). When the neckline of the collar curves in the opposite direction to the curve of the bodice neckline, the roll will be deeper (the set-on tailored collar, Fig. 194b). The straighter the neckline of the collar, the higher the stand (the mandarin collar, Fig. 194c). When the collar neckline is more curved than the neckline of the bodice, the outer edge will ripple (Fig. 194d).

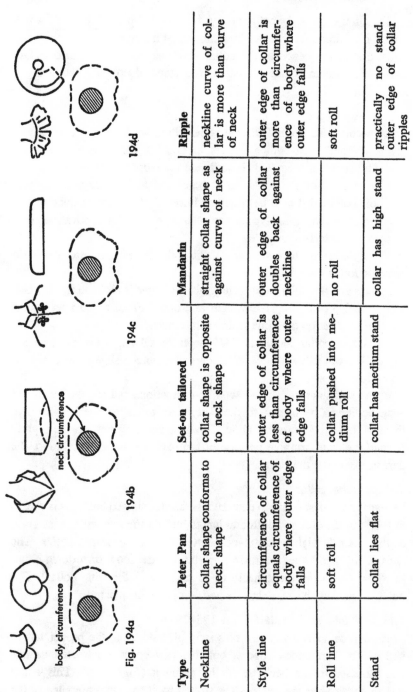

body circumference

neck circumference

Fig. 194a   194b   194c   194d

Type	Peter Pan	Set-on tailored	Mandarin	Ripple
Neckline	collar shape conforms to neck shape	collar shape is opposite to neck shape	straight collar shape as against curve of neck	neckline curve of collar is more than curve of neck
Style line	circumference of collar equals circumference of body where outer edge falls	outer edge of collar is less than circumference of body where outer edge falls	outer edge of collar doubles back against neckline	outer edge of collar is more than circumference of body where outer edge falls
Roll line	soft roll	collar pushed into medium roll	no roll	soft roll
Stand	collar lies flat	collar has medium stand	collar has high stand	practically no stand. outer edge of collar ripples

The outer edge of the collar always falls on that part of the body which equals it in circumference, pushing the rest of it into a stand. As the outer edge, or circumference of the collar shortens, the stand increases. As the collar circumference increases, the stand decreases, producing a soft-roll effect.

Before you begin

Since a collar fits around the entire neckline, we must work with both the front- and back-bodice slopers in drafting the pattern. Trace the neck and shoulder area. This is sufficient for most collars.

The neckline of the bodice must be established before you begin to draft the collar. If it is to be raised or lowered, this must be done first.

Analyze the collar for type, since each type of collar is constructed in its own characteristic way.

The style line of the outer edge of the collar is designed after the basic construction is completed.

Collars are generally faced. They will lie better if also interfaced. Use an interfacing of appropriate weight and body. Facings and interfacings are generally cut on the same grain as the collar.

The upper collar should be ⅛" larger on all edges except the neck edge. This will allow the seam to be rolled under slightly and hidden from view.

In the examples which follow, when directions call for the front and back bodice to be placed so that shoulders touch or overlap, arrange them so they meet at the neckline. The back shoulder will extend slightly beyond the front armhole because of the back shoulder dart. Ignore the dart in designing the collar.

The standing collar

Perhaps the easiest collar to construct is the standing collar. This is a strip of fabric in the desired width and length, cut on the straight or bias grain of the cloth. Straight grain stands better, bias grain drapes better. The ends of this band may meet, overlap, button, tie, loop, turn down either in whole (as in the turtle neck) or in part (as in the wing collar). The outer edge may be straight, shaped, rippled, or pleated.

The bias fold as a collar (Figs. 195–197)

This band collar is made of a bias strip of material in the proper length and width. The folded edge is out, the raw edges are treated as one and attached to the neckline of the garment (Fig. 196a). This collar has an easy roll as the outer edges stretch to fit the circumference of the body at the point where they fall. It may be steamed into a curved

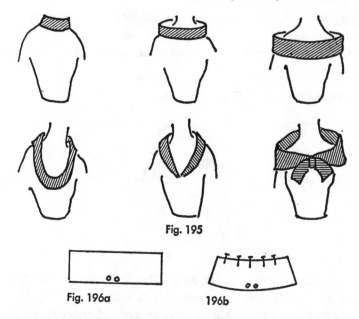

Fig. 195

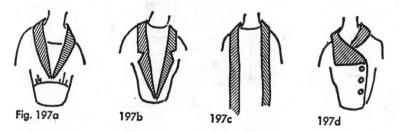

Fig. 196a   196b

shape before stitching by easing in the neckline edge and stretching the outer edge (Fig. 196b).

When attaching the collar to the neckline, a higher stand may be produced by stretching the neck edge of the collar to fit the neckline. A flatter collar may be obtained by easing the neck edge of the collar into the neckline and stretching the outer edge, increasing its circumference.

A shawl-collar effect may be obtained with a bias band by narrowing the band as it approaches the center front (Fig. 197a); or shaping the style line (Fig. 197b); or turning it back in the tuxedo style (Fig. 197c); or shaping the band to form the asymmetric collar (Fig. 197d).

Fig. 197a   197b   197c   197d

There is a difference between this type of shawl collar and a true shawl collar. The true shawl collar is all in one with the front bodice and is seamed at the center back. The roll line, of necessity, must be a straight line. The shawl-effect collars illustrated above are bands stitched to the neckline, which may be shaped. This would permit the collar to roll back in a shape, too. This is a simple way of achieving a shawl-collar look. Directions for making the true shawl collar appear on p. 189 of this chapter.

The Elizabethan collar (Figs. 198–201)

Fig. 198

This is a variation of the standing collar. The Elizabethan collar fits at the lowered front neckline and stands at the back with a slight flare. The style line may be straight or shaped. It must be made of material which will stand—organdy, taffeta, lace. If other materials are used, facing and interfacing will help make the collar stand. Sometimes wiring or boning is used. This is a dramatic collar, rather impractical for ordinary wear (particularly under a coat), but it is quite impressive for formal gowns, wedding gowns, or hostess gowns.

The Elizabethan collar is simply constructed in one of several methods, depending on the fabric used.

Method I

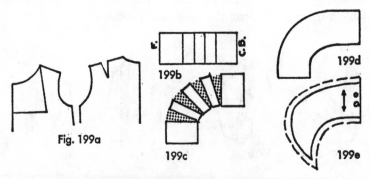

Fig. 199a

1. Establish the bodice neckline (Fig. 199a).
2. Cut a strip of paper of the desired width and equal to the length of the measurement from front to center back (Fig. 199b).
3. Draw several slash lines starting a short distance from the center

back and front. This helps the collar stand at the back and fit without flare at the front (Fig. 199b).

4. Slash and spread for the desired effect (Fig. 199c).
5. Trace the pattern (Fig. 199d).
6. Modify the style line if you wish (Fig. 199e).
7. Add seam allowance, grain, and fold indicator (Fig. 199e).

Method II

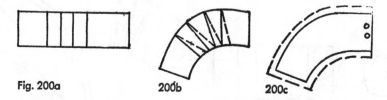

Fig. 200a   200b   200c

A similar final effect may be obtained by starting with a strip of paper of the desired width and length of the outer edge from front to center back (Fig. 200a).

1. Draw slash lines as previously directed (Fig. 200a).
2. Slash and overlap at neckline edge to fit the neckline (Fig. 200b).
3. Trace the pattern (Fig. 200c).
4. Add seam allowance, fold indicator, and grain (Fig. 200c).

Methods I and II produce a shaped pattern piece. If you are using a material like old lace, which you do not want to cut into shape, then use Method III described below.

Method III

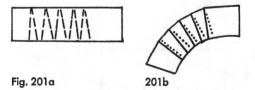

Fig. 201a   201b

1. Draw a band equal in width to your lace and equal in length to the measurement of front to center back at the outer edge (Fig. 201a).
2. Place darts for shaping where the slash lines were placed in Methods I and II (Fig. 201b).
3. When the darts are stitched, the shape of the collar will be like the patterns developed by Methods I and II (Fig. 201b).

NOTE: The front ends may be mitered and stitched to give it shape without cutting.

The fichu (Figs. 202 and 203)

The fichu is related to the Elizabethan collar. It is much wider, generally attached on a deeper neckline, drapes rather than stands, and is joined in some fashion at the center front. It is like the Elizabethan collar in its construction.

Method I

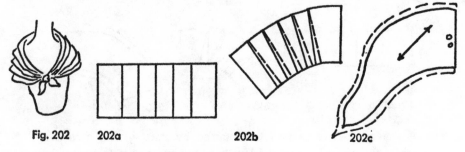

Fig. 202   202a   202b   202c

1. Establish the neckline of the bodice.
2. Start with paper of the desired width (at its widest point) and half the length of the completed outer edge. In this case, long enough to fit around the shoulders (Fig. 202a).
3. Draw slash lines (Fig. 202a).
4. Slash and overlap to fit the neckline (Fig. 202b).
5. Trace the pattern. Draw the style line. Add the extension for the tie or fastening (Fig. 202c).
6. Add seam allowance, grain, and fold indicator. Since this is a draped collar, it would be best to use a bias grain.

Method II

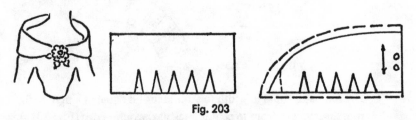

Fig. 203

Substitute for 3 and 4 of Method I:

    3a. Draw darts the length of the desired stand for neckline shaping.
    4a. Use straight grain for this collar. It will stand better. It is also easier to sew darts on straight grain than on bias.

The beauty of the fichu depends on the grace of its proportion and its drape. These are a little difficult to visualize in a flat pattern. A good plan is to make a tentative paper pattern, trace it to muslin, allowing generous margins. Experiment with the muslin to get just the right effect. Make your final pattern from the corrected muslin.

The Chinese, or mandarin collar (Figs. 204–206)

The straight standing Chinese collar, or those many variations based on it are always fashionable.

Though we refer to it as a "straight-standing collar," actually it fits best if somewhat shaped. This will prevent it from poking out at the back. It will also keep the front edges from overlapping. Shaping makes it fit not only the base of the neck but the narrower measurement of the neck where the style line of the collar falls.

This collar may be constructed in either one of two ways.

Method I—Chinese collar with shaped facing.

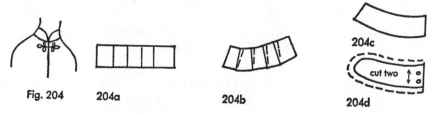

Fig. 204   204a   204b   204c   204d

1. Cut a strip of paper one half the entire length of the neckline and the proper width, not more than 1½" (Fig. 204a).
2. Slash in several places from the outer edge to the neckline edge (Fig. 204a).
3. Overlap the slashed edges until the outer edge fits the neck measurement at a comparable height (Fig. 204b).
4. Trace the pattern (Fig. 204c).
5. Draw any desired style line (Fig. 204d).
6. Add seam allowance, grain, and fold indicator. Cut two, using one for the collar and the other for the facing (Fig. 204d).

Method II—Chinese collar (double collar on a lengthwise or crosswise fold)

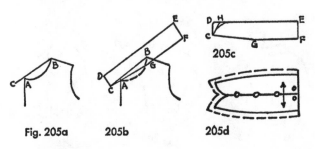

Fig. 205a   205b   205c   205d

1. Trace the neck area of the bodice-front sloper. Label point A at the center front neckline. Label point B at the shoulder neckline (Fig. 205a).
2. Draw a straight line from B to A and extend it to C so that line B–A–C equals the curved front neckline measurement (Fig. 205a).
3. Square a line from C equal to the stand of the collar (not more than 1½″). Mark point D (Fig. 205b).
4. Square a line from D equal to the neckline measurement from center front to center back. Label point E (Fig. 205b).
5. From E square a line down equal to the stand of the collar plus ⅜″. Mark this point F (Fig. 205b).
6. Square a line from F to the shoulder. Label point G (Fig. 205b).
7. Connect G with C at center front (Fig. 205b).
8. Trace the collar (Fig. 205c).
9. Correct line C–G–F with a slightly curved line (Fig. 205c).
10. From D on line D–E measure over ½″. Label point H (Fig. 205c).
11. Connect C and H with a straight line (Fig. 205c).
12. If you wish, you may draw a curved style line for the front end of the collar (Fig. 205c).
13. Fold on line H–E and trace the collar (Fig. 205d).
14. Add seam allowance, grain, and fold indicator (Fig. 205d).

NOTE: The shaping of the collar neckline will make it fit more snugly against the neck. The angle of the center front will prevent the front ends from overlapping.

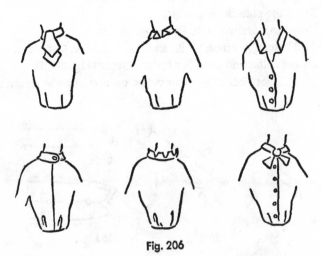

Fig. 206

The directions in Method II can be used for the many style variations of the mandarin collar which require a straight outer edge rather than a shaped one. It is also useful when the fabric layout can utilize a fold of material rather than the shaped facing of Method I.

Extended bands which tie in a bow at center front also fit better when drafted by Method II.

Figure 206 shows some variations of the Chinese collar. It is easy to see why it is such a popular collar.

FLAT COLLARS

Collars which lie flat around the neck may go from tiny ones of 1" or so to the bigness of a cape collar. Big or little, they are constructed in much the same way.

The simulated collar—a collar that really isn't

Fig. 207

The flattest and simplest collar effect is the simulated collar (Fig. 207). It isn't really a collar at all. It is a shaped facing applied to the right side of the garment and top-stitched.

The plastron collar—a temporary attachment

The plastron is a separate collar attached to the dress—between frequent launderings—by pins, tabs, snaps, buttons, bastings, or the law of gravity. It is a flat, facing-type collar, raised slightly at the neckline so the dress beneath doesn't show. It can be made of any interesting material in decorative shapes and garnished with trimming.

1. Place the front- and back-bodice slopers together, shoulder seams touching and meeting at the neckline (Fig. 208a). Trace.

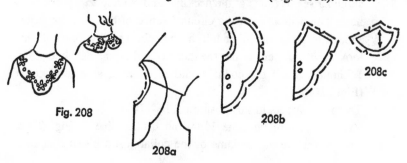

Fig. 208

208a

208b

208c

2. Raise the neckline slightly (the broken line in Fig. 208a).
3. Draw the style line of the plastron (Fig. 208a).
4. Trace the plastron in one piece (Fig. 208b). If there is more than the usual slope to the shoulders, join the front and back sections with a shoulder seam. In that case the grain line of the plastron back is parallel to the center back.
5. Add seam allowance, fold indicator, and grain.

The gilet—a fill-in

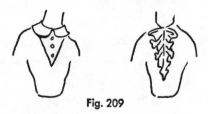

Fig. 209

The gilet is a fill-in for a neckline (Fig. 209). It is made like the plastron but generally has a collar or jabot attached. It is made deep enough to tuck into the neckline of the garment.

The Peter Pan collar—memories of childhood
The Peter Pan remains one of the prettiest of collars. No wonder it appears in so many variations.

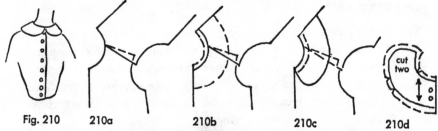

Fig. 210   210a   210b   210c   210d

1. Place the front- and back-bodice slopers together so that the shoulder seams touch at the neckline and overlap ½″ at the armhole. This will shorten the circumference of the outer edge just enough to push the collar into a low roll. The low roll not only looks a little softer but has the merit of hiding the neckline seam. Without the roll the collar would resemble a simulated collar (Fig. 210a).
2. Trace the slopers in this position (Fig. 210a).
3. Raise the entire neckline ⅛″—the broken line in Fig. 210b. This will make the neckline of the collar just a bit smaller than

the neckline of the bodice. Stretching the collar to fit the neckline of the bodice will also help produce the soft roll of the Peter Pan collar.

4. From the neckline measure down in a number of places the width of the collar (Fig. 210b).
5. Draw the style line connecting these points (Fig. 210c).
6. Trace the pattern. Add the grain line parallel to the center back, notches at the neckline, seam allowance, and fold indicator (Fig. 210d).

The Peter Pan collar is sometimes termed a flat-fitted collar because of its fit around the neckline and shoulders. The same type of fit and construction may be applied to a lower neckline as illustrated (Fig. 211). Simply lower the neckline first, then proceed as for the Peter Pan collar.

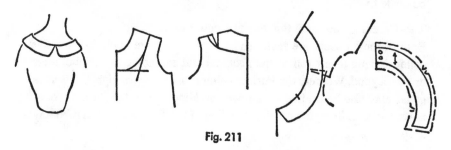

Fig. 211

The sailor collar

This is a flat collar similar in construction to the Peter Pan collar and designed on a dropped neckline, as in the previous exercise.

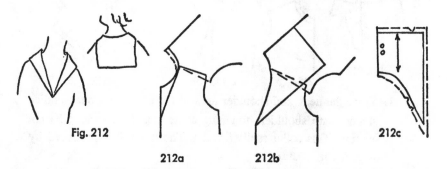

Fig. 212

212a   212b   212c

1. Trace the neck and shoulder area of the front- and back-bodice slopers. Place the shoulders so they touch at the neckline and overlap ½″ at the armhole (Fig. 212a).
2. Lower the front neckline in a V shape—low enough to slip your

head through. A higher V neckline will need a center front opening (Fig. 212a).

3. Raise the back neckline ⅛". Ease this line into the front neckline. (This will shorten the back neckline slightly. When stretched to fit the bodice neckline, it will produce a slight roll. Remember?) (Fig. 212a).

4. Draw the style line (Fig. 212b).

5. Trace the collar. Add seam allowance, notches, grain (parallel to the center back), and fold indicator (Fig. 212c).

(It is impossible to resist the temptation to add: trim with braid and put a star in each corner.)

NOTE: As previously noted, if there is a more than usual slope to the shoulders, this collar looks better if seamed at the shoulder, where it can be made to fit.

The Bertha collar and the Puritan collar

Both of these collars are really short capes. They are made like the flat collar, having a soft roll at the neckline and extending to the shoulders or just beyond. Whereas the Puritan collar is always worn high, the Bertha collar may also be drafted on a lower neckline. While the Puritan collar never varies in its style line, the style line of the Bertha collar can be any shape you wish.

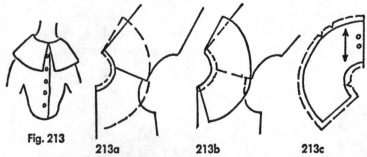

Fig. 213

213a   213b   213c

1. Trace the neck and shoulder area of the front- and back-bodice slopers with shoulders touching at neck and armhole. (Do *not* overlap. This collar really lies flat. The tiny roll is produced by step 2. Fig. 213a).

2. Raise the neckline ⅛" to shorten length (Fig. 213a).

3. From the neckline measure down in a number of places the depth of the collar (Fig. 213a).

4. Extend the collar at the center back style line ⅛" and taper to the center back neckline. This slight addition will help the cape-

like collar fall better around the shoulders (Fig. 213a).

5. Draw the style line (Fig. 213b).
6. Trace the pattern. Add seam allowance, notches, grain (parallel to the center back), and fold indicator (Fig. 213c).

NOTE: If the shoulders slope more than usual, use a shaped shoulder seam to produce a better fit.

The cape collar

The cape collar hangs below the shoulders. It will hang better if center front and center back are located on the straight grain. To do this the cape collar may be drafted in either of the following ways.

Method I produces a rippled, circular collar

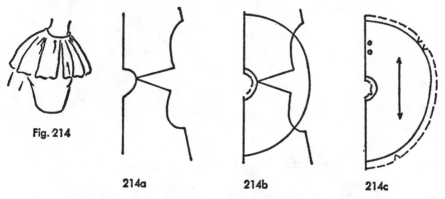

Fig. 214

214a   214b   214c

1. Trace the neck and shoulder area of the front- and back-bodice slopers so that center front and center back are in a straight line. The shoulders touch at the neckline (Fig. 214a).
2. Raise the neckline ⅛″ to shorten it for a slight roll (Fig. 214b).
3. Draw the style line below the shoulder (Fig. 214b).
4. Trace the pattern (Fig. 214c).
5. Add seam allowance, grain, notches, and fold indicator (Fig. 214c).

Method II for a fitted cape collar

1. Trace the neck and shoulder area of the front- and back-bodice slopers so shoulders touch at the armhole while center front and center back are at right angles. Raise the neckline ⅛″ (Fig. 215a).
2. Draw the style line (Fig. 215a).
3. Trace the pattern—style line, center front and center back, neckline, and the shoulders to produce a dart (Fig. 215b). This method produces a fitted cape collar. If the shoulders slope more than usual and additional fitting is necessary, use a shoulder seam be-

low the dart. Directions for doing this follow:

a. draw a straight slash line through the center of the dart and continue it to the style line. Notch. Cut out the collar (Fig. 215c).

b. cut out the dart. Cut on the slash line which separates collar front from collar back (Fig. 215d).

c. trace the collar front and collar back patterns (Fig. 215d).

d. correct the angle at the shoulder with a smooth curve (Fig. 215d).

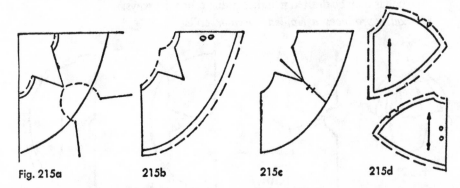

Fig. 215a   215b   215c   215d

4. For both patterns: add seam allowances, grain, notches, and fold indicator.

For either Method I or Method II the neckline and style line may be varied in design. These methods merely present basic construction of the cape collar.

COLLARS WITH A DEEPER ROLL

How to make the flat collar have a deeper roll

By the following method you may change the flat collar to one of medium (half) roll or to one of deep (full) roll.

1. Trace the flat collar. Cut it out.

2. Draw five or six slash lines. Begin the slash lines about 1½" away from the center front and center back (Fig. 216a).

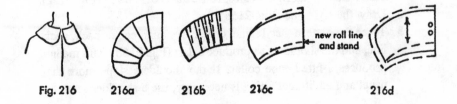

Fig. 216   216a   216b   216c   216d

3. Slash to the neckline. Overlap the style line—more at the back, less at the front until the desired effect has been obtained. This may require some experimentation in muslin (Fig. 216b).
4. When satisfied as to roll, trace the pattern (Fig. 216c).
5. Add to the depth of the collar an amount equal to that used up by the newly created stand. Be sure to make the fall of the collar deep enough to hide the neckline seam (Fig. 216c).
6. Trace the pattern. Add seam allowance, grain, notches, and fold indicator (Fig. 216d).

The amount of overlapping in step 3 will determine the roll. Obviously this could be continued until you get a standing collar. Adding to the depth of the collar, as in step 5, will give you the reefer collar.

The roll-fitted collar

This flattering collar with its medium roll at back and flat fit at the front is a favorite with designers. It may be designed on a straight or shaped neckline which is generally lowered in front.

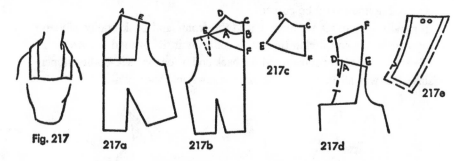

Fig. 217   217a   217b   217c   217d   217e

1. Trace the bodice-front sloper and establish the neckline. Label point A at the shoulder. Draw the style line for the front collar. Label point E (Fig. 217a).
2. Trace the back-bodice sloper. Label point A to correspond to point A on the bodice front (Fig. 217b).
3. Extend the center back line to a distance equal to twice the desired stand. Label point C (Fig. 217b).
4. Draw a slightly curved line from C equal to the back neckline A–B. Label point D (Fig. 217b).
5. On the back shoulder measure up a distance from the armscye equal to the same distance on the bodice front. Label point E to correspond to point E on the bodice front (Fig. 217b).
6. Connect E and D with a straight line (Fig. 217b).
7. From C measure down on the center back line a distance equal

to E–D plus ¼″. Mark the point F (Fig. 217b).

8. Connect E and F with a curved line (Fig. 217b).
9. Trace the back collar E–D–C–F and cut it out (Fig. 217c). This collar is standard in the roll-fitted type. Of course the style line may vary.
10. Trace the bodice front with its new neckline and the style line for the collar (Fig. 217d).
11. Place the collar front and the collar back so that the shoulder seams touch and meet at E. The back collar will extend beyond the front collar at the neckline because of the stand (Fig. 217d).
12. Connect D and the front of the collar with a straight line. Correct the style line with a smooth line if necessary (Fig. 217d).
13. Notch the neckline at the front (Fig. 217d).
14. Trace the entire collar. Add seam allowance, fold indicator, notch, and grain line parallel to the center back (Fig. 217e).

NOTE: In this exercise a straight line is used to connect D with the front neckline because the design indicates it. Were this a curved neckline the connecting line would be curved.

In previous exercises we have placed the front- and back-bodice slopers together so we could plan the entire collar as it fits around the neck. In this exercise we have substituted the back collar for the back-bodice sloper since this was all that was necessary to complete the collar.

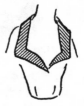

Fig. 218

Sometimes it is difficult to distinguish the roll-fitted collar from others. The test is—does the front collar lie flat? does it have a definite roll at the back? Figure 218 shows several interesting roll-fitted collars for you to try.

The convertible collar—a medium-roll collar

This is the versatile collar which can be worn open or closed and looks equally well both ways. When worn closed, the collar rolls from center back to center front and forms a V shape at center front. This distinguishes it from a high, flat-fitted collar which, because of its structure, follows the curve of the neck. When worn open, the convertible collar forms lapels having a notched effect at the opening extension.

A very simple convertible collar can be made as a variation of the band collar (Figs. 219 and 220).

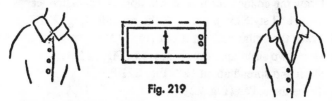

Fig. 219

1. Draw a band double the width of the collar and the length of the neckline from center front to center back.
2. Add seam allowance to the ends and neck edges, the grain parallel to the center back and the fold indicator.

These directions produce a double collar, folded on the lengthwise (or crosswise) grain, folded edge out, neck edge attached to the neckline of the bodice. The front ends may be shaped.

This is a simple and satisfactory collar but has one disadvantage as to fit. When worn closed, it stands away slightly from the neck, particularly at the back. Can you think why? The roll line is larger than the neck circumference at the point of the stand. To make this neckline fit better, use the principle described in drafting the mandarin collar on p. 177. See Fig. 220.

Fig. 220

The mannish shirtwaist collar
This is a convertible collar with a separate stand.

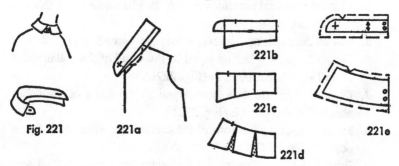

Fig. 221   **221a**   **221b**   **221c**   **221d**   **221e**

The stand
1. The stand is constructed like the mandarin collar (Fig. 221a).
2. Add a front extension so that it can button (Fig. 221a).

The collar

1. Trace the neck band (Fig. 221b).
2. Draw the collar over it as it will appear (neckline, center front, back, and style line). Notch at the neckline (Fig. 221b).
3. Trace the collar and cut it out (Fig. 221c).
4. Draw two slash lines evenly spaced (Fig. 221c).
5. Slash and spread about ⅛″ (Fig. 221d).
6. Trace the collar (Fig. 221e).

Both stand and collar

Add the seam allowance, grain, notches, and fold indicators (Fig. 221e).

The convertible collar with stand and collar in one

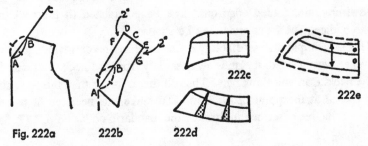

Fig. 222a   222b   222d

1. Trace the neck area of the front-bodice sloper and mark points A and B (Fig. 222a).
2. Connect A and B with a straight line. Extend it so the line equals the measurement of the neckline from center front to center back. Label the end of the line—C (Fig. 222a).
3. Fold the paper on line A–B–C (Fig. 222a).
4. Trace the original neckline curve A–B. Place a notch on this line (Fig. 222a).
5. Unfold the paper and draw in lightly the traced line (Fig. 222a).
6. From C, square a line up equal to the stand of the collar about 1″ to 1½″. Label point D (Fig. 222b).
7. From C, square a line down equal to the stand of the collar plus ⅜″. Label point E (Fig. 222b).
8. From D, square a line toward the center front equal to 2″. Label point F (Fig. 222b).
9. From E, square a line toward the center front equal to 2″. Label point G (Fig. 222b).
10. From F, draw a line to the highest point of the neckline tracing (Fig. 222b).

11. Draw the style line from the center front at A all the way around to G (Fig. 222b).
12. Trace the collar and the roll line A–B–C (Fig. 222c).
13. Draw two slash lines evenly spaced (Fig. 222c).
14. Slash and spread about ⅛″ (Fig. 222d).
15. Trace the new pattern. Trace the roll line (Fig. 222e).
16. Add seam allowance, grain, fold indicator, and notches (Fig. 222e).

The shawl collar

Formerly relegated to the "older set," the shawl collar, in recent years, has undergone a complete rejuvenation. In beautiful shapes and proportions, with high, low, or medium break, both single- or double-breasted, it can be found everywhere in design.

The bias band as a shawl collar was illustrated in Fig. 197 of this chapter. The following directions are for the true shawl collar—that is, a collar cut in one with the bodice and seamed at the center back.

In drafting this collar it is advisable to shift some of the dart control to a center front dart. This slightly lengthens the roll line from the break to the center back and makes the collar fit a little easier. The amount of control shifted varies from very little, about ¼″ if the break is above bust-point height, to ¾″ at bust-point height, to 1″ or more if the break is at the waistline. A shawl collar on a double-breasted garment needs only half these amounts.

Actually the shawl collar is a combination of two types of collars already familiar to you. The front collar, or lapel is an extension of the bodice, folded back in revers and similar in appearance to the flat-fitted collar. The back collar is either one of the two types of convertible collars developed in this chapter. The front collar and back collar are joined at the shoulder line, with an allowance for the stand, at an angle which will make the back collar fit snugly against the back of the neck.

1. Trace the bodice-front sloper. Shift some of the dart control to the center front (Fig. 223a).
2. Draw the opening extension, break, neckline (now the roll line of the lapel), and style line of the lapel (Fig. 223b).
3. Fold on the roll line and trace the lapel shape. Unfold and draw in the lapel shape (Fig. 223c).
4. Make the pattern for the convertible collar in either of the methods suggested in this chapter. The length of the collar will equal half the back neck measurement—that is, from shoulder to center back. Be sure to draw in the roll line (Fig. 223d).

5. Slash the bodice front on the roll line from the shoulder to the break. Spread to an amount equal to the stand of the collar (Fig. 223e).
6. Attach the collar to the lapel, matching necklines, stand, and style line (Fig. 223f).
7. Spread the collar at the style line so that it joins the shoulder at an angle of 75° (75° is ⅚ of your right angle. Since figures and fabrics vary, this may require some experimentation in muslin to find just the right angle for your garment Fig. 223g).

Note that this position of the collar throws the center back seam off grain. This is characteristic of the shawl collar.

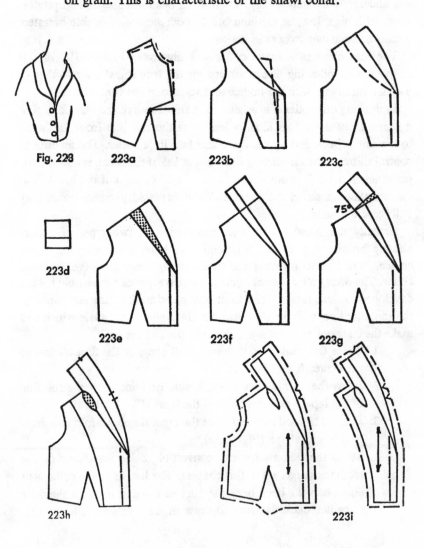

Fig. 223   223a   223b   223c

223d   223e   223f   223g

223h   223i

8. Trace the bodice, lapel, and collar all in one (Fig. 223h).
9. On the original neckline of the lapel make a shaped dart 3″ long, ½″ at the center, and tapering to nothing at the ends (Fig. 223h). This dart helps shape the neckline and improve its fit. This, too, is characteristic of the shawl collar.
10. Locate the facing (Fig. 223h) and trace it.
11. To both bodice pattern and facing add the seam allowance, grain, notches, center front, buttonholes, and roll line of collar and lapel (Fig. 223i).

The notched collar

This style, too, in endless variety of style line and proportion is a traditional favorite. In construction it is very similar to the shawl collar with the exception of its set-on collar.

1. Trace the bodice-front sloper. Shift some of the dart control to the center front (Fig. 224a).
2. Draw the opening extension, break, roll line, style line of the collar and the lapel, the point at which they join, and the shape of the seam which joins them (Fig. 224b).
3. Fold on the roll line and trace the lapel and the collar to the shoulder. Unfold and draw in the tracing. Mark the point at which the collar and lapel join (Fig. 224c).
4. Cut out the pattern. Cut away the collar portion to use when drafting the set-on collar (Fig. 224d).
5. Draft the set-on collar. This is a convertible collar. Its length is equal to half the back neck measurement plus that portion of the collar which you have just cut away in step 4. Its width and stand are determined by your design as sketched in step 2. Place the front collar against the back collar. Add the stand to the front portion. Trace the completed back collar. Trace the roll line. Correct the style line. Mark the point (o) at which it will join the lapel (Fig. 224e).
6. On the bodice front, slash the roll line to the break. Spread to an amount equal to the stand of the collar (Fig. 224f).
7. Trace the front bodice. Trace the new roll line. Mark the point at which it will join the set-on collar. Correct the neckline with a curved line (Fig. 224g).
8. Locate the facing (Fig. 224g).
   a. trace the facing for the bodice.
   b. trace a facing for the collar. (The under collar, or facing, is generally cut on the bias.)

9. To all pieces: add the seam allowance, grain, notches. Mark the center front and buttonhole placement. Mark the point at which collar and lapel join. Mark the roll line on the collar and lapel (Fig. 224h).

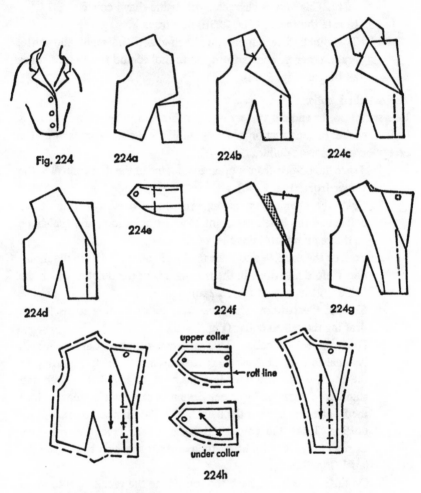

Fig. 224   224a   224b   224c

224d   224e   224f   224g

upper collar

← roll line

under collar

224h

CHOOSE YOUR COLLAR

"Push button" collars

The most difficult thing about drafting a collar is deciding which type it is—convertible or flat-fitted, shawl or roll-fitted, notched or shawl, etc. If you are copying a picture or a model or a sketch of your own, analyze it for neckline shape, roll, and style line. This will enable you to classify it as to type. Once you've done this, the rest is easy. Simply find the directions for that particular type of collar and follow them.

Add a little decoration

Each of the basic collars described in this chapter can be modified. Perhaps you would like to add a little decoration. There is a world of trimming to choose from—pipings, cordings, lace, ruffling, pleating, beading, embroidery, appliqués, and all sorts of interesting edgings.

Or perhaps some fullness

Or perhaps you would be happier to leave the trimming off and add some fullness. There is the collar with pleats (Fig. 225a); or a gathered collar (Fig. 225b); or one with godets (Fig. 225c). You could have rippled revers (Fig. 225d); or a jabot (Fig. 225e); or complete circles added to a band to give a bow effect (Fig. 225f).

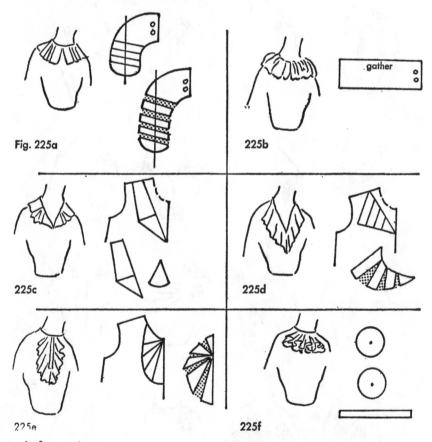

Fig. 225a

225b

225c

225d

225e

225f

A few notes:

If your design calls for a double-breasted closing for either a shawl or a notched collar, follow the directions for making the double-breasted pattern on p. 189.

Current fashion features collars of all types on lowered necklines. In drafting the patterns for these collars, be sure the neckline is lowered first. Then draft your collar.

You really cannot tell how a collar will fit just by looking at half a flat pattern. It is wise to cut a full collar in muslin and carefully fit it around the neck. Make any adjustments which are necessary in the muslin and transfer corrections to the pattern.

A thousand and one ways to design a collar! Keep a scrapbook of interesting collar treatments. Here are a few to get you started.

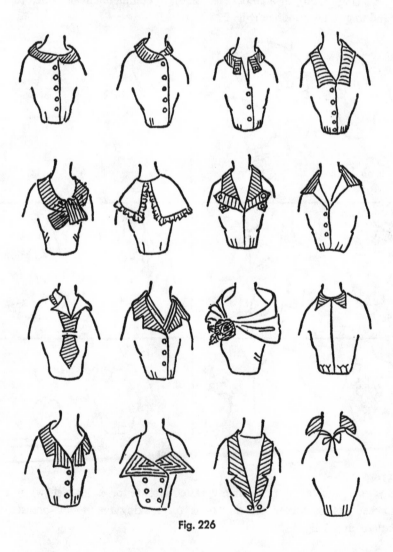

Fig. 226

CHAPTER *8*

The set-in sleeve and its cuff

FAMILIAR PRINCIPLES—NEW APPLICATIONS

One of the really satisfying aspects of pattern making is the fun of taking a few big principles and applying them in an infinite number of variations to create new designs. This is as true of the sleeve and its cuff as it was for the bodice, the skirt, the collar, and the pocket.

Sleeve types are classic—fitted, peasant, bishop, kimono, to name a few. Pattern principles are constant. The newness or todayness of a sleeve is your fresh approach to line, proportion, and detail.

In this chapter you will find no new pattern principles. There will be many applications and variations of what you already know.

Sleeves may be long, short, or any length between. They may be set into the bodice or they may appear all in one with the bodice. The dart control may be shifted or divided; it may appear in a seam; it may be converted into multiple darts. Fullness may be added by way of gathering, shirring, smocking, pleating, or circularity. The sleeve may have a yoke or a cowl. Opening extensions may be added and all sorts of interesting fastenings may be used. Decorative tabs or bands may be applied. Interesting cuffs may be the big interest.

Does this sound like old stuff to you? It is. You have been over it all in previous chapters. Now let us see how all of this applies to a sleeve.

DESIGNING WITH DART CONTROL

The little finger control

Dart control in the sleeve may be shifted as it was in the bodice and the skirt. Most often it is shifted to the little finger control. Directions for this are on p. 26 of Chapter 1. The space created by this shift is frequently utilized for design detail (Fig. 227).

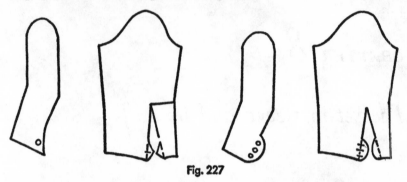

Fig. 227

If your design calls for a more centered style line, extend the elbow dart to the center of the sleeve. Shift the dart control to the center of the wrist line (Fig. 228).

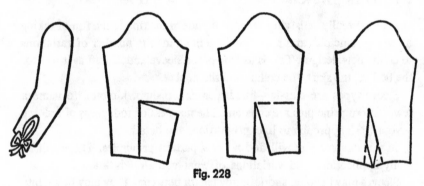

Fig. 228

If you need more room in this area for any design detail, use this sloper with the centrally located wrist dart. Slash from the dart point to the shoulder. Lap out some of the ease at the shoulder, making the dart area larger. Draw your style line in this space (Fig. 229).

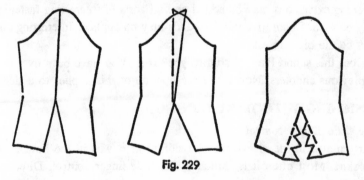

Fig. 229

The shoulder dart

The elbow dart control may be shifted to the shoulder. Used so, it provides the basis for fullness in the cap of the sleeve. The leg-o-mutton sleeve may be built on this dart control (Fig. 230).

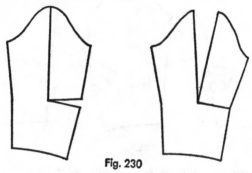

Fig. 230

The dart control may be divided
between cap and wrist (Fig. 231)

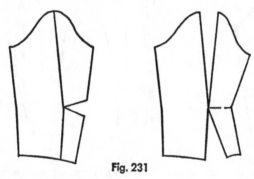

Fig. 231

between elbow and wrist (Fig. 232a)

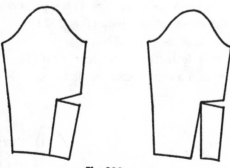

Fig. 232a

A semi-fitted sleeve may have dart control divided between elbow dart and wrist dart. The dart at the elbow remains as a smaller dart. The

dart control at the wrist makes a wider (and easier fitting) wrist.
into multiple darts (Fig. 232b)

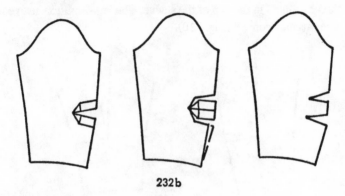

232b

The dart control may appear in a center seam

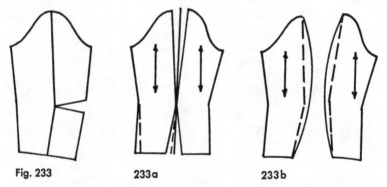

Fig. 233   233a   233b

1. Divide the dart control between shoulder and wrist at center (Fig. 233a).
2. Establish the grain in each section. This is parallel to a line drawn through the center of the darts (Fig. 233a).
3. Separate the sections (Fig. 233b).
4. Add any style features to the center seam (Fig. 233b).

In the short sleeve with a center seam no dart control is involved (Fig. 234).

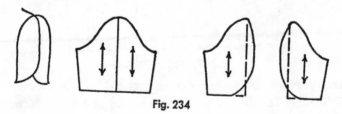

Fig. 234

"Single-" or "double-breasted" sleeve types

Extensions, both "single-" or "double-breasted" type, may be added to this center seam (Fig. 235).

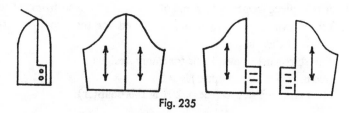

Fig. 235

A kind of "double-breasted," or asymmetric effect may be obtained in the following manner.

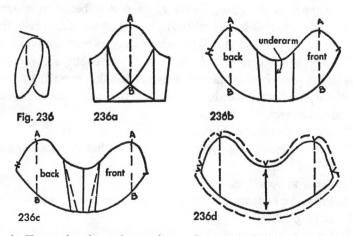

Fig. 236   236a   236b

236c   236d

1. Trace the short-sleeve sloper. Remove all but ½" ease in the cap. See p. 200 of this chapter.
2. Draw the style lines (Fig. 236a).
3. Draw slash lines from the notches at the cap to the hem of the sleeve. Draw line A–B from shoulder notch to hem (Fig. 236a).
4. Trace the front sleeve section. Trace the back sleeve section (Fig. 236b).
5. Join the sections at the underarm seam (Fig. 236b).
6. Slash on the slash lines and overlap, removing some of the fullness at the hem (Fig. 236c).
7. Trace the new sleeve pattern. Both sections will appear in one piece (Fig. 236d).
8. Add seam allowance, grain, notches, and mark the underarm (Fig. 236d). In closing, match lines A–B.

THE LONG AND SHORT OF IT—SLEEVE SLOPERS

Sleeves may be designed on a variety of slopers suitable to the design:
1. The one-piece sloper developed for your basic pattern.
2. A one-piece sloper with some of the ease removed from the cap.
3. The sleeve sloper and bodice adjusted for the sport shirt (see p. 204 of this chapter).
4. The shirtwaist sleeve, basis for many designs (see p. 205 of this chapter).
5. The two-piece sleeve (see p. 201 of this chapter).

Removing some of the ease from the sleeve cap

The ease in the cap of the sleeve, usually 1½" to 2", is necessary to accommodate the curve and fleshiness or muscle of the upper arm. There are many times in designing, however, when it is better to eliminate most of this ease. This is true when the design of the sleeve calls for a smooth fit at the armscye and some extra fullness across the upper arm (Fig. 237). It is also true when constructing a sport shirt, a cowl sleeve, or any sleeve with circular fullness. You will find that removing the ease is a useful device for fabrics which are difficult to ease into the armscye.

To remove the ease:
1. Draw a line across the cap of the sleeve (Fig. 237a).
2. Draw a line at right angles to this that touches the shoulder notch (Fig. 237a).
3. Slash on both lines.
4. Place the underarm of the cap in the usual position and keep it so (Fig. 237b).
5. Overlap the slashed edge at the shoulder, removing all but ½" ease. You will have to compare the length of this new cap with the armscye. Make any necessary adjustments (Fig. 237b).

Fig. 237a   237b   237c

NOTE: The ease may be converted into a dart, providing some shaping at the shoulder (Fig. 237c).

The two-piece sleeve

It is often easier to design an intricate sleeve pattern on the two-piece sleeve sloper rather than the one-piece sloper. The design variations may then be worked out on the upper sleeve, while the under sleeve retains its simple, slender fit.

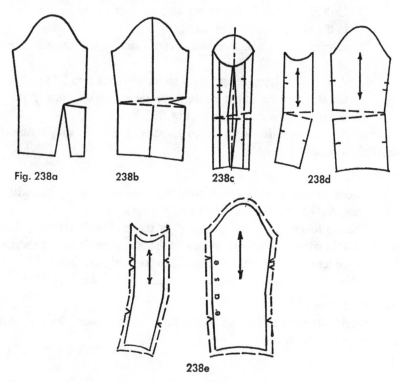

Fig. 238a   238b   238c   238d

238e

1. Trace the one-piece sleeve sloper.
2. Shift some of the elbow dart control to the wrist to widen it (Fig. 238a).
3. Draw a vertical line through the center of the sleeve from cap to elbow and from elbow to wrist (Fig. 238b).
4. Extend and fold out the elbow dart across the width of the sleeve (Fig. 238b).
5. Fold each side of the sleeve so that the underarm seam touches the vertical line (center) at armscye and wrist. Tape sleeve in this position (Fig. 238c).
6. Locate new seam lines in the underarm section in from the fold at sides—1″ at the armscye, ¾″ at the elbow, and ½″ at the wrist. The underarm section is generally one third of the total

width of the sleeve. Adjust the above measurements accordingly (Fig. 238c).

7. Notch these new lines and trace the center line which becomes the grain line.
8. Cut away the underarm section (Fig. 238d).
9. Unfold the dart in the upper section. Unfold the dart to ¼" in the under section (Fig. 238d).
10. Correct the seam lines of both sections with slightly curved lines (Fig. 238e).
11. Add seam allowance, notches, grain; mark an area 2" to 3" at the elbow of the upper sleeve to be eased into the corresponding area of the under sleeve (Fig. 238e).

NOTE: If you would like a two-piece sleeve with a more snugly fitted wrist, then omit step two.

Set-in sleeves

While more difficult to handle in sewing than the sleeve all in one with the bodice, the set-in sleeve has certain advantages.

The sleeve follows the natural "hang" of the arm while retaining its freedom of movement. There is no bulk at the underarm. Whether short, medium, or long, it has limitless possibilities for design variation.

The sleeves which follow in this chapter are all set-in sleeves.

The short sleeve

How short a sleeve is to be varies with the current fashion, the season, and the age of the wearer.

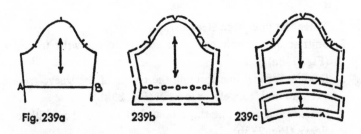

Fig. 239a   239b   239c

1. Trace the basic sleeve pattern above the elbow dart. Trace the grain line and notches (Fig. 239a).
2. Measure down an equal distance from the base of the sleeve cap on both underarm seams—points A and B (Fig. 239a).
3. Connect A and B with a straight line (Fig. 239a).
4. Add hem, seam allowance, notches, and grain (Fig. 239b).

Variations

For step 3, substitute: connect A and B with a slightly curved line. This curved lower edge requires a shaped facing or a bias binding (Fig. 239c). If the previous directions produce a sleeve which is a little too wide, the width may be reduced by any amount you wish on the underarm seam (Fig. 240a). Any interesting shape may be added to the sleeve edge (Fig. 240b).

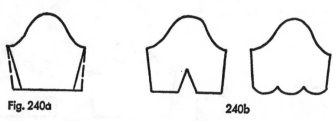

Fig. 240a   **240b**

If you are fond of this type of sleeve, it would be a good idea to make a short-sleeve sloper to keep handy for future patterns. Incorporate all the features you like in this sloper.

The three-quarter length sleeve

The three-quarter length sleeve, ideally, should be placed halfway between the wrist and the elbow. But there are many fine gradations in length, all of which pass as the three-quarter sleeve. Whatever the length, the way to arrive at the pattern is the same.

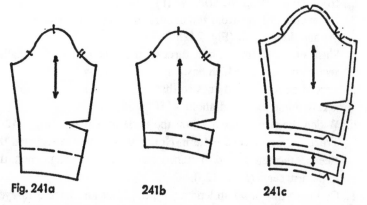

Fig. 241a   **241b**   **241c**

1. Trace the basic sleeve pattern. Trace the grain and the notches.
2. Measure *up* from the wrist in several places the desired amount.
3. Connect these points with a slightly curved line parallel to the wrist (Fig. 241a).
4. Make the facing for the new sleeve length (Fig. 241b).

5. Add the seam allowance, notches, and grain (Fig. 241c). Interesting shapes may be added to the edge of this sleeve length, also.

The sport-shirt sleeve

Shirts, dresses, and uniforms designed to be used in action require a sleeve which will not pull or ride up while in motion. To provide greater movement, the sleeve cap is shortened and widened and the underarm seam is lengthened. The armscye of the bodice is adjusted to fit. Such a sleeve may be either long or short.

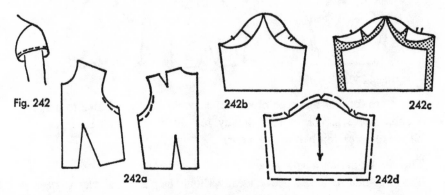

Fig. 242   242b   242c

242a   242d

1. Trace the front-bodice, back-bodice, and sleeve slopers.
2. Lower the armscye about 1" (this may vary with your design or need) on both bodice front and bodice back. The lowering starts from the notch on the armscye (Fig. 242a).
3. Draw curved lines from the underarm seam of the sleeve cap to the shoulder notch (Fig. 242b).
4. Slash on these lines. Slash through the center of each winglike section of the cap which has just been cut away.
5. Spread on all slashed lines so that underarm seam tip of the cap is raised and extended about 1" (Fig. 242c).
6. Widen the sleeve about 1" on the underarm seams (Fig. 242c).
7. Trace the new sleeve pattern. Notice that you have widened the sleeve, shortened and flattened the cap, and lengthened the underarm seam (Fig. 242d).
8. Compare this new cap length with the front and back armscyes. (There should be some ease in the sleeve cap—from ½" to ¾".) Make any necessary adjustments.
9. Relocate the notches to fit the bodice armscye. Add the seam allowance and grain (Fig. 242d).

This sleeve looks best in action; it was for action that it was designed.

When the arm is at rest, the sleeve wrinkles under the arm. The vertical grain fits as usual, but the horizontal grain cannot. It will droop to the front and back so that the sleeve pokes away somewhat at the center. Remember the emphasis in this sleeve is comfort in action rather than beauty at rest. You can't have everything.

The shirtwaist sleeve

1. Trace the basic sleeve pattern. Trace the grain.
2. Shift the elbow dart to the little finger position. The sleeve placket will be placed here (Fig. 243a).
3. Drop two vertical lines parallel to the grain from the sleeve cap to the wrist (Fig. 243a).
4. Draw a curved line at the wrist, making it about 1" deeper at the placket and curving it gradually to the underarm seam (Fig. 243a).

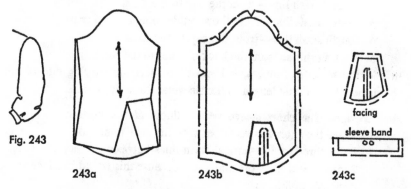

Fig. 243

facing

sleeve band

243a   243b   243c

5. Trace the pattern (Fig. 243b).
6. Mark the sleeve placket. This is usually about 3" in length. Mark perforations (or stitching line) ¼" on each side and top of placket. The placket is generally finished with a facing or a continuous lap (Fig. 243b).
7. Mark the grain, notches, seam allowance (Fig. 243b).
8. Construct a wrist band. The length of the band equals the wrist measurement plus ½" to 1" ease plus a buttonhole extension. The width equals 1"—usually made double (Fig. 243c).

MORE FULLNESS

Slash and spread

Additional fullness is created by the slash-and-spread method. Study the slash lines in Fig. 244.

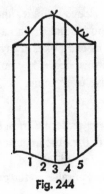

Fig. 244

line drawn across the sleeve cap
lines drawn at right angle to it

1. front slash line—from the front notch to the wrist
2. second slash line—from the cap to the wrist
3. center slash line—from the shoulder notch to the wrist
4. fourth slash line—from the cap to the wrist
5. back slash line from the back notches to the wrist

In addition to more fullness, it is possible to create varying effects of "blousiness" by adding length to the sleeve at these five points.

How to make the short sleeve with fullness at the bottom

1. Trace the short-sleeve sloper with the ease removed.
2. Draw three to five vertical slash lines between the notches (Fig. 245a). Never alter the underarm because this would produce undesirable bulkiness.
3. Slash and spread the hem line to the desired fullness (Fig. 245b).

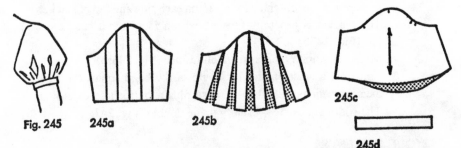

Fig. 245   245a   245b

245c

245d

4. Add length for "blousiness" by drawing a freehand curved line, slightly longer at the sleeve back and eased into the hem line at the underarm. Square off a short distance at each underarm seam so that the line will be a smooth continuous line, gently eased

into the underarm (Fig. 245c). "Blousiness" calls for extra length as well as width.

5. Add grain, notches, seam allowance, and a sleeve band to stay the fullness (Fig. 245d).

How to make the short sleeve with fullness at the cap

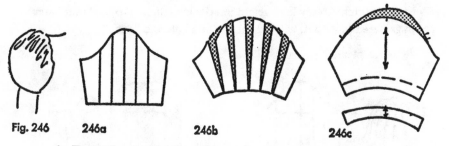

Fig. 246   246a   246b   246c

1. Trace the short-sleeve sloper with the ease removed.
2. Draw three to five vertical slash lines between the notches (Fig. 246a).
3. Slash and spread the cap to the desired fullness (Fig. 246b).
4. Add length to the cap for puffiness. Draw a freehand curve across the top so the back curve is slightly deeper than the front curve. Make the hem facing (Fig. 246c).
5. Add grain, notches, seam allowance, and hem facing.

NOTE: The amount of "blousiness," or puffiness can be determined only by experiment. Try out the pattern in muslin.

How to make the short puffed sleeve with fullness top and bottom

1. Trace the short-sleeve sloper with ease removed.
2. Draw vertical slash lines between the notches (Fig. 247a).
3. Draw a horizontal guide line across the cap (Fig. 247a).
4. Draw a horizontal guide line on paper.
5. Slash and spread to desired fullness, matching the guide lines (Fig. 247b).

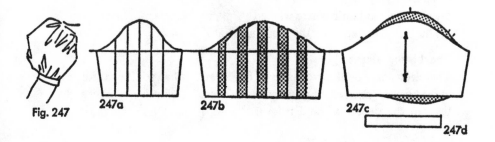

Fig. 247   247a   247b   247c   247d

6. Add a curved line to the cap for puffiness. Add a curved line to the hem for "blousiness." Be sure that curves are slightly deeper at the back of the sleeve (Fig. 247c).

7. Add seam allowance, notches, grain, and a band to stay the fullness at the hem (Fig. 247d).

NOTE: Any sleeve with puffiness requires a fabric with sufficient body to sustain the puff. A very lightweight interfacing, applied to the "puff" area and gathered in with it, will help shape and hold the "puff."

The short pleated sleeve

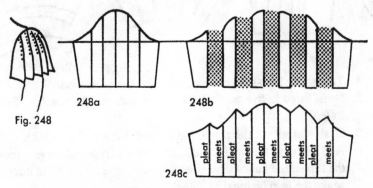

248a   248b   248c

Fig. 248

1. Trace the short-sleeve sloper with the ease removed.
2. Draw vertical slash lines where pleats are desired (Fig. 248a).
3. Draw a horizontal guide line on the sleeve and on fresh paper.
4. Slash on the pleat lines and spread to the desired depth, matching guide lines (Fig. 248b).
5. Fold the pattern in pleats as desired. Trace the sleeve cap. (Sometimes it is easier to place the cap of the sleeve sloper over the cap of the sleeve pattern and trace.)
6. Unfold the pattern (Fig. 248c).
7. Add the seam allowance, grain, notches, and pleat markings.

NOTE: For fabrics which require special pleating effect because of plaids or stripes:
lay pleats in the fabric where wanted
lay the sleeve pattern over the fabric and trace

The bishop sleeve

This sleeve may be three-quarter or full length. It has additional fullness at the bottom gathered into a wrist band. There is "blousiness" only at the back of the sleeve. Viewed from the front, it looks like the shirtwaist sleeve.

 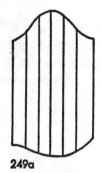

Fig. 249   249a

1. Trace the shirtwaist sleeve. Remove all but ¼" ease in the cap (Fig. 249a). (Cut to the desired length by drawing a line parallel to the wrist.)
2. Draw the five slash lines described on p. 206 of this chapter.

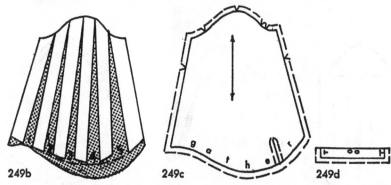

249b   249c   249d

3. Cut out the pattern. Cut on the slash lines.
4. Spread to desired fullness, adding somewhat more fullness at the sleeve back. Pin the sections to paper (Fig. 249b).
5. Add length for "blousiness" as follows (Fig. 249b):
   add some length in equal amounts at underarm seams
   keep front (1) as is
   add more length at center (3)
   add most length at back (5)
   Connect these points with a compound curved line.
6. Trace the pattern, notches, grain, and perforations to make the opening. (The opening is at the underarm.) Add the seam allowance (Fig. 249c).
7. Make a narrow wrist band as previously directed (Fig. 249c).
NOTE: If you wish a uniform "blousy" effect—front as well as back—use the method for the bell sleeve in the following exercise.

The bell sleeve

This sleeve, with added fullness at the bottom, generally hangs free in the characteristic bell shape which gives it its name. Unlike the bishop sleeve, it has a balanced fullness front and back. When worn unconfined by a wrist band, it does not need any extra length for "blousiness." This sleeve may be shortened.

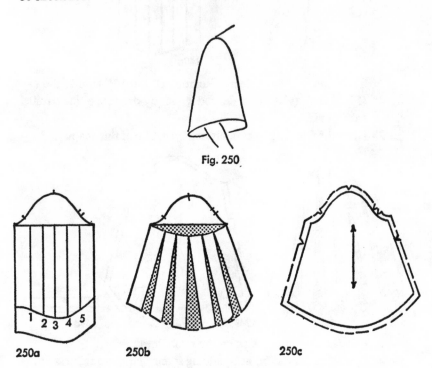

Fig. 250

250a   250b   250c

1. Trace the shirtwaist sleeve pattern. Remove all but ¼" ease in cap. Shorten in length if you wish (Fig. 250a).
2. Draw a line across the sleeve cap (Fig. 250a).
3. Draw the slash lines only to the sleeve cap (Fig. 250a).
4. Cut out the pattern. Cut away the cap. Cut on the slash lines.
5. Pin the cap to paper (Fig. 250b).
6. Pin the slashed sections for spread as illustrated (Fig. 250b). The underarm seam touches the cap. Spread the sections to the desired fullness. The center slash may be spread somewhat more. The underarm seams should have the same degree of bias.
7. Connect the wrist line with a smooth curved line (Fig. 250b).
8. Trace the pattern, notches, and grain. Add the seam allowance (Fig. 250c).

Have you noticed that the slashes in this pattern went only to the sleeve cap? This produces a smooth fit across the upper arm. The fullness was added below. The drop between the cap and the rest of the sleeve provides some extra length. This method produces a nicely proportioned bell shape. It can also be used whenever a less full upper sleeve is desirable. On the other hand, should you wish fullness to start at the very top of the cap, use the method of slashing and spreading described in the previous exercise.

The peasant sleeve
Long or three quarter with fullness top and bottom

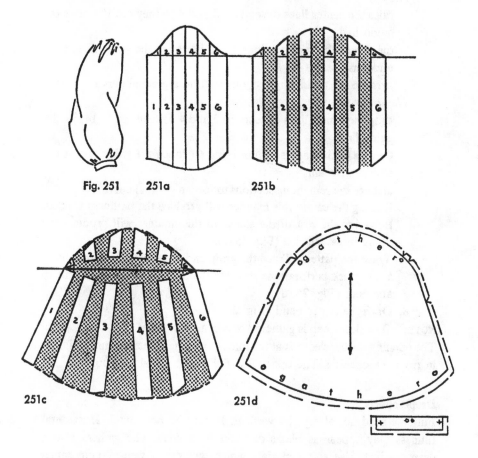

Fig. 251   251a   251b

251c   251d

1. Trace the shirtwaist sleeve pattern. Remove all but ¼″ ease in the cap.
2. Draw five vertical slash lines. Draw a horizontal slash line across

the cap of the sleeve. Label sections 1 to 6 in both cap and lower sleeve (Fig. 251a).

3. Cut out the sleeve pattern. Cut the cap away from the lower sleeve. Cut on all vertical slash lines.

4. Draw a guide line on paper.

5. Using the guide line, spread the entire sleeve as for balanced fullness, matching the amount of spread in the cap and the lower sleeve (Fig. 251b).

6. Then spread as for circularity in both cap and lower sleeve as follows:

The cap

raise the center lines of sections 3 and 4 so they are 1″ above the guide line

the tips of the cap (sections 1 and 6) touch the guide line at the underarm seams

arrange the remaining sections to form a gradual curve

The lower sleeve

drop the center lines of sections 3 and 4 so they are 1″ below the guide line

the tips of the cap (sections 1 and 6) touch the guide line at the underarm seam

arrange the remaining sections to form a gradual curve

Raising the cap in this manner will produce the puffiness needed. Lowering the rest of the sleeve in this manner will produce the "blousiness" needed (Fig. 251c).

7. Trace the pattern. Trace the grain and notches. Add seam allowance. Mark perforations showing the area to be gathered on cap and hem (Fig. 251d).

8. Draft the sleeve band (Fig. 251d).

NOTE: The sleeve cap is gathered between the notches.

The opening for the sleeve is at the underarm. The gathering starts slightly in from the opening. The opening is finished in usual fashion.

Drape effects

Fullness need not always be vertical. It may be horizontal. Horizontal fullness may appear as pleats or tucks or gathers. The gathers give a draped effect. Use soft materials which will drape well. Where much draping is used, it is wise to hold the drapery in place with a very light-weight or sheer lining. Here are a few construction patterns which show how to get these effects (Fig. 252).

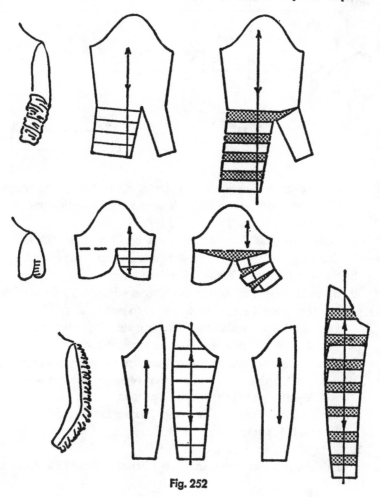

Fig. 252

FROM CAPS TO CAPES

The short set-in cap sleeve

This sleeve with its short, wide cap has the appearance of a cap sleeve but has the "no-strain" advantage of a set-in sleeve.

1. Trace the short-sleeve sloper without cap ease.
2. Measure down a short distance (from 1″ to 1½″) on both under-arm seams (Fig. 253a).
3. From the shoulder notch measure down the desired length of the cap (Fig. 253a).
4. From both front and back points on the sleeve cap, measure down a somewhat shorter distance (Fig. 253a).

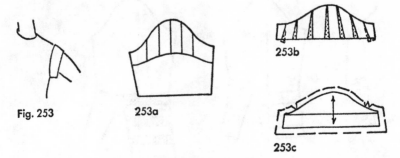

Fig. 253   253a   253b   253c

5. Connect these points with a graceful curve. Be sure to square off a short distance at the underarm so the hem line will be a continuous smooth line (Fig. 253a).

6. Draw five slash lines in the usual position (Fig. 253a).

7. Draw a guide line large enough to accommodate the spread.

8. Cut out the sleeve. Slash on the slash lines.

9. Spread the sections so that the bottom edges touch the straight line (Fig. 253b). It may be necessary to make a slight correction here. Slash and overlap the underarm sections to bring them in line. The bottom of this sleeve is a straight line.

10. Trace the new sleeve. Note how the shape of the cap has flattened out. The length of the cap, however, remains the same so that it will fit easily into the armscye (Fig. 253c).

11. Draw a line across the sleeve cap. Draw a line at right angles to it. This is the grain line.

12. Add seam allowance and notches.

NOTE: This sleeve looks better and hangs better if the entire sleeve is faced.

The short set-in cape sleeve
This sleeve hangs in the armscye like a little cape. It may have varying degrees of fullness as illustrated in Figs. 254–258.

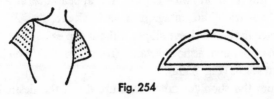

Fig. 254

This first cape sleeve is rather like the short set-in cap sleeve (Fig. 254). The hem is a straight line, the cap is a curved line, not quite the curve of the original armscye. You have seen in the previous exercise how the shape of the cap can be altered without changing its length or, we may add, its fit.

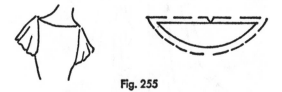

Fig. 255

Sleeve 2 has more fullness. Here the shape is reversed. The cap becomes a straight line while the hem line curves (Fig. 255).

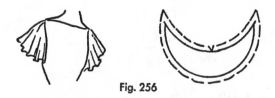

Fig. 256

Sleeve 3 has still more fullness. So much so that the cap and the hem line curve. The curve of the cap is the reverse of the usual cap curve (Fig. 256).

This process can be continued until, like the circular skirt, the sleeve becomes a full circle (Fig. 257). The inner circle remains the length of the armscye.

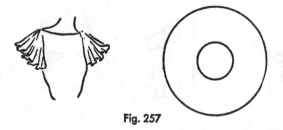

Fig. 257

In all of the foregoing sleeves the length of the armscye remained constant though its shape changed. The shape of the hem line changed as more fullness was added.

Any sleeve length may be treated in the same way. A long circular sleeve produces a dramatic effect suitable for negligees, hostess gowns, and angels in Sunday school plays (Fig. 258).

Fig. 258

NOVELTY SLEEVES

The lantern sleeve—sometimes called a balloon sleeve

The lantern sleeve is made of two circles stitched together.
One circle is for the upper section of the sleeve and one is for the lower.

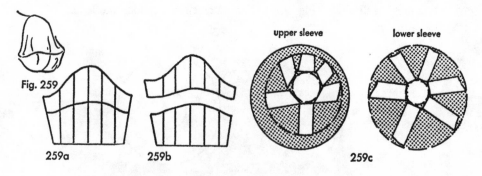

upper sleeve   lower sleeve

Fig. 259

259a   259b   259c

1. Trace the short-sleeve pattern. Remove the ease.
2. Shape the sleeve by narrowing each side of the underarm at the hem line. Taper to the armscye (Fig. 259a).
3. Divide the sleeve into upper and lower sections. Use a curved line (Fig. 259a).
4. Divide the sleeve into six equal parts by drawing vertical slash lines (Fig. 259a).

5. Cut out the sleeve. Cut the upper and lower sections apart (Fig. 259b).

6. Slash and spread each section into a circle. Lay the larger circumference over the smaller. Make the circumference of both sections match for size and shape. The inner circle of the upper section is the armscye. The inner circle of the lower section is the finished edge of the sleeve (Fig. 259c).

7. Trace the pattern. Add seam allowance and notches on the circular edges which join.

This sleeve is best made of some stiff material so that it will hold its shape. It may be trimmed with piping, cording, lace, or braid at the circular seam. Or the circular seam edge itself may be modified into interesting shapes (Fig. 260).

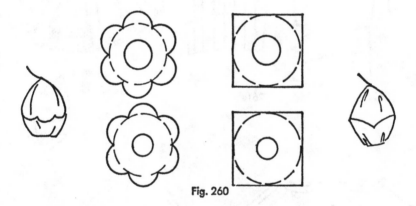

Fig. 260

Variations of the lantern sleeve

While the complete circle is very effective, there are times (and materials) when less-than-a-circle flare is more desirable. In this modified form the sleeve may be either long or short.

1. Trace the basic sleeve pattern. Remove all but ¼" ease in the cap.

2. Shorten the sleeve to the desired length (Figs. 261a and 261d).

3. In a three-quarter or long sleeve, fold out the elbow dart by a tuck starting at the elbow and coming to nothing at the front (Fig. 261d).

4. Divide the sleeve into upper and lower sections. This may be done with a straight or slightly curved line (Figs. 261a and 261e).

5. Divide each section into eight equal parts (Figs. 261a and 261e).

6. Cut out the sleeve. Cut upper and lower sections apart.

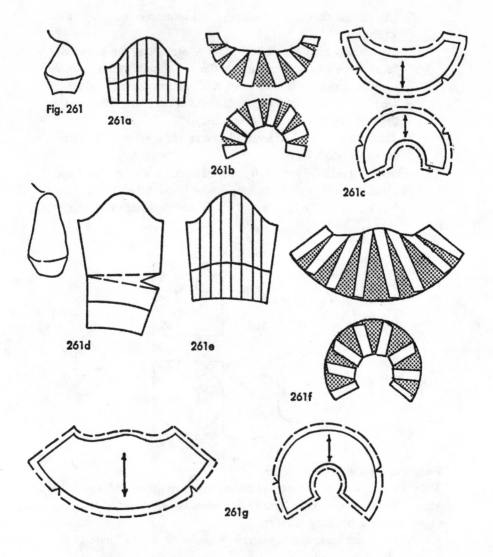

Fig. 261

261a

261b

261c

261d

261e

261f

261g

7. Slash and spread each section to the desired fullness. Circumferences of upper and lower sections must be made to match since the sleeve is stitched together at this seam line. If necessary, overlap at the cuff or finished edge of the sleeve to remove the ease. This will make the sleeve fit more snugly around the arm (Figs. 261b and 261f).

8. Trace the pattern. Add seam allowance and notches (Figs. 261c and 261g).

By way of parenthesis (*the lantern, or balloon skirt*)
This method of producing a lantern, or balloon effect works just the same
way for a skirt as for a sleeve.

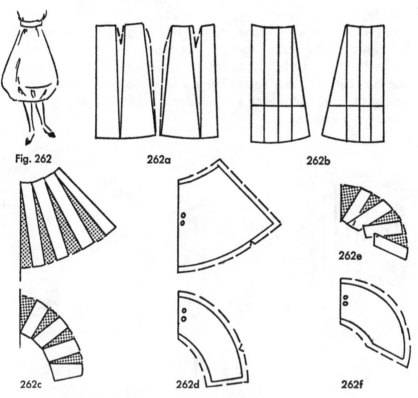

Fig. 262   262a   262b   262c   262d   262e   262f

1. Trace the skirt-front and skirt-back slopers.
2. Fold out the skirt darts, front and back (Fig. 262a).
3. Straighten the side seams (Fig. 262a).
4. Divide the skirt into upper and lower sections (Fig. 262b).
5. Divide each section into four equal parts (Fig. 262b).
6. Cut out the skirt. Cut upper and lower sections apart.
7. Slash and spread sections to desired fullness. This may be from
   very little to a complete circle. Begin spreading a little way in
   from the center line so there will be some spread at the center
   front and center back when the pattern is unfolded. Match the
   circular joining seams (Fig. 262c). Front and back are worked
   alike.
8. Trace the pattern. Add the seam allowance, notches, and fold
   indicator (Fig. 262d).

NOTE: The sweep of the skirt may be shortened by overlapping at the hem as in Fig. 262e. The completed pattern (Fig. 262f) shows the shortened sweep but retains the circumference to match the upper skirt.

The leg-o-mutton sleeve

The leg-o-mutton sleeve comes and goes in fashion. In construction it is the reverse of the bishop or bell sleeves. The sleeve is slim and fitted below the elbow, while bulk or fullness appears above. For this sleeve use the sloper with little finger control. Part of the dart control may be shifted to the shoulder, adding some fullness in that area to begin with, but this is not necessary.

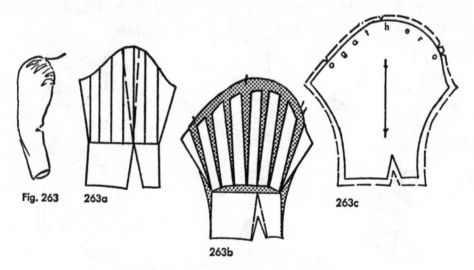

Fig. 263   263a

263b

263c

1. Trace the appropriate sleeve sloper (Fig. 263a).
2. Draw a horizontal slash line at the elbow (Fig. 263a).
3. Draw slash lines from elbow to cap (Fig. 263a).
4. Slash and spread the upper section of the sleeve to the desired fullness (Fig. 263b).
5. Some additional length is automatically added by the separation of the upper and lower sections of the sleeve. More puffiness may be added by raising the cap. Draw a freehand line (Fig. 263b).
6. Shorten the little finger dart. Correct the angle at the elbow with a slightly curved line (Fig. 263b).
7. Trace the pattern. Add grain, seam allowance, notches, perforations, and gather between the perforations (Fig. 263c).

NOTE: Interfacing is often used in the puffed area to produce a firmer stand.

A modification of the leg-o-mutton sleeve is achieved by adding height and some fullness only in the upper part of the sleeve cap. This results in a slender sleeve with height rather than bulk at the shoulder.

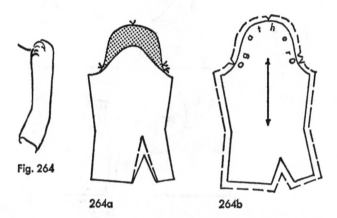

Fig. 264

264a   264b

1. Trace the sleeve sloper with little finger control.
2. Raise the shoulder cap, adding some width by drawing a freehand line (Fig. 264a). The new cap line joins the original cap at the notches.
3. Shorten the little finger dart (Fig. 264a).
4. Trace the pattern; add seam allowance, grain, notches, perforations; gather between the perforations (Fig. 264b).

The amount of the rise of the sleeve cap can be determined only by experimentation. Test the pattern in muslin. It is usually necessary to interface or pad the puffed area to make it stand properly.

FOR A SQUARED LOOK

The darted sleeve cap

Fullness in the cap of the sleeve does not always appear as gathers. It may appear as darts. These give an interesting square shape to the sleeve cap. A number of illustrations follow:

1. Trace the short-sleeve sloper.
2. Draw a horizontal slash line across the cap (Fig. 265a).
3. From the shoulder notch draw a slash line at right angles to the cap line (Fig. 265a).
4. Locate points A and B equidistant from the shoulder notch where you would like the darts (Fig. 265a).
5. Draw slash lines from A and B as illustrated (Fig. 265b).

6. Slash on all the slash lines and spread evenly for the darts (Fig. 265c).

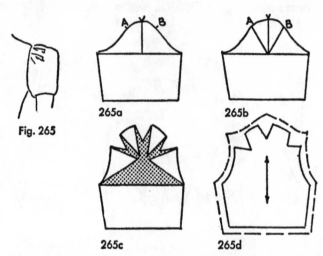

Fig. 265

265a   265b

265c   265d

7. Raise the cap from the horizontal slash line an amount equal to the desired extension at the shoulder, usually about 1″ to 1½″ (Fig. 265c). Raising the cap adds length for puffiness, as well as creating the spread for the darts.

8. Draw darts in the spread. These are usually the amount of the sleeve extension, 1″ to 1½″ (Fig. 265c).

9. Trace the pattern. (Don't forget to fold out the darts before tracing.) Add the seam allowance, grain, and notches (Fig. 265d).

More darts in the sleeve cap require more fullness in the sleeve below the cap.

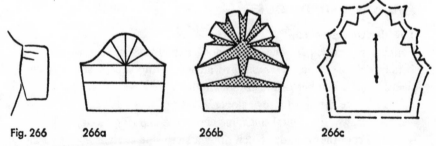

Fig. 266   266a   266b   266c

1. Trace the short-sleeve sloper.
2. Draw slash lines as illustrated (Fig. 266a).
3. Slash and spread cap to desired fullness (Fig. 266b).
4. Raise both cap and middle section an equal amount (Fig. 266b).

5. Draw darts in the cap spread (Fig. 266b).
6. Trace the pattern; add seam allowance, grain, and notches (Fig. 266c).

A crescent shape for a square look

This is a kind of "kissin' cousin" to the lantern sleeve. There are many similarities in construction. The sleeve extends out from the shoulder in a shelf-like arrangement, giving it a squared look.

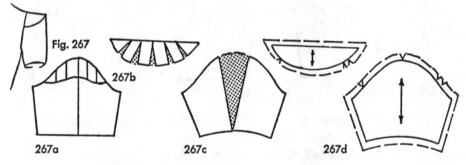

Fig. 267   267b

267a   267c   267d

1. Trace the short-sleeve sloper.
2. Draw a curved line across the upper part of the cap. This shaped section will become the extension, or upper portion of the sleeve (Fig. 267a).
3. Draw a vertical slash line in the extension as illustrated (Fig. 267a).
4. Continue the center slash line to the hem (Fig. 267a).
5. Trace the extension section and its slash lines to paper. Cut it out.
6. Slash on the slash lines and spread against a straight line (Fig. 267b).
7. Use the entire sleeve of Fig. 267a as the lower portion of the sleeve.
8. Slash on the center line. Spread so that the new cap equals the curved line of the extension. This is similar to matching the sections of the lantern sleeve (Fig. 267c).
9. Trace the pattern of the upper and lower sections. Add seam allowance, notches, grain (Fig. 267d).

Corner pleats

A squared look can be created by unpressed, unstitched corner pleats.

1. Trace the short-sleeve sloper. Draw a vertical grain line down the center of the sleeve. Fold the sleeve on the grain line and correct the cap so that front and back are equal in size and

shape. Trace the corrected sleeve sloper (Fig. 268a).

2. Extend the center line (grain line) to the amount of the sleeve extension, usually about 1″ to 1½″ (Fig. 268a).

3. Draw a line perpendicular to the center line (Fig. 268a).

4. Locate points 1 and 2 on the sleeve cap equally distant from the center line (Fig. 268a).

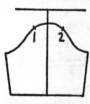
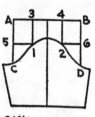
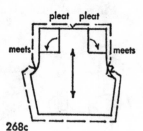

Fig. 268   268a   268b   268c

5. Draw squares from points 1 and 2 which touch the perpendicular line at 3 and 4 (Fig. 268b).

6. Label points 3, 4, 5, 6, A and B as illustrated (Fig. 268b).

7. Extend lines A–5 and B–6 to the sleeve cap. Mark points C and D (Fig. 268b).

8. The corner 5–1–3 is folded into a pleat; the corner 6–2–4 is folded into a pleat. The line C–5–3–4–6–D becomes part of the new sleeve cap.

9. Correct the sharp corners at C and D with a slightly curved line (Fig. 268c).

10. Trace the pattern; add seam allowance, grain, notches. Mark folds for corner pleats.

HEM OR FACING?

The edge of the sleeve is finished off with a hem, facing, or cuff. If the edge is a straight one, the easiest thing to do is to allow for a turned-up hem. If the edge is shaped, it will require a shaped facing. You use the same procedure for this which you used to obtain the neck facing.

The shaped facing

1. Draw a vertical guide line (this may be the grain line or a line parallel to it) passing through the point at which the shaping of the edge changes direction (Fig. 269a).

2. Measure up an equal distance from the edge in a number of places. Make sure that the point of the facing is directly over the point of the shaped edge on the vertical guide line (Fig. 269a).

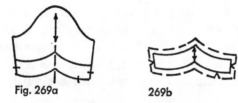

Fig. 269a   269b

3. Draw the facing line. Notch the edge and the underarm seams. Mark the grain of sleeve and facing (Fig. 269a).
4. Trace the facing. Trace the grain and the notches (Fig. 269b).
5. Add the seam allowance (Fig. 269b).

Facing for the sleeve with little finger control

1. Locate the facing in the usual manner (Fig. 270a).
2. Trace the grain of the sleeve and the facing. Notch the sleeve edge and underarm seams (Fig. 270a).
3. Label sections A and B (Fig. 270a).

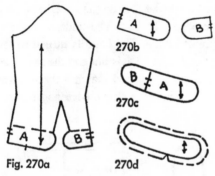

270b

270c

270d

Fig. 270a   270d

4. Trace sections A and B. Trace the notches and the grain. Cut them out (Fig. 270b).
5. Place sections A and B so that the underarm seams match (Fig. 270c). Fasten them in this position.
6. Trace the sleeve facing all in one piece. Trace the notches and the grain (Fig. 270d).
7. Add the seam allowance (Fig. 270d).

This one-piece facing eliminates the necessity and bulk of an underarm seam in the facing.

CUFFS

The band as a cuff

The simplest type of cuff is a band between 1″ and 2″ in width attached to the lower edge of the sleeve. It is cut double on a straight piece of fabric. In length it is equal to the wrist (or arm) measurement plus such ease as is desirable (Fig. 271a). If an opening is used, add the amount necessary for the extension (Fig. 271b). The band may also be extended long enough to tie in a bow (Fig. 271c). The narrow band used as a cuff is really very much like the narrow band used as a collar.

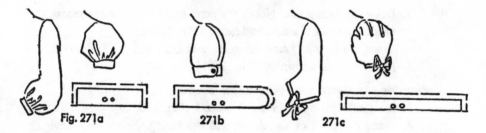

Fig. 271a   271b   271c

The straight band as a turnback cuff

A straight band may be used in another way as a cuff (Fig. 272). In this instance it is a somewhat wider fold on the straight of the goods and is the length of the sleeve edge plus ½″. The underarm seam of the band is stitched first and pressed open. The band is turned to the right side and folded lengthwise. The folded edge is out and the raw edges are treated as one. The underarm seam of the cuff matches the underarm seam of the sleeve. The cuff is eased into the sleeve edge and folded back.

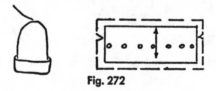

Fig. 272

The bias fold as a cuff

Like the straight fold, the bias fold, too, may be used as a cuff (Fig. 273). It has the advantage of an easy roll. In a striped or plaid material it is a very decorative finish for a sleeve.

It is made exactly as the straight band is, except that it is on bias grain.

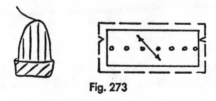

Fig. 273

The wide fitted-band cuff

If the band to be used is more than 2″ in width, it is designed on the lower portion of the sleeve sloper. This provides both the size and shape best suited for the wide fitted cuff. The lower portion of the sleeve sloper which is cut away from the rest of the sleeve is, by definition, really a yoke. And it does what many yokes do: it provides a trim, fitted look to the yoke area which contrasts with the fullness above it.

Most of the ease is removed from this sleeve yoke so that it is quite fitted. We saw this same principle work in the case of the midriff yoke.

This wide fitted-band cuff may be either straight or shaped.

The straight fitted-band cuff

1. Use the sleeve sloper in the predetermined length.
2. Mark the style line of the cuff (Fig. 274a).
3. Mark the grain of the sleeve and the cuff (Fig. 274a).
4. Notch the style line. Indicate by perforations where gathers are to begin and end (Fig. 274a).
5. Cut the cuff from the sleeve (Fig. 274b).

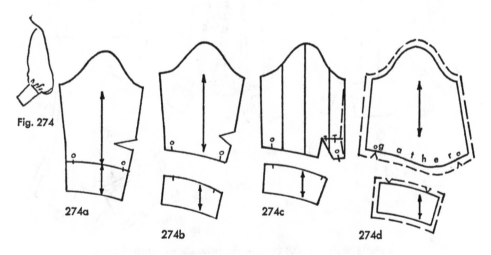

Fig. 274

274a   274b   274c   274d

6. Remove any excess ease from the cuff (Fig. 274c).
7. Shift the dart control in the upper portion of the sleeve to the little finger position (Fig. 274c).
8. Add the desired amount of additional fullness and "blousiness" as previously directed (Fig. 274d).
9. Complete the pattern: add seam allowance, grain, notches. Cut a facing for each cuff (Fig. 274d).

The shaped yoke cuff is constructed in like manner (Fig. 275).

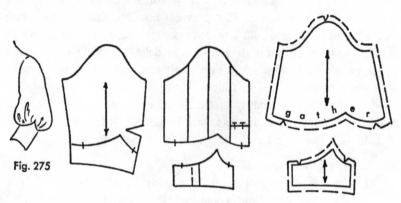

Fig. 275

The simulated cuff

Here is a band cuff cut in one with a sleeve which has additional fullness above its partial yoke. It is like the simulated bodice yoke in Chapter 2.

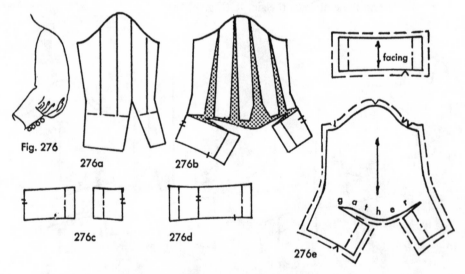

Fig. 276

276a   276b

276c   276d

276e

1. Trace the sleeve sloper with the little finger control (Fig. 276a).
2. Mark the style line for the simulated cuff and the vertical slash lines as illustrated (Fig. 276a).
3. Slash the cuff style line and continue cutting to the underarm seam. Slash the vertical slash lines.
4. Spread to the desired fullness. Add length for "blousiness" (Fig. 276b).
5. Add any extension necessary for closing the cuff (Fig. 276b).

6. Notch the sleeve edge and the underarm seams.
7. Locate the facing for the cuff. This will be a straight band as long as the entire lower portion of the sleeve and the width of the cuff (Fig. 276b).
8. Trace the facing sections. Cut them out (Fig. 276c).
9. Join the facing sections at the underarm as previously directed (Fig. 276d).
10. Trace the sleeve and cuff pattern all in one. Trace the facing (Fig. 276e).
11. Complete the pattern: add seam allowance, grain, and notches.

The simulated fitted cuff on a fitted sleeve

Fig. 277

This simulated cuff is no more a cuff than the simulated collar was a collar. It is actually a shaped band, or facing applied to the right side of the garment and top-stitched (Fig. 277).

The fitted cuff on a fitted sleeve

While this cuff lies fairly flat against the sleeve, it has just enough ease to make it stand away slightly.

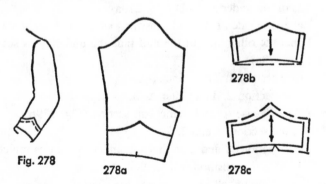

Fig. 278

278a

278b

278c

1. Trace the sleeve sloper.
2. Draw the style line of the cuff (Fig. 278a).
3. Trace the cuff pattern (Fig. 278b).
4. Add ¼″ ease on each underarm seam (Fig. 278b).

5. To establish the grain: draw a straight line connecting the ends of the cuff. The grain line is at right angles to this line (Fig. 278b).
6. Trace the cuff pattern and the grain (Fig. 278c).
7. Add seam allowance. Cut a facing for each cuff.

NOTE: In sewing, match the underarm seam of the cuff to the underarm seam of the sleeve. Ease the cuff edge into the sleeve edge.

The fitted cuff with a closing extension

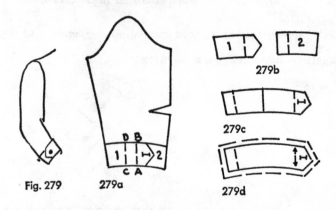

Fig. 279   279a   279b   279c   279d

1. Trace the sleeve sloper.
2. Locate the cuff in the usual manner. Draw in the shaped extension. The dotted line A–B indicates the place where the extension starts (Fig. 279a).
3. An opening extension needs an underlap as well. Draw in the line of the underlap C–D (Fig. 279a).
4. Label one side of the cuff plus the extension as section 1. Label the other side of the cuff plus the underlay as section 2 (Fig. 279a).
5. Trace section 1. Trace line A–B.
   Trace section 2. Trace line A–B.
6. Add ¼″ ease to each underarm section (Fig. 279b).
7. Cut out sections 1 and 2.
8. Place sections 1 and 2 so that the underarm seams match. Fasten in this position (Fig. 279c).
9. Trace the cuff all in one piece (Fig. 279d).
10. Add the seam allowance and the grain. In a separate cuff the grain is usually centered over the top of the hand. In this case line A–B meets that requirement so we shall use it as the grain. This cuff should be faced. In closing, match lines A–B.

The flared cuff

The flared cuff starts out like the fitted cuff. But it is slashed and flared.

1. Trace the sleeve sloper.
2. Locate the cuff parallel to the sleeve edge. Notch the sleeve edge (Fig. 280a).
3. Trace the cuff and the notch. Cut out the cuff.
4. Draw several slash lines on the cuff (Fig. 280b).
5. Slash and spread to the desired fullness. Add some flare to each end of the cuff to balance the fullness (Fig. 280c).
6. Trace the flared cuff (Fig. 280d).

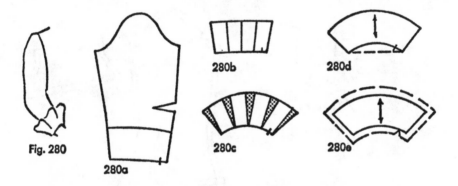

Fig. 280

280a   280b   280c   280d   280e

7. Establish the grain: draw a straight line connecting the ends of the cuff. The grain line is at right angles to this (Fig. 280d).
8. Trace the pattern, notch, and grain. Add the seam allowance. Face (Fig. 280e).

The turnback cuff

This is a simple but effective cuff. It is cut all in one with the sleeve pattern as an extension of the lower edge, which turns back to form the cuff.

1. Trace the sleeve sloper. Trace the grain (Fig. 281a).
2. Make the wrist line a straight line. You cannot turn back a curved line (Fig. 281a).
3. Mark the width of the cuff on the sleeve (Fig. 281a).
4. Draw a line from the elbow dart to the little finger position (Fig. 281a).
5. Fold on the wrist line and trace the cuff and the little finger line (Fig. 281b).
6. Cut out the pattern. Shift the elbow dart control to the little finger control. Shorten the dart (Fig. 281c).

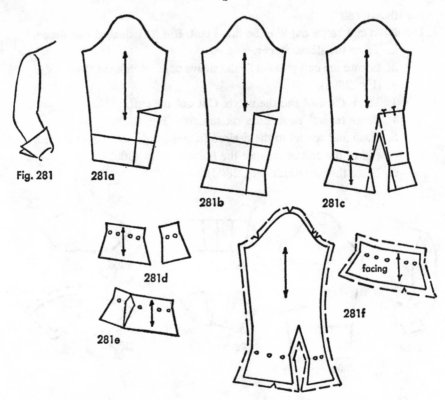

Fig. 281   281a   281b   281c   281d   281e   281f   facing

7. Add a shaped extension for design interest in the opening created by the dart (Fig. 281c).

8. Trace the new sleeve pattern with the extended cuff. Mark the wrist line which becomes the fold line for the turnback. Notch the cuff edge (Fig. 281c).

9. Locate the facing. Make it deep enough so that the facing edge will not show when the cuff is turned back (Fig. 281c).

10. Mark the grain line of the facing parallel to the sleeve grain line (Fig. 281c).

11. Trace the facing. Trace grain, notch, and fold line (Fig. 281d).

12. Join the facing sections at the underarm as you did in the previous exercises. The very small amount of fullness resulting from the shaped space at the underarm will be useful ease when the cuff turns back (Fig. 281e).

13. Trace the completed facing. Trace the completed sleeve (Fig. 281f).

14. Add the seam allowance (Fig. 281f).

The French cuff

The French cuff is a wide band which turns back to form a double cuff. It is generally designed for a shortened sleeve. There are four buttonholes on each cuff through which the cuff links may be passed.

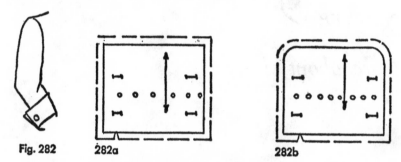

Fig. 282   282a   282b

1. Make the length of the cuff equal to the wrist or arm measurement plus a 1″ extension for the fastening.
2. Make the width of the cuff twice the desired width plus ½″. This extra ½″ is added to that part of the cuff which turns back in order to hide the seam line which attaches the cuff to the sleeve.
3. The edges of the turnback may be square (Fig. 282a) or rounded (Fig. 282b).
4. Make the facing exactly the same as the cuff.
5. Place the buttonholes an equal distance from the fold line.
6. Notch the sleeve edge to match the sleeve.
7. Mark the grain.
8. Add the seam allowance.

CHAPTER 9

More about sleeves

DOLL CLOTHES AND DEFINITIONS

In the days before one went to a store to buy elaborate and expensive doll's clothing, millions of little girls busily stitched away making dresses for their dolls from scraps of material. There were two universal requirements—a hole for the neckline and kimono sleeves. Altogether a highly satisfactory garment for a doll to wear and a little girl to make. Remember?

The kimono sleeve

Stripped of all nonessentials, these childish creations best illustrate the true definition of a kimono sleeve—a sleeve that is cut all in one with the bodice.

The primitive kimono was made of rectangles of material stitched together. The sleeve and shoulder line were placed at right angles to the center front and center back like this:

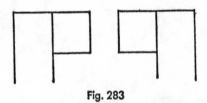

Fig. 283

The kimono sleeve was easy to make (it still lures beginners); it was easy to store (just fold flat and tuck away in box or drawer); it was comfortable to wear (still one of its greatest assets).

WRINKLES—OLD AND NEW

The gusset

The rectangular construction of the kimono had one drawback. When the arms were at the side (a much more natural position than keeping them at right angles to the body), there was considerable wrinkling under the arm. While a deep kimono sleeve avoids some of this, it hardly seems practical for our present-day active lives.

A recent solution to this problem was to design the kimono sleeve at an angle that would bring it into a more natural arm position; but what it gained in naturalness it lost in freedom of movement. To correct this defect a gusset was added to the underarm.

There is still a certain amount of wrinkling which is inherent in the design of the kimono sleeve. Therefore, it is best to use a soft fabric so the wrinkling under the arm doesn't become too bulky or uncomfortable.

To eliminate the wrinkling entirely the sleeve would have to be placed so that it hangs at the side of the body. If such a sleeve were to be cut in one with the bodice, it would permit no movement at all. A large enough gusset to provide the movement would restore the wrinkling. (You can see why the set-in sleeve was invented.) Still, there is a certain "easy" look and "easy" fit to the kimono which will always make it desirable.

Between the right angle shoulder-sleeve placement of the original kimono sleeve and the vertical placement of the set-in sleeve are a whole group of kimono-raglan-dolman sleeves with varying degrees of angle. The angle at which sleeve joins shoulder is determined by the way in which the bodice front, bodice back, and sleeve are placed to produce the pattern. The following exercises illustrate this.

SLEEVES ALL IN ONE WITH THE BODICE

The kimono sleeve

1. Trace the bodice-front, bodice-back, and sleeve slopers.
2. Shift the back shoulder dart to the back neckline.
3. Cut out the slopers.
4. Place the bodice slopers so that the shoulder seams touch at the neckline and are spread ½" apart at the armhole (Fig. 284a).
5. Fold back the cap on the sleeve pattern and place it so that the ends of the cap extend an equal distance below the front and back armscyes on the side seams. Trace (Fig. 284a).
6. Connect the center of the wrist and the point at which shoulder seams touch the neckline with a straight line. Place a notch on

this line. This may be a curved line if necessary to divide the sleeve accurately or if you prefer it (Fig. 284a).

7. Cut the sleeve pattern apart lengthwise on this line (Fig. 284b).
8. Trace the pattern. Complete it by adding seam allowance, notches, grain, and fold indicators (Fig. 284b).

NOTE: If you wish, you may extend the elbow dart to the lengthwise seam and close it (Fig. 284c).

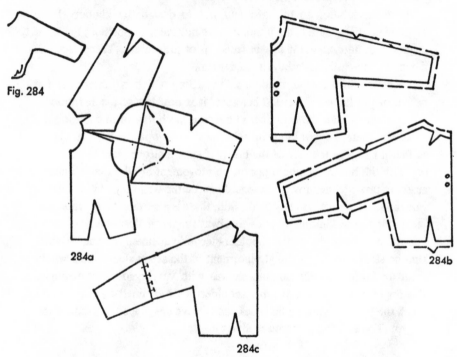

Fig. 284

284a

284b

284c

Variations of underarm styling

A. If sleeve is to have a gusset, it is designed for this angular underarm.

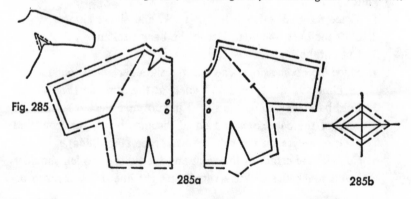

Fig. 285

285a   285b

1. Draw a line from the underarm to the shoulder at the neckline.
2. On this line measure up a distance equal to the length of one side of the gusset, usually 3″ to 4″. The pattern will be slashed on this line to this point. Mark the end of the slash (Fig. 285a).
3. On separate paper draw two lines perpendicular to each other. Draw a diamond-shaped gusset so each side is the same length as it touches these lines (Fig. 285b). Add seam allowance.

B. *If no gusset is used*

1. Draw short identical curved lines from the side seams of the bodice to the underarm seams of the sleeves, both front and back (Fig. 286). This underarm curve may be dropped as low as your design requires it. A very low curved line, approaching the waistline, produces the batwing sleeve.

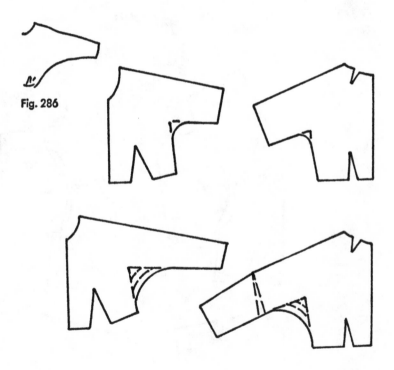

Fig. 286

By slightly changing this basic arrangement of bodice front, bodice back, and sleeve, different effects may be obtained. The diagrams in Fig. 287 illustrate this.

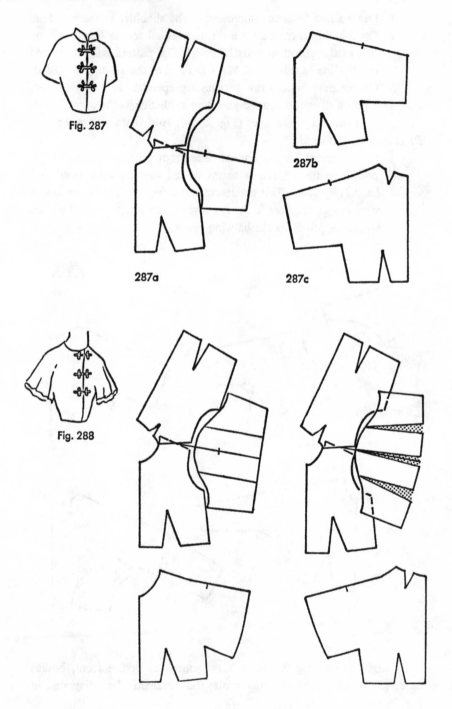

Fig. 287

287a

287b

287c

Fig. 288

The short kimono sleeve

1. Use the slopers developed for the shirt sleeve in Chapter 8, p. 204.
2. Place the slopers so that the shoulder seams overlap at the neckline and spread 1″ at the armhole. Trace (Fig. 287a).
3. Draw a line from the point of overlapping through the center of the sleeve (Fig. 287a).
4. Trace the bodice front and the sleeve front (Fig. 287b).
5. Trace the bodice back and the sleeve back (Fig. 287c).
6. Correct the angularity at the shoulder with a curved line (Figs. 287b and 287c).

To make the pattern for the design illustrated:

7. Add an opening extension and a collar.
8. Complete the pattern: add seam allowance, grain, notches, and fold indicator.

The short kimono sleeve with flare

This pattern is developed from the same slopers and in much the same way as the short kimono sleeve of the previous pattern. To add the circular fullness: draw slash lines through the sleeve; slash and spread to the desired circularity (Fig. 288). To complete the pattern follow steps 4 to 8 of the directions for the short kimono sleeve.

The close-fitting kimono sleeve

1. Trace the bodice-front, bodice-back, and sleeve slopers so that shoulders touch at the armhole and are spread open at the neckline. Both center front and center back are on straight grain. The sleeve and bodice overlap in the manner illustrated in Fig. 289a. Make certain that the side seams are equal in length.
2. Connect the shoulder and the center of the wrist with a straight line (Fig. 289a).
3. Trace the front bodice and sleeve front. Trace the back bodice and sleeve back (Fig. 289b).
4. Locate the opening for the gusset. Construct the gusset (Fig. 289b).
5. Correct the angularity at the shoulder with a curved line (Fig. 289b).
6. Add seam allowance, grain, notches, and fold indicator (Figs. 289b and 289c).

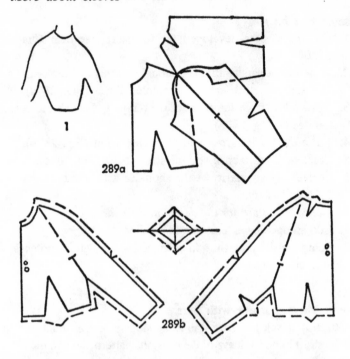

A semi-fitted kimono sleeve on a surplice-front bodice

Here is another all-in-one-piece pattern making effective use of the grain.

Use the kimono-sleeve pattern developed on p. 235 of this chapter.

1. Trace the bodice-back pattern with the center back on straight grain. Extend the center back line as illustrated in Fig. 290a.
2. Shift the waistline dart control of the bodice-front pattern to a French underarm dart.
3. Place the bodice-front pattern so the shoulders touch at the neckline and are spread at the wrist (Fig. 290a). Trace.
4. Fold the center front and trace the waistline (Fig. 290a).
5. Drop a straight line from the neckline to the waistline, parallel to the extended center back line (Fig. 290a). This becomes the line of the surplice. As you can see, it is on the straight grain as is the center back.
6. Add a little extra length to the sleeve. (This is more for shaping than length, so take it easy.) Draw a compound curved line, deeper at the back than the front and tapering to nothing at the underarm seam (Fig. 290a).

7. Complete the pattern: add seam allowance, grain, notches, fold
   indicator, and center front (Fig. 290b).

NOTE: Sketch 2 illustrates the interesting effect obtained when striped
material is used.

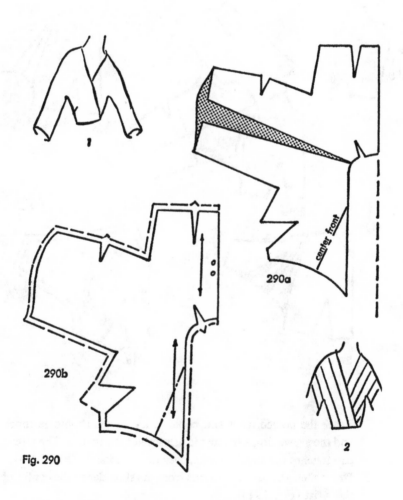

Fig. 290

The burnoose sleeve

There is a charming perversity to this sleeve. The wrinkles under the arm which we have been trying so hard to minimize emerge here triumphantly and dramatically as great drapes. The moral of this story is that, designwise, practically any defect can become a great attraction when exaggerated with a flourish.

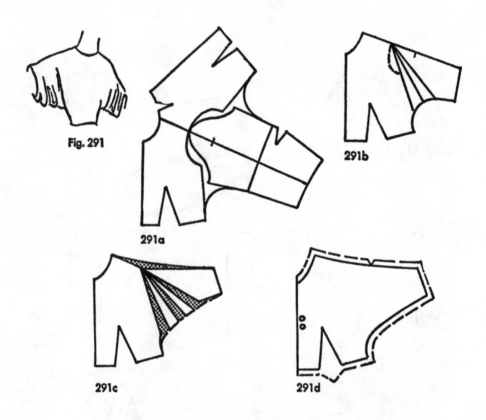

Fig. 291

291a

291b

291c

291d

1. Trace the bodice front and bodice back so the shoulders touch and the sleeve drops below the armscye of the bodice. The sleeve cap touches the shoulder whenever this is possible (Fig. 291a).
2. Draw a lengthwise straight line from the shoulder to the center of the wrist (Fig. 291a).
3. Draw underarm curved lines, front and back, from the side seams of the bodice to the underarm seams of the sleeve. Some fullness

will result by this placement of bodice and sleeve slopers and by these underarm curved lines (Fig. 291a).

4. Shorten the sleeve with a slightly curved line. (Of course this could be a long sleeve if you wished.) (Fig. 291a.)

5. Trace the bodice front and sleeve front in one. Trace the bodice back and sleeve back in one. Mark the shoulder point (Fig. 291b).

(Only the illustration for the front pattern appears here. The back pattern is made in exactly the same way.)

6. Draw slash lines from the shoulder point to the underarm on both front and back (Fig. 291b).

7. Slash and spread for additional fullness (Fig. 291c).

8. Correct the underarm curve. Correct the shoulder curve (Fig. 291c).

9. Trace the new pattern. Add seam allowance, notches, and fold indicators (Fig. 291d).

The kimono sleeve with dropped shoulder

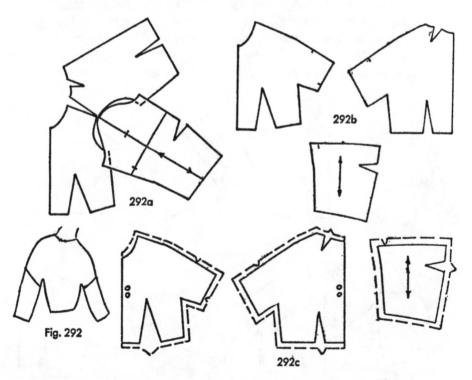

292a

292b

292c

Fig. 292

1. Trace the bodice-front, bodice-back, and sleeve slopers so that shoulders touch at the armhole and spread open at the neckline,

but the spread is not as great as in the close-fitting kimono sleeve in Fig. 289. This means that the center back will *not* be on the straight grain. The sleeve and bodice overlap in the manner illustrated in Fig. 292a. Make certain that the side seams are equal in length.

2. Connect the shoulder and the center of the wrist with a straight line (Fig. 292a).

3. Measure down an equal distance on both underarm sleeve seams.

4. Connect these points with a slightly curved style line (Fig. 292a).

5. Notch the lengthwise shoulder seam and the style line (Fig. 292a).

6. Trace the bodice front with the short kimono sleeve. Trace the bodice back with the short kimono sleeve. Trace the lower sleeve in one piece. The center line of the lower sleeve is the grain line (Fig. 292b).

7. Add the seam allowance, grain, notches, and fold indicator (Fig. 292c).

There is not much point in cutting a pattern apart merely to join it again, unchanged, with a seam line. Make the separation meaningful by adding some design features: perhaps a band of trimming (Fig. 293); or some flare (Fig. 294) or some additional fullness (Fig. 295). Here are several designs and construction patterns. Can you follow them?

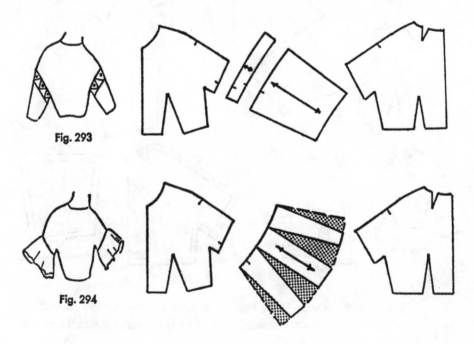

Fig. 293

Fig. 294

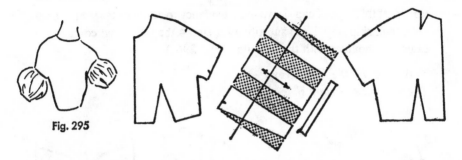

Fig. 295

Juggle the pieces

The varied effects of all the foregoing designs are dependent on the relative placement of the bodice-front, the bodice-back, and the sleeve slopers. Glance back over the chapter and note the effect created by the placement of front and back slopers with:

1. shoulders touching at the neckline and spread at the armhole
2. shoulders overlapping at the neckline and spread at the armhole
3. shoulders touching at the armhole and spread at the neckline
4. shoulders touching at the neckline and spread at the wrist
5. shoulders touching at the neckline and armhole while the sleeve cap is dropped below the bodice armscye

It's like a game to juggle these three pattern pieces until you arrive at an interesting design.

The cap sleeve

The cap sleeve is a very short version of the kimono sleeve.

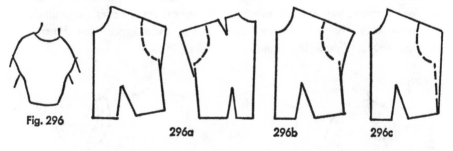

Fig. 296

296a   296b   296c

1. Trace the bodice-front and the bodice-back slopers (Fig. 296a).
2. Extend the shoulder lines to the desired length of the cap (Fig. 296a).
3. Lower the armhole 1″ to 2″ (Fig. 296a).
4. Connect the extended shoulder to the lowered armhole. You may use either a straight line (Fig. 296a) or a curved line (Fig. 296b).

NOTE: If this type of cap sleeve has a tendency to strain or tear at the armhole, then skip step 3 and substitute for step 4 the following: connect the extended shoulder with the waistline (Fig. 296c).

Variations of the cap sleeve
The cap sleeve with shaped style line

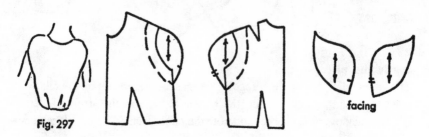

Fig. 297

facing

The shoulder of this cap sleeve is stitched to the shoulder point. The shaped cap requires a shaped facing. This sleeve looks prettier if the entire cap is faced. The facing extends to the dotted line on the diagram (Fig. 297). If this is done, the edge of the facing will be hidden from view.

The sleeveless dress
Are you surprised to find this here? Actually the sleeveless dress is not just one with the sleeves left out. It looks better when the shoulder line is slightly extended beyond the normal armscye for the set-in sleeve. Hence this puts it in the class of cap sleeves.

In a set-in sleeve the armscye is deep enough to provide ease of movement. This is not necessary where there is no sleeve. Furthermore, the deep armscye exposes too much of the armpit area, never particularly noted for its beauty. In some cases it may even expose the lingerie. Obviously a slight adjustment is needed here, too.

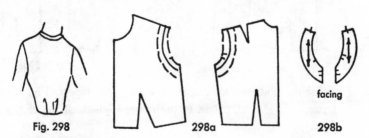

Fig. 298   298a   298b

facing

1. Trace the bodice slopers, front and back.
2. Raise the armscye at the underarm in the necessary or desired amount (Fig. 298a).

3. Extend the shoulder slightly (Fig. 298a).
4. Redraw the armscye, connecting the extended shoulder with the raised armscye (Fig. 298a).
5. Mark the facing (Fig. 298a). Trace it (Fig. 298b).

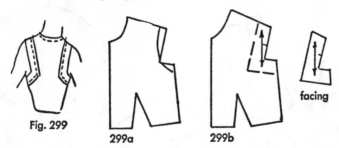

Fig. 299

299a

299b

facing

NOTE: For variety: the underarm may be squared off (Fig. 299); the facing may be top-stitched for a decorative effect.

Modified cap sleeve

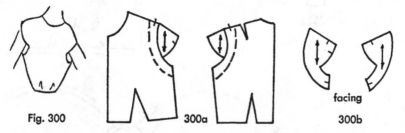

Fig. 300

300a

300b

facing

This sleeve has the good features of both the cap sleeve and the sleeveless dress. The style line of the upper portion gives the effect of a cap, while the lower portion retains the freedom of movement of the sleeveless dress. This eliminates the area of strain in the cap sleeve.

1. Extend the shoulder line as for the cap sleeve (Fig. 300a).
2. Raise the armscye as for the sleeveless dress (Fig. 300a).
3. Draw the style line of the cap, bringing it to the raised armscye (Fig. 300a).
4. Mark the facing (Fig. 300a). Trace it (Fig. 300b).

PART OF THE BODICE JOINED WITH THE SLEEVE

Sometimes, instead of joining the entire bodice with the sleeve, only parts of the bodice are joined with the sleeve. A whole new group of sleeves stem from this procedure—the dolman sleeve, the raglan sleeve, the saddle sleeve, the sleeve and yoke in one, the dropped shoulder. Each type of sleeve in this grouping can in turn be varied endlessly.

The dolman sleeve

The dolman sleeve is a set-in sleeve which has *part* of the bodice cut in one with the sleeve. The sleeve, itself, is in one piece.

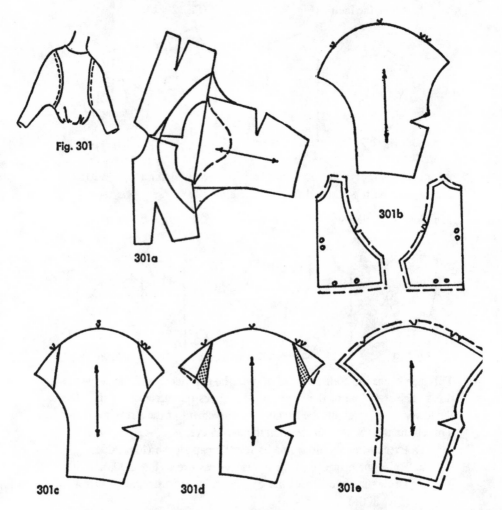

Fig. 301

301a

301b

301c   301d   301e

1. Trace the bodice-front, bodice-back, and sleeve slopers. Place these slopers so shoulders touch at the neckline and are ½" apart at the armhole. Fold back the sleeve cap and place the sleeve so that the ends of the cap extend an equal distance below the front and back armscyes on the side seams. Trace the grain of the sleeve (Fig. 301a).

2. Draw the style line for the new armhole shape on bodice and underarm, both front and back. Curve the style line across the

spread at the shoulder. Make sure the underarm curves match. Notch at front and back (Fig. 301a).

3. Move the back shoulder dart to the new style line so that one dart leg becomes part of the line (Fig. 301a).
4. Cut the sleeve away from the bodice at the style line. Cut out the bodice front and bodice back. Correct the line of the remaining dart leg so it becomes continuous with the style line of the back bodice (Fig. 301b). The waistline dart control can be used as gathers to emphasize the looseness and "blousiness" associated with this style. Designwise, the line of a stitched dart might detract from the line of the dolman sleeve (Fig. 301b).
5. Divide the armhole line of the sleeve into quarters. Divide the underarm curve in half. Draw slash lines connecting the quarter mark at each sleeve end with the center point of the underarm curve (Fig. 301c).
6. Slash the sleeve pattern on these slash lines and spread about 1½" to 2". This lengthens the underarm seam and provides more grace to the sleeve as well as more ease of movement (Fig. 301d).
7. Trace the new sleeve pattern. Trace the grain and notches.
8. Complete the pattern: add seam allowance, grain, notches, and fold indicators (Figs. 301b and 301e).

The strap-shoulder or saddle sleeve

Use the shirt-sleeve sloper for this sleeve. The ease has been removed from this sleeve cap, making it easier to fit the strap sleeve into the armhole.

1. Trace the bodice-front, bodice-back, and sleeve slopers.
2. Draw the style line of the strap, as you would a yoke, across the shoulder of front- and back-bodice slopers. The total width of the strap should not be more than 3". If it is wider, it will not fit the cap of the sleeve very well. Notch the strap front and back. Notch the shoulder seam (Fig. 302a).
3. Cut the yokes away from the bodice (Fig. 302b).
4. On the sleeve pattern draw a lengthwise guide line passing through the shoulder notch and extending the length of the bodice shoulder above the sleeve cap (Fig. 302c).
5. Place the front and back yokes so the shoulder seams meet on this extended line and the armhole ends touch the sleeve cap. Fasten in this position with pins or tape (Fig. 302c). As you can now see, these combined yokes form the strap which is attached to the sleeve cap.

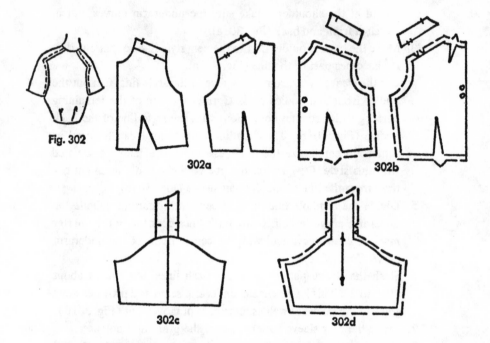

Fig. 302

302a

302b

302c

302d

6. Trace around the sleeve and strap, making the pattern one piece (Fig. 302d).
7. Complete the pattern: add seam allowance, grain, notches, and fold indicator.

The raglan sleeve

In the strap-shoulder sleeve we joined the sleeve to a back and front shoulder yoke. The raglan sleeve uses exactly the same idea in a slightly different way.

There are two types of raglan sleeve. Type A is similar in construction to the strap-shoulder sleeve. Type B is made with a shoulder dart for shaping. The bodice pattern is the same for each type.

Part I—Both types

1. Trace the bodice-front and bodice-back slopers.
2. Draw a diagonal guide line from the neck to the lower armscye (Fig. 303a).
3. Slightly above this guide line to its center and slightly below this guide line from its center, draw a compound curve which eases into armscye (Fig. 303a). This is the style line for the raglan sleeve.
4. Notch the style line and the shoulder seam (Fig. 303a).

5. Cut the bodice yokes away from the rest of the bodice on the style lines (Fig. 303b).
6. Trace the sleeve sloper.
7. On the sleeve pattern draw a lengthwise guide line, passing through the shoulder notch and extending the length of the bodice shoulder (Fig. 303c).

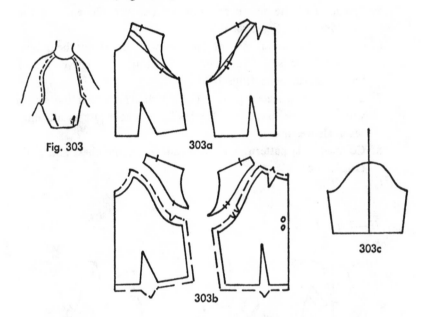

Fig. 303   303a

303c

303b

Part II—Type A

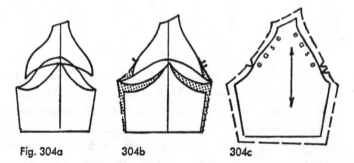

Fig. 304a   304b   304c

1. Place the front and back yokes so that shoulder seams meet on the extended vertical line and the armhole ends overlap the sleeve cap about ½″ at the shoulder (Fig. 304a). This forms the strap.
2. Draw curved slash lines from the shoulder notch of the sleeve to the point of the cap at the underarm seam (Fig. 304a).

3. Cut out the sleeve and strap construction pattern. Cut the sleeve from the strap. Slash on the curved slash lines of the sleeve cap.

4. Draw a vertical guide line. Place the strap over it, guide lines matching. Fasten. Place the sleeve in position under the strap, guide lines matching and touching at the shoulder. Fasten (Fig. 304b).

5. Spread until the sleeve cap touches the armhole ends of the shoulder strap (Fig. 304b).

6. Connect the raised ends of the cap with the sleeve hem line. Correct the ends of the style line of the strap with a curved line to the underarm seam (Fig. 304b).

7. Trace the new sleeve pattern (Fig. 304c). Note that the sleeve will have to be eased into the bodice armhole just as all other set-in sleeves are.

8. Complete the pattern: add seam allowance, notches, and grain (Fig. 304c).

Part II—Type B

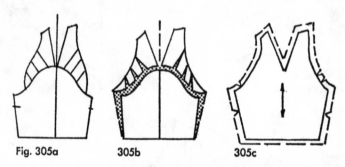

Fig. 305a   305b   305c

1. Place the front and back yokes so that the armhole ends fit over the sleeve cap. A dart will form at the shoulder (Fig. 305a).

2. Draw several slash lines from the armhole of the shoulder yokes to the front and back style lines (Fig. 305a).

3. Slash and spread so the shoulder yokes fit the entire cap of the sleeve. Slightly raise and extend the ends of the sleeve cap (Fig. 305b).

4. Connect the tips of the yokes with the hem line of the sleeve. Correct the style lines with a smooth curve (Fig. 305b).

5. Trace the new sleeve pattern (Fig. 305c).

6. Complete the pattern: add seam allowance, grain, and notches.

Dart control variations

The dart control which forms at the shoulder of the Type B raglan sleeve can be used in the same way as all other dart control.

> 1. It can be shifted. The resulting dart control may be used as full-
> ness (Fig. 306).

Fig. 306

> 2. It can be divided. The dart control may appear in a shaped seam
> (Fig. 307).

Fig. 307

> 3. It can be made into multiple darts (Fig. 308).

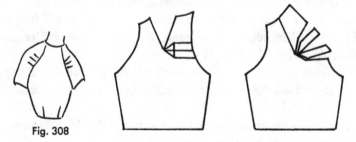

Fig. 308

You see the same principles work in the same way wherever the same conditions prevail.

Shape for the style line

The style line need not always be the curve used here for illustration. It may have an interesting shape. Ofttimes a dropped neckline or a yoke may cut off the upper portion of the raglan sleeve. The characteristic shape and construction will remain below (Fig. 309).

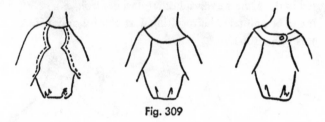

Fig. 309

More attachments

Sometimes the entire raglan sleeve is attached to the back as one piece and seamed only at the front (Fig. 310). Or it may be attached to the front as one piece and seamed only at the back.

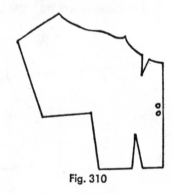

Fig. 310

The sleeve and yoke in one

The strap-shoulder and the raglan sleeves are examples of the use of sleeve and yoke in one piece. This combination of sleeve and yoke is frequently used in design. The yoke may be small, as in the strap sleeve, or it may be large, as in Figs. 311, 312, 313.

1. Trace the bodice-front, the bodice-back, and the sleeve slopers.
2. Draw the yoke style line on bodice front and bodice back (Fig. 311a).
3. Draw a lengthwise slash line which will divide the sleeve into front and back sections (Fig. 311a).
4. Notch the yoke style line and the sleeve slash line (Fig. 311a). Notch the front and back underarm below the yoke. Notch sleeve underarm to match (Fig. 311a).
5. Cut out the front, back, and sleeve. Cut apart the bodice on the yoke lines. Cut the sleeve apart on the slash line.

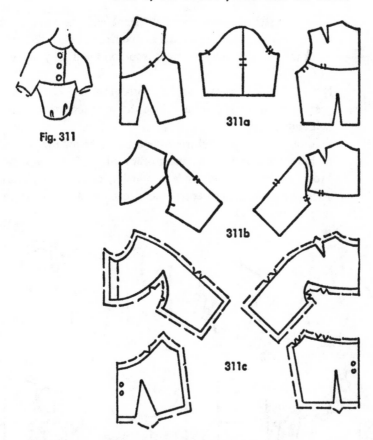

Fig. 311

311a

311b

311c

6. Place the front yoke and the front sleeve so they touch at the yoke point and spread at the shoulder, making the sleeve lie at a suitable angle to the yoke, as developed in the kimono sleeve. Do the same for the back, making sure that the angle of the back sleeve matches the angle of the front sleeve (Fig. 311b).

7. Trace around the yoke and sleeve, connecting them at the shoulder with a smooth, continuous curved line (Fig. 311c).

8. Trace the bodice front and bodice back (Fig. 311c).

9. To complete the design illustrated here: add the opening extension to the yoke front, seam allowance, grain, fold indicator, and notches.

The cape sleeve and yoke in one

Here is an interesting cape sleeve, all in one with the yoke, which demonstrates still another way to develop the pattern.

1. Draw the front- and back-bodice slopers.

2. Draw the style line for the yoke front and the yoke back. Notch the yoke style line. Notch the underarm below the yoke. Mark the grain, parallel to center front, on the front yoke (Fig. 312a).

3. Draw a fold line parallel to the center front and center back, passing through the point at which the yoke touches the armhole (Fig. 312a).

4. Fold on the fold line and trace the armhole below the yoke on both front and back. Trace the notches (Fig. 312b).

5. From the newly traced underarm point, draw the underarm seam parallel to the center front and center back to any desired length (Fig. 312c).

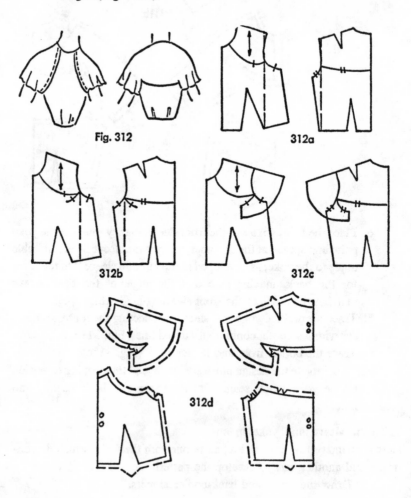

Fig. 312

312a

312b

312c

312d

6. Extend the shoulder line to the desired length for the cape sleeve just as you would for a cap sleeve (Fig. 312c).

7. Connect these points with a graceful curve for the cape (Fig. 312c).

8. Trace the front yoke and cape sleeve in one. Trace the notches and the grain line. Trace the lower bodice front from the yoke style line down (Fig. 312d).

9. Trace the back yoke and cape sleeve in one. Trace the notches. Trace the lower bodice back from the yoke style line down (Fig. 312d).

10. Add seam allowance, grain, notches, and fold indicators (Fig. 312d).

The dropped, or extended shoulder on a yoke

The dropped, or extended shoulder on a yoke is an example of part of the sleeve in one with part of the bodice. (Another type of extended shoulder where part of the sleeve is all in one with the entire bodice is illustrated in Fig. 292.)

1. Trace the bodice front, bodice back, and sleeve.

2. Draw the style line for the yoke front and the yoke back. Make them end an equal distance down from the shoulder on the armscye. Notch the style line. Notch the underarm below the yoke (Fig. 313a).

3. Measure the length of the armscye from the shoulder to the style line of the yoke.

4. From the shoulder notch on the sleeve, measure down on both front and back sleeve cap an amount equal to the length measured in step 3.

5. Connect these two points on the sleeve cap with a horizontal slash line. This will divide the sleeve into upper and lower sections (Fig. 313a).

6. Draw a vertical slash line perpendicular to the horizontal slash line. This will divide the sleeve in half—a front section and a back section (Fig. 313a).

7. Cut the sleeve apart into upper and lower sections. Set the lower section aside for the time being (Fig. 313b).

8. Cut the upper sleeve section apart into front and back (Fig. 313c).

9. Divide the front and back sleeve sections into three equal parts each. Slash on these lines (Fig. 313c).

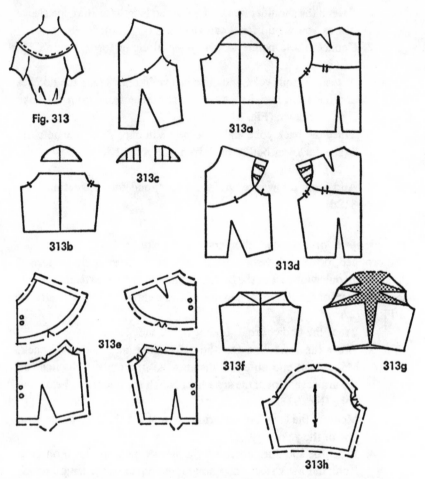

Fig. 313

313a

313b

313c

313d

313e

313f

313g

313h

10. Attach the front sleeve section to the bodice front, the sleeve cap and bodice armscye touching from shoulder to yoke. In doing so, the cap will spread automatically to the right amount. Do the same with the back (Fig. 313d).

11. Trace the yoke and sleeve cap in one, connecting the sleeve cap and yoke with a smoothly flowing curved line (Fig. 313e).

12. Trace the lower front bodice and the lower back bodice (Fig. 313e).

Actually this much of the pattern makes an interesting design all by itself. But if this were all you wanted, it could be constructed much more simply by following the directions for making the modified cap sleeve on p. 247 of this chapter. The bodice yoke could be a continuation of the line of the sleeve cap.

To complete the pattern for this design you will need to adjust the lower sleeve so that it fits the yoke sleeve cap.

13. On lower sleeve divide front armscye and back armscye in half. Connect these points with a horizontal slash line (Fig. 313f).

14. Draw two diagonal slash lines from the corners of the lower section to the intersection of the vertical and horizontal slash lines (Fig. 313f).

15. Slash and spread *all* slash lines as illustrated in Fig. 313g. The amount of the spread across this lower sleeve cap equals the length of the yoke front and yoke back sleeve caps combined.

16. Correct all angularity resulting from the spread with gently curving lines (Fig. 313g).

17. Trace the lower sleeve section. Mark the shoulder notch at the center of the cap (Fig. 313h).

18. To all pattern pieces, bodice front, bodice back, and sleeve: add seam allowance, notches, grain, and fold indicators (Figs. 313e and 313h).

NOTE: This business of cutting off a section of one part of a pattern and joining it to another opens up all sorts of interesting possibilities in creating new designs. The following are frequently used. There are many others.

The shirtwaist with front yoke extension

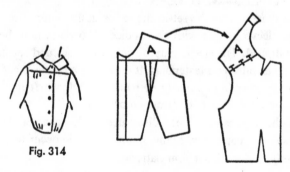

Fig. 314

A bodice back which wraps around to front

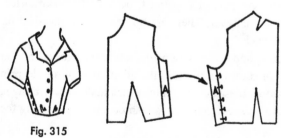

Fig. 315

The skirt with a raised waistline

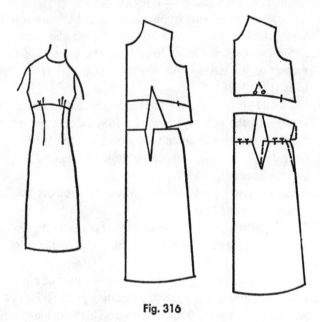

Fig. 316

OLD PRINCIPLES—NEW USES

All that was done to vary the set-in sleeve for design interest may also be done to the sleeve in one with the bodice. The darts may be shifted, divided, multiplied. The sleeve may be cut in sections and seams. It may have extensions, tabs, and fastenings. It may have a facing, a cuff, a yoke. It may have fullness in circularity or balanced fullness. It may be long, short, or in-between. It may be trimmed or plain.

Some of these ideas have been illustrated in this chapter. Some have been suggested for you to try. Many, many more will occur to you as you observe, study, and work out your patterns.

As you can see, we always come back to the same few principles which work alike on any part of a pattern, be it bodice, skirt, sleeve, collar, cuff, pocket, or whatever. There are no new principles—just new ways of using the old ones.

The selection and combination of details, the proportion and grace of line, the use of color and texture, the adaptation of an old principle to a new conception—these are the things which make a design say it is "You." This is the creativeness that makes fashion such a satisfying form of self-expression.

CHAPTER *10*

Let's make the pattern

E FOR EFFORT

The first nine chapters of this book are concerned with showing you how the pattern principles work to achieve certain individual effects. Each exercise deals with the development of a specific detail. These are the ABCs of pattern making. Were you never to make a complete pattern of your own, this much learning would still be valuable. Thoughtful performance always deepens your understanding and appreciation of the problems involved in any activity. You understand paintings a little better when you have tried to paint; or music a little better when you have tried to play an instrument; or farming a little better when you have struggled with a vegetable patch. Undoubtedly, in the future you will regard all patterns, both your own custom-made ones and commercial ones, with a little more appreciation and respect for the time and know-how that go into their creation.

This chapter is particularly for those of you who, by now, are eager to put all this new-found information together to see how it works out when making the complete pattern.

A FOR ART

It has been the primary purpose of this book to provide the tools by which the home sewer can convert her design ideas into working patterns rather than to dwell on the designing of clothes. The art principles which govern design constitute a separate and extensive field of study. However, as you have undoubtedly observed, the two are so interrelated that it is quite impossible to disengage them completely. Some reference to designing appears inevitable.

Where do design ideas come from?
Designing a dress, like any other creative activity, deals with the expression of an idea—not just any idea, but *your* idea. That is not to say that if you want to design a pattern for a dress you must invent something absolutely brand new, something never seen before. All of us, even as great designers do, build on what has gone before.

Actually, for the few famed giants of design—those who lead the way—there are countless others who, with less acclaim, make very significant contributions to fashion. And there are literally millions of women who have worth-while and original ideas.

The same sources of inspiration are there for all. Some are more able by talent, by training, and by the very habit of creating to view, to select, to interpret, to adapt, to organize, to present as much of the past, as much of the present, and as much of themselves as will give their work their own unmistakable imprint.

You've heard it said that there is nothing really new. There are only new ways of looking at old ideas. Creative as Dior was, even his most widely heralded contribution was only a "New Look." It is this "new look" which any of us can take from past styles or existing trends. When filtered through our own individuality, this gives us the right to say, "This is my idea." This is as true of creating a design for a dress as of creating a poem or a song or a picture.

Well then, where do the design ideas come from? Anywhere, everywhere. A picture in a magazine and a painting in a museum. A glimpse in a window and a glance at a book. A candid camera shot of a celebrity or an unknown girl hurriedly crossing the street. Some yardage of irresistible fabric and a piece of jewelry that needs a proper setting. A fashion report in the newspaper and an overheard description on the bus. A memory out of the past of a dress that made you feel beautiful and a dream of "taking a flyer" at that daring new thing from Paris.

Fashion trends and you
Study the fashion trends, but also study yourself. How would you really like to look if you could? What features are you proud of and which would you rather forget? What, in your experience, have you found to be becoming to you? What made you look a sight? What activities fill your days? How often do you go out at night? From the many current fashion ideas, select what is right for you and for your way of life.

A PATTERN FROM A PICTURE

A working sketch

Clip pictures of designs which appeal to you for color, line, and detail. Make a sketch of something you've seen that you particularly like. You don't have to be an artist to do this. Have you noticed that the sketches throughout this book are not professional fashion sketches? They are such as any woman could jot down—a kind of pictorial shorthand that shows style line, proportion, seams, darts, and decorative details. For you, a work of art is not important; a working sketch is. Note the silhouette, the proportion and relationship of its various parts, the important style lines, or any special features which attract you to the design.

Information, please

Now go back and analyze the design for details. In drafting a pattern a general observation is not enough. Every aspect must be specifically and carefully considered.

1. Where is the shaping? How is the dart control used? Is there one dart or several darts? Are the darts straight or curved? What direction do they follow? Do any of the style lines conceal the dart control? Which are the decorative seams and which the control seams? Do any of the darts enter a control seam? Do any of the darts enter other darts? How much dart control for a "relaxed look?" What is the best place for additional dart control for a very fitted garment? Does the dart control appear as a dart, a tuck, a dart tuck, a pleat, gathers, shirring, smocking?

2. Is there fullness in addition to the dart control? Where is the fullness? How much fullness is there? In what form does the fullness appear? Where should the pattern be slashed? How much shall the slashes be spread?

3. Which are the important style lines? Where do they start and where do they end? How much above the waistline? How far from the center line? How much in from the side seam? How much below the neckline? How far above the knee, below the knee? Where in relation to the hip? Where in relation to the armscye? Where on the shoulder seam? Does the style line of the bodice continue into the skirt? Does it include any part of the sleeve? Are the style lines curved or straight? Are they simple lines or complex lines? What direction to the line? Is it repeated in any way?

4. Where is the straight grain? (If you are copying a picture or dress,

the grain line is an important clue to its construction, especially if there are several sections to the pattern.) Where is the straight grain on each piece? Where is the straight grain on the sleeve? Is the sleeve on the bias (a recent trend)? Where is the straight grain on the collar and cuffs, the pockets, the peplum, the panel, the decorative band?

5. Are there any decorative features of special interest? Are there buttons or bows? Where are they placed? How large are they? Is there any trimming? How much trimming? What kind of trimming? How is it applied?

6. What kind of neckline does the garment have? Is it raised or lowered? Is it asymmetric or formally balanced? What neckline for front, what for back? Is there a collar? What type of collar? How large is the collar? How much stand? What is the style line of the collar? Is it made of contrasting material or self-fabric?

7. What kind of sleeves, if any? Are they short, long, or in-between? Are they set-in, kimono, raglan, dolman? Are they fitted, puffed, bell, full, rippled, cape?

These features are by no means all that could be noted, but they will serve to give you some idea of the kind of detailed observation which is required to determine the type of construction for each part of your pattern. As you train yourself to see these many necessary things, you will have the happy experience of discovering just how much there is to see when you look at a design.

You will find that by the time you have completed gathering the information you need for your pattern (as nearly in your judgment as you can at this stage; more questions will pop up as you work along), you will have a pretty good idea of how to proceed.

DECIDE THE DRESS TYPE

Decide the dress type. Present-day clothes fall into five major types.

1. There is the one-piece dress which really isn't one piece at all. It is a dress with bodice and skirt joined by a seam at the normal waistline. But since you slip it over your head or step into it in one piece, that seems to qualify it as one-piece.

2. There is the two-piece garment that we are accustomed to call "separates." Often these are but two parts of the same garment— a skirt and a blouse, or a skirt and a jacket. The number of different effects it is possible to achieve by the interchange of parts in several sets of "separates" has made this a great favorite.

Fig. 317a

317b

317c

317d

3. There is the chemise garment, a truly one-piece garment with no waistline seam. It can be fitted, as it is in the sheath dress; it can be semi-fitted—like the "relaxed look" of 1958; it can be unfitted to hang free as a duster or a smock; again, it can be unfitted, its fullness "cinched" in by sash or belt—in the Claire McCardell manner.

4. There is the princess-type garment, a one-piece, no waistline affair. This is quite fitted by seams and darts through the bodice, while the skirt flares out in graceful lines.

5. There is the one-piece dress with a "waistline" seam where you would not expect to find it. It may appear anywhere below the normal waistline for a long torso effect. Or it may appear anywhere above the normal waistline for the Empire or Directoire styles.

Sometimes these types may be combined. For instance a design can have bodice front and skirt front joined at the waistline while the back is chemise—fitted, semi-fitted, or unfitted (Fig. 317a). The front can be chemise while the back bodice and skirt are joined at the waistline (Fig. 317b). A one-piece back and two-piece front make for an interesting effect (Fig. 317c). Some dresses play it safe by having two—one waistline high, one low (Fig. 317d). Many other combinations are possible.

DECIDE THE SILHOUETTE
Each of these types may be modified by silhouette. Silhouettes change—sometimes subtly, sometimes drastically. The history of costume design indicates that three main silhouettes recur in the fashion cycle—the straight, or columnar (Fig. 318a), the bell, or bouffant (Fig. 318b), and backswept fullness (Fig. 318c). In recent years we have seen dress designs based on all three silhouettes (Figs. 318d, e, and f).

LET'S GO!

The one-piece and two-piece dresses
The patterns for these dresses should present no new problems for you. The pattern exercises throughout the book have dealt with bodice and skirt. These could be either seamed at the waistline or worked out as "separates."

The problem here is more likely to be design. Developing the parts separately can give opportunity for great variety—slim bodice, slim skirt; full bodice, full skirt; fitted bodice, full skirt; full bodice, slim skirt. Skirt and bodice should have some harmonious relationship—colors of one family (or at least on friendly terms), style lines that flow easily from

Fig. 318a

318b

318c

318d

318e

318f

Fig. 319

bodice to skirt, design details that are related or repeated in bodice, skirt, or sleeve. However "separate" the parts really are, they should give the appearance of belonging together (Fig. 319).

The chemise dress
A chemise, shaped to a sheath, can be produced in the following way:
1. Trace the front and back hip-length slopers (Fig. 320a).
2. Extend the slopers to skirt length (Fig. 320a).

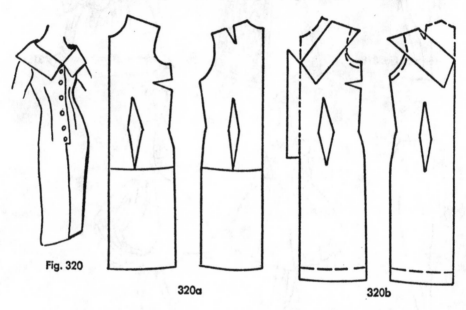

Fig. 320

320a   320b

3. Draw the style lines on the full-length slopers (Fig. 320b).
4. Adjust the dart control accordingly. Since this is a fitted style, you will preserve all the dart control. Perhaps the fitting will reveal the need for more dart control.
5. Develop the pattern as previously directed for neckline, sleeves, extensions, facings, collars, etc.

(The finished pattern for the chemise dress will be found in Fig. 323.)
If the chemise is semi-fitted, follow this procedure:
1. Trace the hip-length slopers, front and back (Fig. 321a).
2. Extend the slopers to skirt length (Fig. 321a).
3. Lessen or do not stitch the waistline darts. Retain the underarm or shoulder dart. Some dart control is necessary for shaping the bust line (Fig. 321b).
4. Straighten the side seam from armscye to hem, touching at the hip (Fig. 321b).

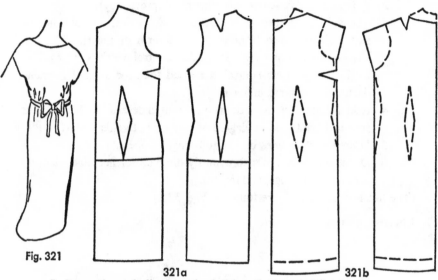

Fig. 321

321a   321b

5. Draw the style lines on the full-length slopers (Fig. 321b).

6. Develop the pattern as previously directed for neckline, sleeves, extensions, facings, collars, etc.

(The finished pattern for this dress will be found in Fig. 324.)

If the chemise is unfitted (Fig. 322), use the following procedure:

1. Trace the hip-length slopers, front and back.

Fig. 322

2. Extend to skirt length (as illustrated previously).

3. The waistline dart remains unstitched. Some dart control is necessary on the bodice front at the underarm or the shoulder for shaping the bustline. Choose the dart control which is most suited to the design. Less control is needed than for a fitted garment darted in the same manner.

4. Add fullness on the side seam from underarm to hem. Make sure to have the same degree of bias on both side seams.

5. Draw the style lines on the full-length slopers.

6. Develop the pattern as previously directed for neckline, sleeves, extensions, facings, collars, etc.

(The finished pattern will be found in Fig. 325.)

Chemise patterns

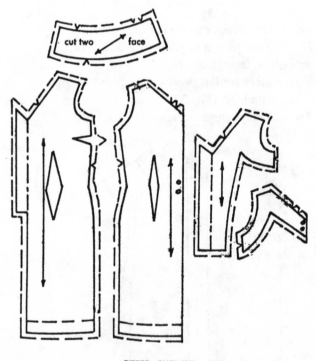

FITTED CHEMISE

Fig. 323

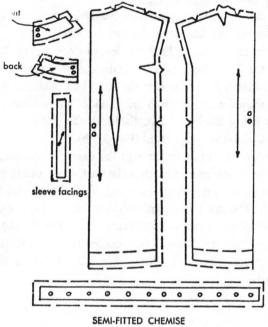

back

sleeve facings

SEMI-FITTED CHEMISE

Fig. 324

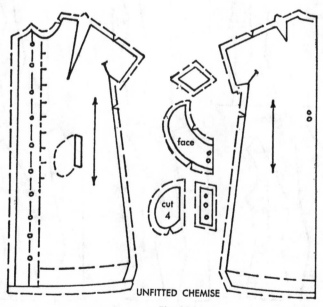

face

cut 4

UNFITTED CHEMISE

Fig. 325

The French dart hip-length sloper

The French dart hip-length sloper is the basis for any princess-type design. Directions for making this sloper follow:

1. Trace the front and back hip-length slopers (Fig. 326a).
2. On the front sloper shift the underarm dart control to the shoulder. Match the position of the front and back shoulder darts on the shoulder seam. Notch the shoulder and waistline darts above and below the bust point. Establish the grain on the side front parallel to the center front (Fig. 326b).
3. Cut the pattern apart through the darts (Fig. 326c).
4. To get a little more ease over the bust, draw a slash line from the bust point to the underarm seam. Slash and spread from ¼″ to ½″. (The side front seam between the notches is eased into the corresponding seam of the center front Fig. 326d.)
5. Correct the seam lines of both center front and side front sections with curved lines (Fig. 326e). Fig. 326f shows the finished front sloper.

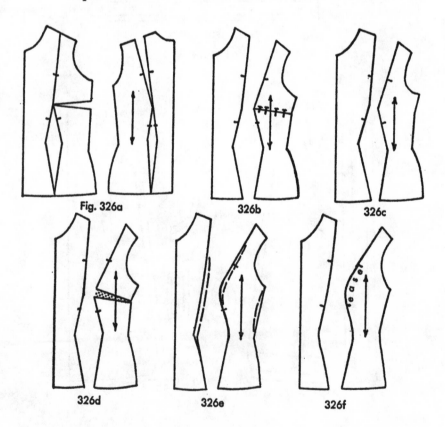

Fig. 326a   326b   326c

326d   326e   326f

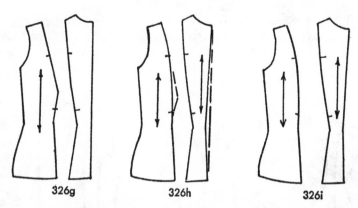

326g   326h   326i

6. On the back sloper extend the shoulder dart to the waistline dart. Notch both darts above and below the shoulder blade. Establish the grain of the side back section parallel to the center back (Fig. 326a).

7. Cut the pattern apart through the darts (Fig. 326g).

8. Correct the seam lines of both center back and side back sections with curved lines. These lines remove the angularity at the shoulder blade and also some of the ease, which is desirable (Fig. 326h).

9. Shape the center back seam, identing it at the waistline. Fig. 326i shows the finished back sloper.

The French dart hip-length sloper extended to skirt length, without flare, may be used as the basis for tubular or raised waistline designs (Fig. 327).

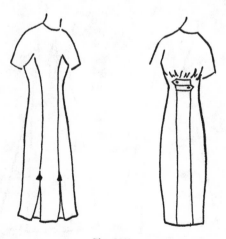

Fig. 327

The princess style dress

  1. Trace the French dart hip-length slopers (Figs. 326f and 326i).

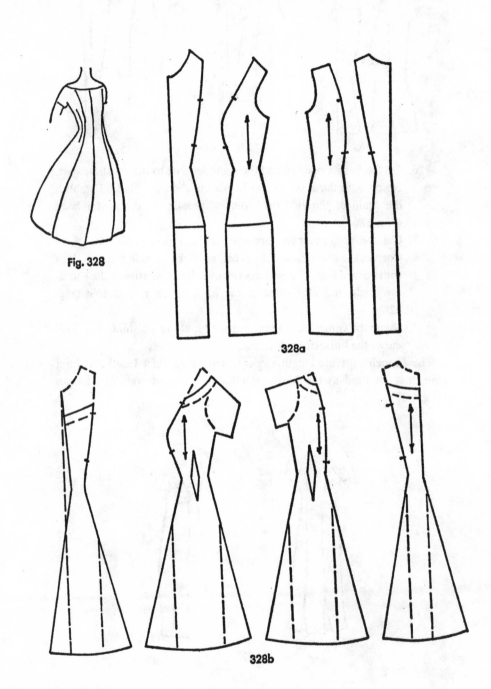

Fig. 328

328a

328b

2. Extend each section to skirt length. Make the seam lines parallel to the grain (Fig. 328a).

3. Add as much flare as is desired to each section starting either at the waistline or at the hip. The new flared seam line should be equal in length to the straight seam line. (This will make the hem line somewhat curved.) An equal amount of flare is generally added to all sections. However, more flare may be added wherever the design requires it (Fig. 328b).

4. Many princess designs call for more shaping through the waistline area. To provide this extra shaping do the following (Fig. 328b):

   a. add darts

   b. use a center back and center front seam rather than the usual fold of the fabric; indent the seams slightly (about ½″) at the waistline

5. Draw the style lines (Fig. 328b).

6. Develop the pattern as previously directed for neckline, collar, sleeve, cuffs, extensions, facings, etc.

   (Complete pattern in Fig. 329.)

The completed pattern for the princess dress

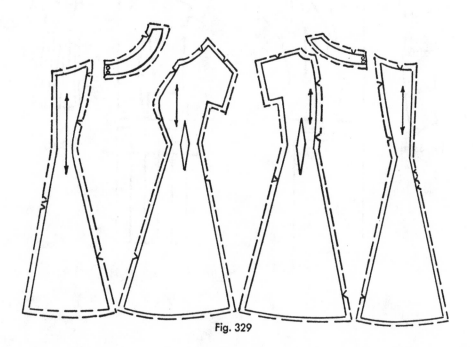

Fig. 329

The one-piece long torso dress

When the long torso dress is fitted, it is drafted from the French dart hip-length sloper (Fig. 330a). When it is unfitted, like a middy, it is drafted from the regular hip-length sloper (Fig. 330b).

1. Trace the appropriate hip-length slopers.
2. Trace the skirt slopers from hip to hem line.
   If the horizontal style line of the bodice is either longer or shorter than the hip-length sloper, the skirt must be lengthened or shortened accordingly.
3. Develop the pattern for the bodice and the skirt as previously directed.

(Construction of the patterns for the dress fronts are illustrated below. The pattern for the dress backs are developed in the same way.)

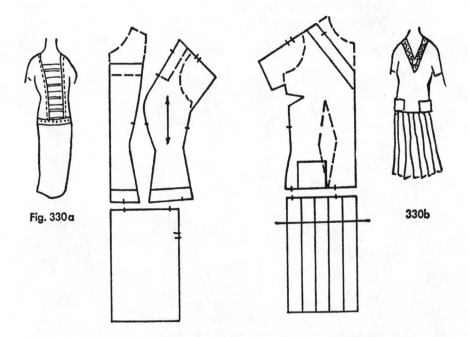

Fig. 330a   330b

The dress with shaped, lowered waistline

The bodice of a dress frequently drops below the normal waistline. Often it is shaped. The pattern for a dress of this type is based on the hip-length sloper.

1. Trace the hip-length slopers, front and back.
2. Extend the slopers to skirt length (Fig. 331a).
3. Draw the style line (Fig. 331a).
4. Cut the sloper apart on the style line (Fig. 331b).
5. Develop the pattern for the bodice (Fig. 331c).
6. Develop the pattern for the skirt (Fig. 331d).

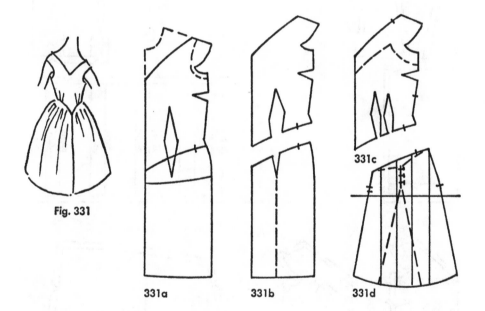

Fig. 331

331a   331b   331c   331d

(Construction of the dress front is illustrated. The back is done in the same way. The completed pattern for the dress front is in Fig. 332.)

The completed dress-front patterns for the lowered waistline (long torso) dresses in Figs. 330a, 330b, and 331.

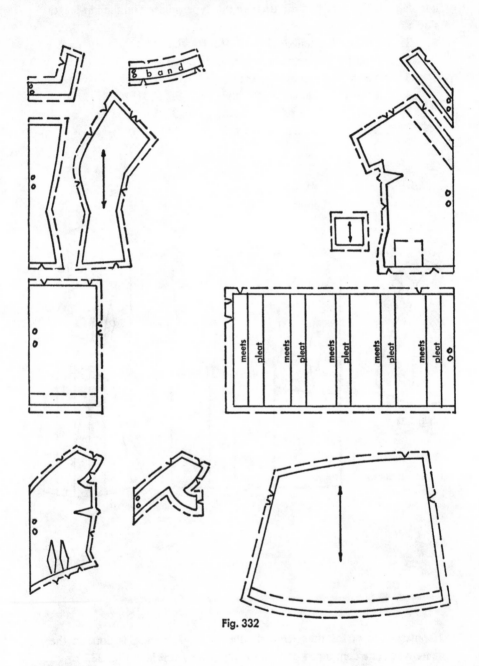

Fig. 332

The basque-bodice dress

A dress with a lengthened or shaped basque bodice is designed on the French dart hip-length slopers. The pattern for the back of this dress is done in similar manner (Fig. 333).

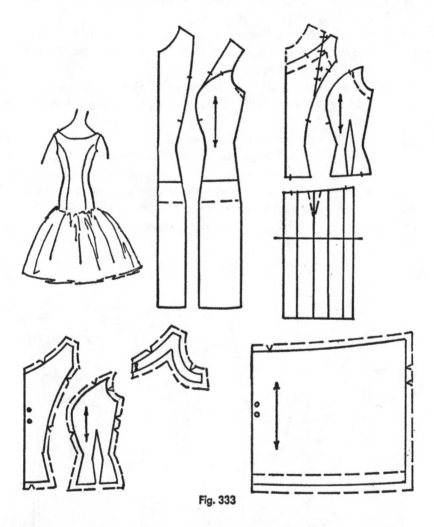

Fig. 333

The one-piece dress with the raised waistline (*Directoire or Empire*)

It is easy to understand the popularity of this beautiful and very feminine line. Each time it appears in the fashion cycle its simplicity and grace come as a relief to a period when clothes display a studied clumsiness.

The Empire line may be developed from either the regular hip-length sloper or from the princess dress, depending, of course, upon the design.

These illustrations are for the dress front. The back is developed in the same way. Directions for both follow.

The Empire line

1. Trace the hip-length slopers, front and back.
2. Extend the slopers to skirt length.
3. Draw a horizontal line below the bust point. Some of the waist-line dart control is left in the bodice for shaping over the bust line. The underarm dart is optional.
4. Cut the pattern apart on the horizontal style line.
5. Add length to the bodice front, tapering to nothing at the side seam.
6. Add the style line for neckline, sleeve, etc.
7. Develop the pattern for the bodice as previously directed.
8. Develop the pattern for the skirt as previously directed.

The same procedure is followed when the designs call for the French dart hip-length slopers as a basis. This is illustrated in Fig. 335. The back of the dress is developed in the same way.

Fig. 334

Fig. 335

The completed front pattern for the Empire-line dress based on the princess pattern

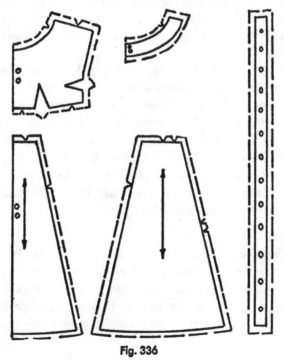

Fig. 336

When you have decided the dress type and selected the appropriate slopers, collect all the materials you will need to draft the pattern—the paper, tools, sketch, and any pertinent information. Work out each part of the pattern as directed in the first nine chapters of this book. You may use this book as you would a cookbook. Open to the proper page for the recipe.

Often it is helpful to work out a quarter-scale pattern until you have solved all the pattern problems. Then tackle the full-scale pattern. It is quite a thrill to see this complete full-scale pattern materialize.

TRIAL RUN

Muslin model

In industry every new model gets a trial run. This is essential in order to get all the "bugs" out of the design. You, too, will need to give your pattern a trial run. Your test is a muslin (or batiste, if your design involves drapery) model made from your completed pattern.

The muslin will give you a good idea of how your dress will look when made up. It will reveal whether your pattern produces the effect you have in mind and whether that particular style is flattering for you.

Drape the muslin on your dress form or on yourself. Usually half a muslin garment is sufficient for testing. Sometimes, however, you cannot judge the effect unless you have a complete muslin—a collar, for instance, a sleeve, a double-breasted, or asymmetric garment, fullness for any special effect.

You may be tempted to skip this step, but don't, particularly at the beginning of your pattern-making experience. You may find that you want to make changes in your design as well as in your pattern. Perhaps the pattern is too wide or too skimpy. Maybe the sections don't match. It could be that the darts or seams don't line up. Perhaps the fit would be improved if parts were cut on the bias rather than the straight grain. You may find the proportions are not pleasing. Or that a style line needs shifting. You may sadly discover that while the original was perfectly enchanting the style looks dreadful on you.

Try, try again

Don't be discouraged. Practically no one hits it right the first time. Some correction is almost always necessary. This is the stage in which your pattern is perfected. Pattern companies and manufacturers spend a great deal of time on this muslin sample. If they're lucky, they perfect it after a second or third time. Sometimes it takes even a fourth and fifth try.

All of this entails many consultations among the stylist, the fashion artist, the draper, the pattern maker, and the sample maker. An error could be very costly for these people. It could be for you, too. A test muslin may save you an expensive or favorite length of fabric or many hours of finished sewing on a garment that turns out to be a dud.

It's a pattern!

Make the corrections on your pattern which the muslin fitting indicates. Trace the perfected and completed pattern. Add the seam allowance and all the necessary symbols. Make any notations on the pattern which will help in assembling the garment. You may want to jot down some sewing directions for any particularly difficult or tricky part.

A JIGSAW PUZZLE

Commercial patterns give you a layout chart and the yardage requirements, in addition to the pattern and the sewing directions. When you make your own patterns, you will have to work these out for yourself. A study of commercial patterns can be quite helpful in this matter.

Lay out the pattern pieces

Laying out the pattern pieces is like playing with a big jigsaw puzzle. All of the pattern pieces must be so placed that the various shapes fit (reasonably) against each other, with a proper respect for the grain. All this must be accomplished in the least amount of material, for economy's sake.

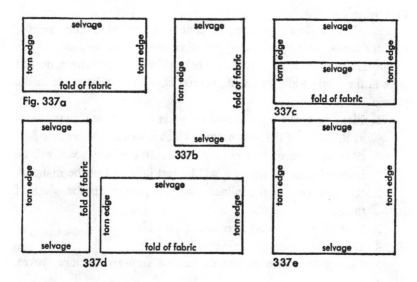

Fig. 337a

337b

337c

337d

337e

On a fold where possible

It is always easier if you can cut two of any pattern piece at the same time. This makes for more accurate cutting and marking. It also saves time. Whenever possible, lay out the pattern on a fold so that the material is double. Several folding arrangements are possible: a lengthwise fold (Fig. 337a); a crosswise fold (Fig. 337b); a partial fold (Fig. 337c); any combination of folds (Fig. 337d). When pattern pieces are to be cut one at a time, place them on the right side of the fabric which is opened to its full width (Fig. 337e).

How much yardage?

It is a good idea to keep on hand several lengths of wrapping paper cut to the standard widths of fabric—35", 39", 44", 54". Have them long enough to test the yardage necessary for your design. Mark the edge which corresponds to the selvage. Fold the paper in the appropriate manner. Lay out the pattern pieces with the grain parallel to the selvage. Place the largest pieces first. Arrange the smaller pieces around the larger ones in the spaces left along the selvage, along the fold, and in the area between.

When the fabric has a nap, pile, or directional weave or print, arrange all the pattern pieces so they go in the same direction, that is, the top of the garment to the bottom. (The nap runs *up* for pile fabrics like velvet, corduroy, and velveteen; *down* for the nap fabrics like wool broadcloth or the many new long-haired woolens. The repeat of the design units on prints, weaves, plaids, or stripes must match just as they do on drapes and slipcovers.)

They've got to fit!

You may have to do a bit of juggling to fit all the pieces in economically, with due regard for the grain, nap, pile, direction of fabric design—all this within the confines of the standard fabric widths. If the pattern doesn't quite fit the fabric width or length, several changes may be made in the pattern.

1. Piece the pattern. Make sure the grain of the "piece" is the same as the grain of the section from which it was cut. Whenever possible try to piece in some place where the joining seam will be inconspicuous or where it will be lost in a fold of the material.
2. Remove some of the fullness until the pattern fits the width of the fabric.
3. Shorten the pattern where and if possible.
4. Eliminate any expendable detail.
5. Change the grain on certain pattern sections. Facings, yokes,

pockets, collars, cuffs, sleeves—all are possibilities.

6. Combine the fabric with other fabric for contrast of color or texture. This may be done for facings, insets, yokes, panels, or wherever consistent or effective in your design.

These changes involve a certain amount of restyling. Sometimes interesting ideas emerge because of limitations. Often the result is an improvement over the original. (At least you can try to persuade yourself that this is so.)

When your pattern and layout chart are completed, fold them neatly or roll them up. Store them in any manner convenient for you. It is well to attach a picture or sketch of the design so you will know just what that precious bundle of paper represents when you finally do get around to using it.

"I MADE THE PATTERN FOR THIS MYSELF!"

Now your pattern is really complete. Between you and your astonished public remain only those comparatively slight details involved in assembling your materials (fabric and findings) and assembling your dress (the sewing-fitting-ripping-sewing). Just think how proud you will be when you announce, "I designed and made this myself." And while your friends are clucking admiringly, you can further stagger them with a certain ostentatious modesty when you say quietly, "I made the pattern for this myself, too." You are sure to be the center of attention from that moment on whenever you make an appearance.

Bargain patterns

The experience of making your own patterns will unquestionably affect your attitude toward commercial patterns. While freeing you from your dependence upon them, your new knowledge also serves to make you more appreciative of what they have to offer.

You get in each pattern envelope a style created by a talented and sometimes big-name designer. It is the fruit of much experimentation, much consultation, much perfecting by a staff of experienced technicians. It includes a listing of all the materials necessary for production, step-by-step directions for sewing, suggestions for suitable fabrics, and even, in some cases, a label to add prestige. You certainly must agree that you are getting a bargain.

Freedom of choice

Will what this book offers you make you abandon the use of commercial patterns? Of course not. Make your own patterns when you wish. Use commercial patterns when the designs appeal to you. You now have the freedom that comes with choice.

Often you can start with a pattern that basically has the features you want. That can be a timesaver. Then change any features which will bring the design closer to your own ideas. Change any features which will make the design more becoming to you. The knowledge of pattern construction will provide you with new confidence in handling commercial patterns. You will find that you are no longer fearful of changing the position of a dart or the line of a seam or of eliminating a detail or adding or removing some fullness. Your knowledge of patterns will even help in the actual sewing. You will understand why and how pattern pieces are joined in a particular way. You will be emancipated from that little sheet of printed instructions.

There is a great deal you can learn from a commercial pattern. Study the shapes of the pattern pieces and try to analyze how they were arrived at. Note any particularly ingenious use of pattern principles. Examine the layout charts carefully for hints on the best use of space. Build up a library of commercial patterns which have interesting design details you may want to incorporate with your own ideas. Handle the commercial pattern as you would any other piece of research material. It has important information which you can use creatively.

You'll never be the same!
The experience of making your own patterns will inevitably result in your seeing fashion with a new eye. It will be difficult for you to be merely a passive observer. No longer will you just sit quietly daydreaming on trolley, bus, or subway. You will be trying to figure out how to make the pattern for dress after dress that you see and admire on others. A new fashion book will send you flying to your paper, pencil, and scale models. Watching a movie or a television show will become a mental exercise as you trace the lines and solve the problems of pattern construction of the heroine's dress long before she solves her own problems. You will enjoy a wonderful new sense of power that comes with discovering that you can produce just what you want in clothes!

Pattern making, fascinating as it is in itself, is merely a means to an end. The larger end is the creation of works of beauty. In this instance, happily, that beauty may adorn you.

APPENDIX

Revised measurement chart for all pattern companies

Approved by the Measurement Standard Committee of the Pattern Industry

Select your size by the bust measurements on this revised chart. That size, then, is your correct size for all patterns even though the bust measurement on the envelope may be different. These are actual body measurements, not garment measurements.

MISSES'	10	12	14	16	18	20	
If Bust is	31	32	34	36	38	40	
Waist	24	25	26	28	30	32	
Hip	33	34	36	38	40	42	
Back Waist Length	15¾	16	16¼	16½	16¾	17	

JUNIOR MISSES	9	11	13	15	17
If Bust is	30½	31½	33	35	37
Waist	23½	24½	25½	27	28½
Hip	32½	33½	35	37	39
Back Waist Length	15	15¼	15½	15¾	16

TEENS	8	10	12	14	16
If Bust is	29	30	32	34	36
Waist	23	24	25	26	28
Hip	31	32	34	36	38
Back Waist Length	14½	14¾	15	15¼	15½

CHILDREN	½	1	2	3	4	5	6
If Chest is	19	20	21	22	23	23½	24
Waist	19	19½	20	20½	21	21½	22
Hip						25	26
Back Waist Length							10½

GIRLS	7	8	10	12	14
If Breast is	25	26	28	30	32
Waist	22½	23	24	25	26
Hip	27	28	30	32½	35
Back Waist Length	11	11½	12¼	13	13¾

SUB-TEEN	8s	10s	12s	14s							
If Bust is	28	29	31	33							
Waist	23	24	25	26							
Hip	31	32	34	36							
Back Waist Length	13½	13¾	14	14¼							

WOMEN	40	42	44	46	48	50					
If Bust is	42	44	46	48	50	52					
Waist	34	36	38½	41	43½	46					
Hip	44	46	48	50	52	54					
Back Waist Length	17⅛	17¼	17⅜	17½	17⅝	17¾					

HALF SIZES	12½	14½	16½	18½	20½	22½	24½				
If Bust is	33	35	37	39	41	43	45				
Waist	27	29	31	33	35	37½	40				
Hip	37	39	41	43	45	47	49				
Back Waist Length	15¼	15½	15¾	16	16¼	16½	16¾				

SKIRTS, SLACKS, AND SHORTS

Teens

Waist	23	24	25	26	28						
Hip	31	32	34	36	38						

Jr. Misses

Waist	23½	24½	25½	27	28½						
Hip	32½	33½	35	37	39						

Misses and Women

Waist	24	25	26	28	30	32	34	36	38½	41	
Hip	33	34	36	38	40	42	44	46	48	50	

BOYS	1	2	3	4	5	6	8	10	12	14	16
If Chest is	20	21	22	23	23½	24	26	28	30	32	34
Waist	19½	20	20½	21	21½	22	23	24	25½	27	29
Hip					24	25	27	29	31	33	35
Neck Base Girth						11½	12	12½	13	13½	14

MEN											
Chest	32	34	36	38	40	42	44	46	48	50	
Waist	28	30	32	34	36	38	40	42	44	46	
Neck Base Girth	13½	14	14½	15	15½	16	16½	17	17½	18	
Shirt Sleeve Length	33	33	33	33	34	34	34	35	35	35	

Other Titles from
Echo Point Books
You May Enjoy

How to Make Clothes That Fit & Flatter

by Adele P. Margolis

In the world of fashion, finding the perfect fit is an art. In this timeless guide, acclaimed sewer Adele P. Margolis offers simple instructions for the amateur designer, including how to choose the right size; use color theory and lines to create flattering illusions; alter patterns and fabric to fit your figure; and more.

HARDCOVER ISBN 978-1-63561-089-5

Encyclopedia of Sewing

by Adele P. Margolis

With more than 1,000 alphabetized entries and 3,000 illustrations, this reference combines the convenience of a dictionary with the instructiveness of an encyclopedia to answer all your sewing questions. Covering a wide range of methods and problems, from basic garment construction to inserting zippers, this guide is essential for every home sewer.

HARDCOVER ISBN 978-1-63561-091-8

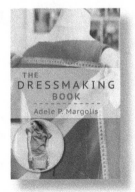

The Dressmaking Book

by Adele P. Margolis

In this essential primer, renowned sewing expert Adele P. Margolis offers step-by-step instructions for creating your own garments. Featuring over 200 how-to line drawings, this guide covers the fundamentals of dressmaking and fashion, including how to select patterns and materials, alter designs, and hand-stitching and sewing machine basics.

HARDCOVER ISBN 978-1-63561-088-8

Our books may be ordered from any bookstore or online purveyor of books, or directly through our Web site, www.echopointbooks.com. Or visit our retail store, located in Brattleboro, Vermont.